Beckett in
Popular Culture

Beckett in Popular Culture

Essays on a Postmodern Icon

Edited by P.J. MURPHY
and NICK PAWLIUK

McFarland & Company, Inc., Publishers
Jefferson, North Carolina

LIBRARY OF CONGRESS CATALOGUING-IN-PUBLICATION DATA

Names: Murphy, P. J. (Peter John), 1946– editor. |
Pawliuk, Nick, 1970– editor
Title: Beckett in popular culture : essays on a postmodern icon /
edited by P.J. Murphy and Nick Pawliuk.
Description: Jefferson, North Carolina : McFarland & Company, Inc.,
Publishers, 2016. | Includes bibliographical references and index. |
Includes bibliographical references and index.
Identifiers: LCCN 2015043158 | ISBN 9780786499595
(softcover : acid free paper) ∞
Subjects: LCSH: Beckett, Samuel, 1906–1989—Criticism and
interpretation. | Beckett, Samuel, 1906–1989—Influence.
Classification: LCC PR6003.E282 Z57185 2016 | DDC 848/.91409—dc23
LC record available at http://lccn.loc.gov/2015043158

BRITISH LIBRARY CATALOGUING DATA ARE AVAILABLE

ISBN (print) 978-0-7864-9959-5
ISBN (ebook) 978-1-4766-2331-3

© 2016 P.J. Murphy and Nick Pawliuk. All rights reserved

*No part of this book may be reproduced or transmitted in any form
or by any means, electronic or mechanical, including photocopying
or recording, or by any information storage and retrieval system,
without permission in writing from the publisher.*

Manufactured in the United States of America

*McFarland & Company, Inc., Publishers
Box 611, Jefferson, North Carolina 28640
www.mcfarlandpub.com*

For HCE
for all those who make their own
contribution to this dialogue:
voxpopbeckett.ca

He's not fucking me about, he's not leading me up any garden, he's not slipping me any wink, he's not flogging me a remedy or a path or a revelation or a basinful of breadcrumbs, he's not selling me anything I don't want to buy, he doesn't give a bollock whether I buy or not, *he hasn't got his hand over his heart.* Well, I'll buy his goods, hook, line and sinker, because he leaves no stone unturned and no maggot lonely.
—Harold Pinter (1967)

The postmodernisms have, in fact, been fascinated precisely by this whole "degraded" landscape of schlock and kitsch, of TV series and *Reader's Digest* culture, of advertising and motels, of the late show and the grade-B Hollywood film, of so-called paraliterature, with its airport paperback categories of the gothic and the romance, the popular biography, the murder mystery, and the science fiction or fantasy novel: materials they no longer simply "quote" as a Joyce or a Mahler might have done, but incorporate into their very substance.
—Fredric Jameson, *Postmodernism* (1991)

A second constant has been a perhaps perverse de-hierarchizing impulse, a desire to challenge the explicitly and implicitly negative cultural evaluation of things like postmodernism, parody, and now, adaptation, which are seen as secondary and inferior.
—Linda Hutcheon, *A Theory of Adaptation* (2006)

But I like to think that all this hubbub of recombination [adaptations of all sorts] is, on balance, a healthy feature of any society that has a robust and living art and is busy arguing with itself on issues large and small. Viewed as such, the works of Beckett, along with what we think we know of Beckett himself, have become, and promise to continue to be, a powerful collection of instruments for art, thought, feeling, judgment, pleasure, and, yes, pain as well.
—H. Porter Abbott, "The Legacy of Samuel Beckett" (2010)

Acknowledgments

Such a complex dialogical exchange as this book intends to be necessarily involves a number of other contributors in addition to the authors of the particular essays. Danielle O'Neill sourced a multitude of Beckett in popular culture echoes and linkages. (Not to mention from her own eclectic reading, such as Dean Koontz's reference to a certain Mr. Godot, gun runner!) Jennifer Murphy and Tanya Pawliuk have over the years raised "Beckett Spotting" to an art form—from cryptic crosswords to fashion magazines and points betwixt and beyond. Their insights have enriched our discussions of numerous points. Our former colleague Martin Whittles was a much appreciated collector of Beckettian references for us in magazines of all sorts, high and low. Our colleague Jeff McLaughlin, whose specialty is philosophy, comics, and the Holocaust, offered insightful suggestions on Beckett and the graphic novel. And, above all, Professor Werner Huber of the University of Vienna, who ever since our work together on *Critique of Beckett Criticism: A Guide to Research in English, French, and German* (1994), has supplied a series of on-going updates around the depiction of Beckett in popular culture, a veritable catalogue of Bakhtinian carnivalesque.

Table of Contents

Acknowledgments vii

Preface 1

Saint Samuel (à) Beckett's Big Toe: Incorporating Beckett in Popular Culture
    P.J. MURPHY 3

Fail Better! Samuel Beckett's Secrets of Business and Branding Success
    STEPHEN BROWN 19

The Strange Case of Detective Fiction
    P.J. MURPHY 33

Far Out Worlds: Sci-Fi and Speculative Fiction
    NICK PAWLIUK 53

Through a Glass, Lightly and Darkly: Depictions on Prime Time Television
    P.J. MURPHY *and* NICK PAWLIUK 69

Screenings for Beckett in Modern Film: Ghostly Presences and Popular Culture Manifestations
    CAMERON REID 85

The Graphic Novel: Another "Stain upon the Silence"?
    NICK PAWLIUK 99

"a mollycoddled little git from Foxrock": Beckett in Irish Pop Music
    CAMERON REID 107

B Is for Beckett: Babies and Baby Naming
    TANYA PAWLIUK 120

In Fashion: Literary Wardrobes and the Marketplace
    JENNIFER MURPHY, TANYA PAWLIUK, P.J. MURPHY
    and NICK PAWLIUK   129

The New Dedalus: Avatars and Identities in Online Social
   Networks
    MARK ROWELL WALLIN   143

Two Quinks for Sam
    ALEXANDER M. FORBES   155

The Sporting Life
    P.J. MURPHY   157

Beckett as Pop Culture Icon
    P.J. MURPHY   169

Addenda: Beckett Cetera: A Pop Culture Miscellany
    P.J. MURPHY *and* NICK PAWLIUK   176

Bibliography   187

About the Contributors   193

Index   195

Preface

This project began with Nick Pawliuk proposing a sequel of sorts to my *Beckett's Dedalus: Dialogical Engagements with Joyce in Beckett's Fiction* (2009): namely, a study of popular culture adaptations of Beckett's work which would in a number of ways complement how Beckett's own work in some decisive ways was an "adaptation" of Joyce's. We had both been collecting for ages (read decades) a host of Beckettian adaptations within popular culture and would periodically compare notes on the incredibly rich diversity of such materials and how they could sometimes shed new light on the so-called "standard" or "accepted" readings of Beckett. We realized that no such study of Beckett's works in popular culture had as yet been undertaken and this was a decisive factor in our deliberations about proceeding with the project.

We began with a series of discussions about the theoretical framework and outlined an early version of what became the introductory essay: "Saint Samuel (à) Beckett's Big Toe: Incorporating Beckett in Popular Culture." The critical focus of our argument was a reassessment of a number of stereotypical assumptions about Beckett and his work. We thought that the shift in perspective afforded by popular culture could be especially productive in this rethinking, and combined we wrote two-thirds of the book. Our next strategic move was to recruit several colleagues with an abiding interest in adaptation theory as well as an extensive knowledge of Beckett: namely, Cameron Reid (modern film; pop music), Tanya Pawliuk (baby naming), Mark Rowell Wallin (social networking) and Alexander M. Forbes (short poems on images of Beckett in popular culture). (See "About the Contributors" for further background information on each author.) That none of them would claim to be a "Beckett specialist" *per se* worked to our advantage in that we asked them to examine afresh a number of popular culture adaptations of Beckett in specific areas and to evaluate the depiction of Beckett and his works in their commentaries.

Over the following three-year period, we held a series of informal seminar-type get-togethers (yes, a few pubs were necessarily pressed into service): various views about the overall development of the project were discussed and constructive criticisms offered about the essay topics we had commissioned. The one major exception was Nick Pawliuk's recruitment of Stephen Brown, University of Ulster marketing guru, who generously allowed us to reprint his informative and provocative "Fail Better! Samuel Beckett's Secrets of Business and Branding Success," which is virtually unknown in Beckett studies and merits a new hearing.

We hope this foundational study will stimulate seminal questions about Beckett's works and new ways in which we might approach them and adapt them.

Saint Samuel (à) Beckett's Big Toe

Incorporating Beckett in Popular Culture

P.J. Murphy

At the end of his inconclusive journey in search of his mother, Molloy invokes Chaucer's "General Prologue" to *The Canterbury Tales*, citing a spring day replete with showers and bird melody; but whereas Chaucer's characters "longen" then "to goon pilgramages," Molloy "longed to go back into the forest. Oh not a real longing."[1] Of course not: at this stage of the game, it can be nothing but a literary longing. Molloy's first memory after noting the birds' music is of the two travelers A and C, perhaps as signs of Author and Character functions, both roles having been played by himself, as necessarily required by the doubling inherent in the "re-presentation" of narrative.

In the midst of these perplexities of the fictional process in terms of determining who is who and what is what, Beckett parodically invokes a number of analogies between himself and his most famous namesake—St. Thomas à Becket. First and foremost is the underlying awareness that both journeys are towards a goal that will never in fact be reached: Chaucer's pilgrims will never arrive at Thomas à Becket's shrine in Canterbury for the elaborate sequence of tales envisaged by their author remained incomplete at the time of Chaucer's death; likewise, Molloy (and indeed his successors) will not resolve the riddle of an historical author-figure behind their stories—and as for Molloy's quest for his mother to sort out questions of origins, it remains forever open-ended: he might be said to at best have replaced his mother in her room, without ever knowing how he got there.

Secondly, in conjunction with such metafictional speculations, there remains inescapably a number of practical considerations about just how does one undertake such a pilgrimage and the expenses thereof (*The Can-*

terbury Tales are full of such details of the profitable business associated with visiting holy shrines). Such aspects are also satirically depicted in the scene which precedes Jacques Moran's return home after having failed in his quest to find Molloy: Moran disarms the threats of the farmer upon whose land he is trespassing by declaring that he is on a "pilgrimage" to "the Turdy Madonna" (173) and implores aforementioned cattle breeding rustic to supply some hot tea as "a small favour to a pilgrim on the rocks" (173), further ingratiating himself by offering a florin for the farmer's poor-box. Moran's last words before he delivers the ending to his narrative underscore an accounting as much as a recounting: "That was how I spent a florin" (174).[2] Hence just prior to the famous literary teaser with which he leaves his reader, "It is midnight" / "It was not midnight," Moran is fixated upon money matters and adds that he had "heavy debts" and "all there was to sell I have sold" (175). And it is not only the petit-bourgeois Moran who is concerned with the material culture contexts of his literary enterprise: Molloy is also enmeshed in the commercial contexts of the literary marketplace as the opening to his narrative underlines—"so many pages, so much money," even if he declares that he does not "work for money" (7).

Consequently, there are indeed ironic dimensions to the later developments within Beckett studies which depict the persona of the author as a veritably "sainted" figure of some sort who is somehow regarded as above such paltry Grub Street concerns as making a living from writing and promoting and advertising such works in the public domain of the marketplace. For far too long such materialistic contexts and the cultural ramifications thereof have been excluded from serious critical consideration within Beckett studies. For those of us who have proceeded upon the assumption that such contexts are ineluctably a factor in determining how any author's work is produced and consumed, Stephen John Dilks' *Samuel Beckett in the Literary Marketplace* (2011) comes as a welcome challenge-cum-corrective to such idealized concepts of "purity" and literary "canonization." Dilks neatly extrapolates a common theme from the host of obituaries by friends of Beckett: namely, how such accounts "have been overwhelming to the point of tedium in their repetition of a narrative of placing Beckett on a pedestal, cut off from market forces, preferring prison-like solitude to publicity and celebrity."[3] Two such representative examples cited by Dilks will give the flavor of this prescribed rhetoric which through its sheer repetition constitutes a veritable advertising slogan: Ronan McDonald summarizes how Beckett has been depicted as "a saintly artist untainted by grubby self-promotion or the coarse business of self-explication"; John Calder, Beckett's English publisher, literally canonizes Beckett in an article published on the author's birthday the year after his death, "A Saint Born on

Good Friday," in which much is made of Beckett's presumed disregard of the "favour of the multitude."[4]

Given such tropes of literary apotheosis, it is hardly surprising that the "Beckett Industry," particularly in the wake of the "Big Business" boom of Beckett's Nobel Prize in 1969, should be somewhat conflicted about how to deal with the highly successful marketing of Beckett's so-called "art of failure" as formulated in 1949's *Three Dialogues with Georges Duthuit*. The most telling example in this regard is, of course, James Knowlson's *Damned to Fame: The Life of Samuel Beckett* (1996). In the authorized biography, Knowlson does deserve more credit than Dilks is willing to grant him for helping establish the contextual frameworks for a better understanding of the historical author-figure of Samuel Beckett (the German Diaries are a telling instance of this); nevertheless, Dilks is justified in emphasizing how these dimensions are not thoroughly critically evaluated since the "damned to fame" title (suggested to Knowlson by Beckett via Pope's *Dunciad*) excludes a full appreciation of the marketing and commercial aspects with which Beckett was also intimately engaged throughout his career. In short, Dilks effectively makes the case that Knowlson's perspective is so fundamentally restricted that we should "challenge the use of '*The*' in the title of Knowlson's biography by putting his art-focused account alongside a more pragmatic account of Beckett's life as a professional writer."[5] To put it another way, Knowlson has in a number of crucial instances been co-opted by Beckett to forward certain views about the aesthetic imperatives behind his works, which, albeit supplying some valuable historical background, still feed into the idea of Beckett as a "sainted" literary figure who against his will has been "damned to fame."

As I have argued elsewhere, Beckett studies has been "directed" to a quite incredible degree by Beckett's own comments on it. The so-called art of failure, the "nothing to express" litany of *Three Dialogues*, is the most obvious example, having generated scores of studies around the "nothingness" theme, from the early days of existentialist criticism through to the post-structuralist ones which still guide most discussions today. A most telling instance in Knowlson's biography is his reading of Beckett's relationship with Joyce in terms of Beckett's own rephrasing to him of what he had earlier said in the very influential "interview" with Israel Shenker in 1956. As I argued in *Beckett's Dedalus* (2009), Beckett's relationship with Joyce is, to say the very least, much more complex than Beckett's own "authorized" versions as conveyed to Shenker, Knowlson, and others.[6] Beckett is clearly engaged in fabricating a certain persona of the author-figure which suits the promotion of his works and indeed their marketing.

But what makes Beckett's work so interesting and rewarding is that such propagandizing about his aesthetic agenda is itself challenged by a complex counterpointing within his own writing. A most revealing sequence in this regard is found at the very center of the "middling" section of Beckett's first novel, the "Und" chapter of *Dream of Fair to Middling Women* (1932). Here are located in concentrated form Beckett's narrator's reflections on author-character relationships and especially how such fictional characterizations are bound to disappoint their author's best laid plans. Such speculations have predictably enough dominated critical commentary on this section (and indeed the novel as a whole), and this is understandable in so far as the first fifteen pages of this chapter focus on the convoluted nature of such relationships, as do the final nine pages of "Und" in which Belacqua theorizes about the kind of novel he would ideally like to write. But in the six pages at the center of "Und" there is a remarkable shift in focus as the narrator comes to recognize that Belacqua is alas "a hotch-potch" (125) who will not carry out his fictional duties as prescribed by his author and that his "portrait" is a hopeless jumble that cannot be neatly delineated and thus presented as a coherent whole with a solid footing. So much so that the next six pages focus fundamentally on Belacqua's feet and his ill-fated quest for boots and shoes which would fit him properly. High-faluting matters such as the equation of the ideal fictional contrivance with "one pure permanent liǔ" (125) are brought thumping down to earth by means of that telling simile par excellence of Belacqua's misfit nature: "Like his feet" (125), which is to say that Belacqua is as much out of joint as a character as his feet on the corporeal plane.

Here we also encounter a concentrated focus upon material culture contexts, the nature of popular culture itself in terms of advertising and consumerism (and indeed value for money, no less), not to mention issues of class, social status, and the questioning of the essential nature of "popularity" itself. In short, we have at the very middle of "Und" all those questions of a pragmatic nature about life in the capitalistic marketplace, which, as Dilks' study foregrounds, Beckett studies has been loath to engage, along with the unresolved issue of how such materialistic concerns relate to the discussion of more "purely" (so-called) literary questions which frame this interlude—a veritable mock-epic excursus on boots and feet.

Beckett's alter ego Belacqua is a strange duck, to be sure, when he ventures out into the "big world," particularly its marketplaces. He tries to avoid recognition by—let alone social intercourse with—those who knew him: as he "waddled forward bowed to the ground or screwed inward to the stores, their kindly sheets of glass, he would not respond" (126). While he might mean something to those who knew him (those who were in effect his social equals), the narrator focuses on the "curious" fact "that never, never by any chance at anytime, did he mean anything at all to his inferiors" (126). He is a duck out of water and recounts how he visits the same stores day after day, year after year for "some trifling indispensable purchase" (such as coffee, tobacco and drink) but is never recognized as a "regular," in the various senses of the word: in short, he stands self-condemned as leaving "no trace, but none of any kind, on the popular sensibility"—to wit, "he had no success with the people, and he suffered profoundly in consequence" (127). All this from the fictional surrogate of a writer who will in the aftermath of his critical success with the famous *Trilogy* and *Waiting for Godot* go on to become one of the most recognizable faces and indeed "personalities" in 20th-century culture—both "high" and "low," and we will in subsequent essays be examining just how his works have been adapted within popular culture.

In a summary one-sentence paragraph of the above descriptions of indifference and virtual excommunication by the *vox populi*, Belacqua, we are duly informed, "never grew accustomed to this boycott" (127). The final word in this self-critique is indeed telling—and goes to the heart of questions of "Irishness" and social class, particularly those of the Protestant minority in the new Republic of Eire. Captain C.C. Boycott was an Irish land agent for absentee English landlords who cared nothing for the welfare of the local inhabitants. Belacqua is not actually refused social or commercial relations with his countrymen and fellow Dubliners but has the status of a veritable nobody. No doubt about it, this Belacqua-Beckett composite could do with a good public relations firm and an advertising campaign to change his image and market it successfully.

There is, however, a brief respite between this nullification of his public image and the full blown discussion of boots and feet and the relations betwixt this odd couple. When in doubt or at a loss where to go next, Beckett, particularly in his early career, nearly always had recourse to Joyce as a handy touchstone. And this is the case here; before the narrator lets his story of Belacqua be "carried away by his feet" (133), there is a short passage which echoes Stephen Dedalus's anti-social behavior in *Portrait*. The narrator in his royal we pose announces that Belacqua "desired rather vehemently to find himself alone in a room where he could look at himself in the glass and pick his nose thoroughly, and scratch his person thoroughly..." (128).[7] Furthermore, Belacqua would lock the door and shut out the public world, thus "being at home to nobody." This might be what Belacqua desired, but this "bash in the tunnel" (to adapt Flann O'Brien's phrase[8]) is a short lived respite, for this "nobody" most definitely does have a body that ties him to the world and keeps his long-suffering feet grounded.

Belacqua gives two main reasons for "the demolition of his feet" (128):

firstly, that as a child he walked upon their outer rim (the description of how "boldly then he stepped off the little toe and the offside malleolus," becoming more progressively arcane in its evocation of medical terminology); secondly, that as a youth "he shod them [...] in exiguous patents." The latter reason incorporates another Joycean reference, calling to mind Knowlson's anecdote about Beckett's mimicking of Joyce's taste for tight-fitting patent shoes at the time that Beckett first met him in Paris.[9] The next two episodes are detailed examinations of boot-buying expeditions in Italy (*Pied*mont, of course) and in Germany with his Smerry. However cosmopolitan the search for the "boot juste" may be, the results are disappointingly similar: alas, just as Belacqua doesn't fit into the social scene or the market place, he doesn't fit properly into his boots or shoes. Indeed, in the Italian hiking reference he dubs his boots bought "for 100 lire or thereabouts" (129) as the "morbid Jungfraülein" (or melancholic "Miss Fit," so to speak) after they have crucified his "bloated" feet and been passed on to a servant who then pawned them for drink. In the second sequence, he pays five Reichmarks for "a stout pair of elastic-sides" (130), over the objections of Smerry, and gets into a convoluted discussion with the salesgirl and her supervisor over the left foot being somewhat larger than the right, Belacqua, however, being that rare bird whose feet were "monstrously symmetrical" (132). This pair is also deemed unsatisfactory, no cure all for Belacqua's "pedincurabilites" (133), and handed down without further ado "to an inferior" (132).

After the ostensibly bootless discussion of the ill-fated quest for right-fitting boots, the narrator invokes a prayer of sorts to the effect that "the only unity in this story is, please God, an involuntary one" (132). But in terms of his self-contained "Tale of Foot and Boots," as it might be dubbed, at the center of the central "Und" section of *Dream*, there resides, arguably, a number of in-built unities one might point to. Certainly, a guiding theme throughout is the relationship between the various classes, between superiors, equals, and "inferiors." Even Belacqua's obsequious bootlicking approach to various shopkeepers and civic employees in the marketplace—"notwithstanding the humility, the timorousness, almost the tenderness, of his approach"—leads only to a "disagreeable passage of arms with the vendor" (127). On another level, the narrator might make claim that a certain verbal booty has been plundered from the futile quest of Belacqua for boots that would fit him properly, but the sad fact remains that Belacqua is "a hotch-potch" and instead of a fully developed portrait of his various body parts (belly, loins, breast, demeanor, face, hands) we are left fundamentally with only his feet which, truth to tell, did—fittingly enough—run away with this would be exposition (or at least hobbled away at a fair pace). The whole interlude is finally summed up by the tag phrase "Cacoethes scribendi, the doom of the best of penmen" (133), namely, all writing is in the final accounting waste matter. Perhaps that big baby Belacqua would have been better off with booties or possibly buskins.

The mock-epic discussion of boots and feet is, however, much more than simply footling nonsense and explicitly points the way toward how Belacqua (and by extension Beckett himself) might find ways of "fitting in" through an expanded understanding of a common humanity. Georges Bataille's remarkable 1929 essay "The Big Toe" has some valuable insights in this regard, foremost of which is the recognition that "the big toe is the most human part of the human body" and plays an important part "in giving a firm foundation of the erection of which man is so proud."[10] Bataille's discussion revolves around the counterpointing of idealist and materialist ways of interpreting our human existence: man has "a light head" and wants to aspire to the purity of the heavens but is pulled back by being forced to admit that he also has a "foot in the mud." Bataille concludes that this fundamental dichotomy leads unfortunately to a world-view in which far too many believe "human life entails, in fact, the rage of seeing oneself as a back and forth movement from refuse to the ideal, and from the ideal to refuse—a rage that is easily directed against an organ as *base* as the foot" (137). Beckett like Bataille does not "rage" against this "back and forth movement" and instead initiates a dialogical engagement between the two in which some type of mutual dependency needs to be recognized.

Beckett would also share Bataille's "spasmodic laugh" at the spectacle of mankind trying vainly to distance itself from terrestrial mud only to see how "its purest flight lands man's own arrogance spread-eagle in the mud" (139). *How It Is* is an epic rendition of this bathetic pratfall. Both would agree that "the human foot is commonly subjected to grotesque tortures that deform it and make it rickety" (see Belacqua's sad testimonials in this regard) and that, concomitantly, there is a "hilarity" which is "commonly produced by simply imagining the *toes*" (138). Witness the comic inventory of Beckett's "First Love" (1945) in which the narrator promises that someday he'll tell his reader in a more comprehensive way about his "strange pains in detail," delineating between those of the mind, the heart and the soul, and finally the "frame proper" from the head to the feet, but it is only with the feet, with the "base" foundation, that we actually get any "details," for it is upon this "pedestal" that the narrator's imagination comes alive. This deployment parallels the would-be attempt to give a fully detailed "portrait" of Belacqua in *Dream* whereas in the final analysis only his feet receive such careful anatomical scrutiny:

all the way down to the feet beloved of the corn, the cramp, the kibe, the bunion, the hammer toe, the nail ingrown, the fallen arch, the club foot, duck foot, goose foot, pigeon foot, flat foot, trench foot and other curiosities [33].[11]

In short, here is the materialist base upon which Beckett grounds his writing. For Beckett as for Bataille the "return to reality" means man's "opening his eyes wide: opening them wide, then, before a big toe."[12]

The literary game is then truly afoot in Beckett (all puns are bound to be lame in this context). The "big toe" is the fitting relic of the deconstruction of the "Saint Samuel" mythology of so much Beckett criticism of a hagiographic bent. It is not for naught but for down-to-earth cultural contexts that the leader of the mob in Shakespeare's *Coriolanus* is dubbed "the great toe of the assembly." And outside of Beckett studies itself, popular culture adaptations of Beckett are the "reliquary" in which we can locate the vital remains of Beckett's legacy in a dialogical engagement with the materialist contexts of literary construction. In *Beckett's Dedalus*, I pursued an in-depth discussion of how Beckett created himself as a writer through a complex rewriting of other writers (a process in which Joyce played the predominant role) and how this parody-travesty process could at some points result in what Bakhtin referred to as *parodia sacra*, that is, works which become in their own right (write) "canonical." It was at this juncture that Nick Pawliuk suggested that we undertake a full-length study of adaptations of Beckett's works in popular culture, pointing out that how these adaptations were carried out was in a number of ways complementary to Beckett's own strategies for artistic development and that such a process would enhance our understanding of how we have made use of Beckett's works. The theoretical framework of *Beckett's Dedalus* could itself be "adapted," as it were, to the rich popular culture materials we had been collecting over the years in terms of Beckettian "reincarnations" in genre writing such as detective fiction and science fiction, the worlds of advertising, TV programming, modern film, popular music and social networking, not to mention the cult of genius and celebrity naming associated with Beckett's "brand" in the marketplace, and so on.

While Beckett criticism has taken notice of some aspects of this cultural traffic, it has not undertaken any investigations of a comprehensive and in-depth nature. Preliminary comments do, however, reveal an underlying ambiguity about the nature and value of these adaptations and what they might reveal about Beckett's works themselves, let alone what is the legacy of those works in the popular imagination. Two revealing instances of these uncertainties about how to go about discussing the "other Becketts" manifested in popular culture avatars are the Introductions to two special issues of the *Journal of Beckett Studies*. In the first instance (*JOBS*, vol. 10, Nos. 1 and 2), the editors (Daniela Caselli, Steven Connor, and Laura Salisbury) attempt to summarize the nature of Beckett studies at the beginning of the new millennium. They posit that "two opinions divided without opposing" those engaged with writing on Beckett: namely, the existentialist-humanist view which "remains the dominant view in popular representations of Beckett's work," particularly those focused on his theatrical productions, and, on the other hand, the post-structuralist views of various critics in the 1980s and 90s (for example, Connor himself, Leslie Hill, Thomas Trezise, et al.) who opposed the idea of the human and instead concentrated upon the "difference" of the deconstruction of the subject.[13] Of particular importance to our discussion of images of Beckett in popular culture is that Connor et al. subsume these "opposing" positions and the critical enterprise of being "a Beckettian" under a series of theological metaphors which essentially support the canonical-doctrinal notion of "Saint Samuel Beckett" as a guiding concept. The editors do point out the ironic dimensions of this, perhaps most strikingly how the "faithful" followers of Beckett cannot do without the iconic images of the author's face (no matter that the author's agency has undergone its own "death" in post-structuralist theorizing). In the editors' view, the opposition between humanist and anti-humanist readings has become "normalized," part of the status quo: "the critical church of the 'friends of Beckett' has proven itself surprisingly ecumenical" (vi). There is something inherently misleading about this quietist approach which supplies, in my opinion, an unjustified warrant to the "nothing to be done" and "nothing new" schools of Beckett criticism—let's just all agree to politely disagree over minor points of a safely academic nature since we all agree on the core values of being "Beckettian."[14] Hence, while the editors point out that critics might develop views of "other Becketts," and they mention in this regard Beckett and popular forms of writing such as detective fiction and science fiction and "the growing interest in new forms of cultural materialist readings of Beckett," any possibilities of an authentic dialogical engagement are quickly nullified: "remaining true here to a certain notion of Beckett, these and other putative 'other Becketts' will smoothly be absorbed into the growing mass of 'discourse on Beckett' without the slightest schism in the ranks of the faithful" (iii). The "certain notion" referred to here is the assumption that we all can agree on the fundamentally negative qualities inherent in Beckett's presumed world view and that humanist/anti-humanist perspectives are only qualifications and variations on this theme.

On the contrary, as I have argued throughout my critique of Beckett criticism, the assumption of such a "consensus" is itself highly debatable: we need in fact to consider a "Copernican Revolution" of sorts in Beckett studies whereby more affirmative dimensions of the Beckettian enterprise need to be taken into account.[15] In our following discussion we show how a popular culture-materialist approach to Beckett's work does indeed necessitate a revisionist critique of such stereotypical critical discourse.

S.E. Gontarski's introduction to a special issue on "Transnational Beckett" in *JOBS* Vol. 16, Nos. 1 and 2 (Fall 2006–Spring 2007) focuses more directly on the commercial images of Samuel Beckett as a "global" author who has taken on a number of prominent roles within popular culture. But Gontarski's review of such issues in the midst of the Beckett centenary year celebrations is undermined by the unresolved ambiguity with his very approach to such popular culture issues. For he regards this situation as at best "something of a mixed blessing" and his own answer to his guiding question: "Are we in the midst of a global triumph of the avant-garde or simply witnessing its reduction to nostalgia or its assimilation into commerce and so into kitsch?,"[16] becomes clear over the rest of his introduction. Namely: that the commercial assimilation of the modernist avant-garde as evidenced by the appropriation of Beckett's image in popular culture and further corroborated by the corporate support of the centenary celebrations is a form of Adorno-type "degradation" that somehow betrays the integrity (if not "purity") of Beckett's aesthetic enterprise, that in the cultural logic of our late capitalism there has occurred a collapse of the distinctions between art and commodity.

Gontarski calls this "the Elvis effect," and by this he means the "later" Elvis who filmed *Viva Las Vegas* (1963) and opened the International Hotel (1969) in the entertainment capital of the world and became "the darling of the blue-haired middle class" (5). Gontarski implies that even though Beckett's name has not yet appeared on a Las Vegas marquee depictions of his works and images within popular culture have undergone this "effect." But the process of such assimilation and adaptation is indeed much more complex than Gontarski's depiction. For example: Gontarski seems unaware that there was until very recently a long-standing Beckett festival of drama on the "fringes" of Las Vegas.[17] Beckett's name was not up there in neon lights, but it was there on a series of playbills. Moreover, even the so-called "Elvis effect" Gontarski refers to is not a linear, monolithic concept and need not necessarily entail "degradation": in Sheryl Crow's video for her "Leaving Las Vegas" there is the central image of a whole series of Elvis impersonators—of the late über-kitsch variety—jumping on trampolines. The diaspora of such simulacra suggests a host of creative possibilities for rethinking the art/commodity nexus. What happens in Vegas doesn't always stay in Vegas.

Gontarski concludes by hedging his bets—so to speak; even though

"Beckett has left the building," Gontarski holds out the affirmative possibilities of "rethink[ing] Beckett against an overt commodity culture," thereby echoing the title of his introduction with a final "Viva! Sam Beckett."[18] But it is obvious from his full title and its qualifying "or"—"Viva, Sam Beckett, or Flogging the Avant-Garde"—that Gontarski is in the final accounting adopting the Adorno-like "degradation" view on the culture-industry. Gontarski might be hedging his bets, but we all know that the house always wins and in terms of his guiding metaphor in his introduction, this means "Las Vegas" as symbol of the entertainment industry will rake in the chips by the end of the night.

There are, however, many more affirmative dimensions to the question of Beckett studies and its popular culture engagements than those allowed by the "nothing to be done" (because it is assumed that it has *already* been done) and the commodification of art schools. Gontarski noticeably fails to give one example of a critically affirmative use of Beckett's work in popular culture. Instead he makes only passing reference to a number of rather trifling instances of so-called "adaptations," such as the "Monsterpiece Theater" production of *Waiting for Godot* (in which the tree seems to think it's in the "Scottish play" and runs offstage), and the equally superficial if less amusing Guinea Pig Theater version of *Godot*. In the same year as the Beckett centenary, Linda Hutcheon in *A Theory of Adaptation* begins her investigation by noting that the popularity of the adaptation phenomenon is invariably accompanied by "the constant critical denigration of the general phenomenon of adaptation—in all its various media incarnations."[19] In her exploration of the "dialogic relations among texts," and the political import thereof, Hutcheon aims "to challenge the explicitly and implicitly negative cultural evaluation of things like postmodernism, parody, and now adaptation, which are seen as secondary and inferior" (3). In sharp contrast with Gontarski's ambiguously suspended argument, she directly engages in a critique of why "we tend to reserve our negatively judgmental rhetoric for popular culture, as if it is more tainted with capitalism than is high art" (30–31). The incredible number of adaptations of Beckett's work throughout popular culture affords the opportunities for a revisionist critique of the ways in which Beckett's oeuvre has been received and to rethink what its legacy for us is; namely, what do *we do* with Beckett—not merely as passive "consumers" but as active participants in the construction of such images?

The theoretical model for our discussions of various areas of popular culture derives from a careful and thorough appraisal of actual practices: that is, a critical-inductive evaluation of the rich array of particular adaptations in popular culture. For example: our discussions of detective fiction and science fiction writing; in both of these genres, there is evident on the superficial level a great deal of name-dropping, what might be termed cultural littering in which the invocation of Beckett's name and works acts as a cultural signifier of status. Beneath such surface referencing, a three-fold pattern, however, emerges: some popular culture adaptations echo or mimic prevalent academic views, sometimes implying the need to challenge such stereotypical or ideologically driven positions; on the other hand, some other popular culture adaptations supply through parody a comic corrective to or subversion of such serious or so-called "high" culture approaches; and—most interesting of all—there are also a number of instances in which adaptations of Beckett incorporate aspects of his works in such a way as to produce new works which are "original" in their own right, engaged as they are in a dialogical rewriting of the source texts. In short, "homage" to such texts by Beckett co-exists with a "contestation" in which the dynamic interplay of textuality leads to the construction of works which can offer new critical illumination.

Popular culture reincarnations of Beckett and his works are the "big toe" of his corpus and can afford new ways of approaching the connections between so-called "higher" and "lower" cultural functions. While there is indeed a growing awareness of the historical-materialist dimensions of Beckett's work, there is, nevertheless, a still prevalent tendency to assimilate such observations to the "Saint Sam" model in which there is an aesthetic detachment from such mundane restraints. This is the case in a number of telling instances in Knowlson's "authorized" biography, and also evident in Andrew Gibson's recent intellectual history of Beckett's life. In his last chapter "Where He Happened to Be: Capital *Triumphans*, 1985–9," Gibson offers many stimulating insights of a cultural-materialistic nature, concluding, however, with the assertion that Beckett in his later works of the eighties is somehow still detached from all this:

> As Capital announced its imminent triumph, Beckett held it at and even greater distance. As it promised to fill every space and make every void substantial, his work ever more irresistibly emptied the world out, becoming more and more phantasmal and wraith-ridden.[20]

As I have argued in *Reconstructing Beckett* (1990) and *Beckett's Dedalus* (2009), I see Beckett's later works (such as *Ill Seen Ill Said*, *Worstward Ho*, and *Stirrings Still*) as complex ontological fables in which Beckett's fundamental concerns are to devise a "syntax of weakness" which will "let being into literature," and that these represent exciting new possibilities for the realigning of word and world. The "spectral" imagery in such texts is part of a much more complex dialogical engagement which we are perhaps only now beginning to fully appreciate and which entails a sense of grounding the spectral within the world, one which still implicitly references those elements which Gibson says Beckett has distanced himself from.

Popular culture manifestations of various sorts afford sightings of Beckett as alive and well (viva Beckett, indeed) within much more down-to-earth contexts of an undeniably commercial nature. Thinking our way through the reception of Beckett's works in popular culture can also assist us in our rethinking of how to approach Beckett's works themselves. In the "Foreword/Manifesto" of *Reconstructing Beckett* (1990), I argued that Beckett belongs to the tradition of the *Avant-Garde, not* as the term is loosely defined so that it is virtually synonymous with the modern-postmodern itself, but in the sense advanced by Peter Bürger in which it is a historically conceived attack on the autonomous status of art and aims instead at a reintegration of art and life. I then added a major qualification: rather than directly trying to integrate art with life, Beckett's literary explorations, particularly in the post–*Trilogy* period, show him trying to bring life to his art. An examination of Beckett *within* popular culture can advance from a different perspective a series of vital questions about the art-life nexus, without being compromised by the either/or cultural baggage of popular culture versus the *avant-garde* (as in Gontarski's title for his introduction—a classic instance of assimilating the term *avant-garde* within a critically vexed to-ing and fro-ing between modernist and postmodernist value systems).

A similar ambiguity about how Beckett should be read, how he should be "classified" in terms of the various antinomies of the modernist-postmodernist debate, is evident in Fredric Jameson's landmark *Postmodernism, Or, The Cultural Logic of Late Capitalism* (1991). And taking center stage in Jameson's exposition of his argument is a series of artistic representations of shoes and boots. Central to Jameson's argument here is the contrast between Van Gogh's high modernist *A Pair of Boots* (with its Heideggerian associations) and Andy Warhol's *Diamond Dust Shoes* which are characterized as in fact lacking all character, "a random collection of dead objects hanging together on the canvas," lacking depth and agency: there is deemed "no way to complete the hermeneutic gesture and to these oddments that whole larger lived context."[21] The Warhol images (which are also used on the paperback cover of Jameson's book) supply then the key items in Jameson's inventory of postmodernist imagery.

Where Beckett would be placed by Jameson in terms of these opposing sets of values is not, however, made clear. In a discussion of the most significant postmodernist authors such as Cage and Warhol and company, Beckett's name comes last (and hence foremost) in the series, "or even Beckett himself." Beckett is here designated the poster-boy or patron saint of postmodernism with its characteristic "textuality, écriture, or schizophrenic writing" (26). That such an astute critic noted for his mastery of the provocative and incisive qualifying phrase should let such a stereotypical gloss of Beckett stand is itself indicative of the problem: certain assumptions about Beckett's vision have become so deeply entrenched that they have become "naturalized" and here we have arguably our foremost Marxist critic endorsing just such an essentially ideological judgment.

In my own Beckett "shrine"-cum-study, I have framed a franked Eire stamp (28 pence) which features Beckett's face on a Euro coin, in honor of his 1969 Nobel Prize for Literature, on the left of the stamp, and on the right—wait for it—a pair of boots.[22] These boots are, of course, emblematic of *Waiting for Godot* and its opening "Nothing to be done" in which Vladimir is commenting on how he (shades of Belacqua) can't seem to make the boots fit. These boots are clearly in the Van Gogh–Heidegger tradition and in terms of their realistic depiction they are most similar to the photograph Jameson includes by Walker Evans entitled "Floyd Burrough's Work Shoes." Beckett's vision indisputably contains elements of the modernist *and* postmodernist, granted, but there are other more interesting and illuminating ways of approaching this admixture than toeing the party-line of the "Church of Friends" of Saint Sam. Would Beckett look down his nose at his commemorative stamp? I do not think so. After all, he would, if nothing else, appreciate the irony of how the issuing of this stamp resolved in a sense two of the problems the young Belacqua of *Dream* wrestled with: the ill-fated quest to find a pair of shoes that actually fit was part of a larger social dilemma in which Belacqua found it excruciating to go to the bank or even to buy stamps. A study which focuses upon various depictions and adaptations of Beckett in popular culture holds out the possibility of finding new and illuminating ways of addressing Beckett's oeuvre and our changing relationships with it.

Notes

1. Samuel Beckett, *Molloy* (New York: Grove Press, 1958), 91. I partially alluded to this point of comparison with Chaucer in *Beckett's Dedalus: Dialogical Engagements with Joyce in Beckett's Fiction* (Toronto: University of Toronto Press, 2009), 189.

2. In this instance, "filthy lucre" does, however, keep a poetic ("flowery") distance from mundane commercial exchange as a florin is definitely redolent of "old money." A florin is a former British coin worth two shillings and possesses a cosmopolitan lineage in its very etymology: Middle English via Old French and Italian *fiorino*, flower, the original coin bearing a fleur-de-lis.

3. Stephen John Dilks, *Samuel Beckett in the Literary Marketplace* (Syracuse: Syracuse University Press, 2011), 3.

4. Ibid., 9.

5. Ibid.

6. See, in particular, the Introduction, "Prolegomenon to Any Future Beckett Criticism" in *Beckett's Dedalus*, 17–19.

7. "Compare this with Stephen's reaction after his efforts to write a love poem about his missed kiss with E—C— in the tram: "he went into his mother's bedroom and gazed at his face for a long time in the mirror of her dressing table" (*Portrait*, 71) and, later, with his mortification of his senses—especially touch—"when he suffered [over] patiently every little itch and pain" (*Portrait*, 135). James Joyce, *A Portrait of the Artist as a Young Man* (Boston: Bedford, 1993).

8. O'Brien's most extended commentary on Joyce depicts his fellow Irishman locked within a privy in a darkened train car in a tunnel, thereby parodying the aesthetic disengagement of Stephen Dedalus. See Flann O'Brien "A Bash in the Tunnel," in *Stories and Plays* (Hammadsworth: Penguin Books, 1973), 201–206.

9. James Knowlson, *Damned to Fame: The Life of Samuel Beckett* (London: Bloomsbury, 1996), 101.

10. Georges Bataille, "The Big Toe," in *Contemporary Critical Theory*, ed. Dan Latimer (New York: Harcourt Brace Jovanovich, 1989), 136.

11. Ulrika Maude in *Beckett, Technology and the Body* (Cambridge: Cambridge University Press, 2009) is the only critic I am aware of who has made any significant connections between Bataille's essay and Beckett's works, with his obsession with "pathologies of the foot" (124).

12. Bataille, "The Big Toe," 140. There is a remarkable literary predecessor of Bataille's essay in Vladimir Nabokov's short story "The Passenger" (first published in Russian in 1927) in which the narrator wakes up on a train to see the foot of his fellow passenger in the compartment above him: "While I looked it tensed, the tenacious big toe moved once or twice; then, finally, the whole extremity vigorously pushed off and soared out of sight" (*The Stories of Vladimir Nabokov* [New York: Vintage, 1997], 184). Nabokov's narrator cannot come to terms with this base and repellent organ and this critical portrait thereby makes a number of points as found in Bataille's essay.

13. Daniela Caselli, Steven Connor, and Laura Salisbury, "Introduction," *Journal of Beckett Studies*, Volume 10, Numbers 1 and 2 (Fall 2000–Spring 2001), i.

14. A particularly telling example of this tendency in Beckett studies to arrive at a consensus, a sort of *summa theologica*, albeit of the *via negativa* variety, is Andrea Oppo's *Philosophical Aesthetics and Samuel Beckett* (Oxford: Peter Lang, 2008).

15. See, for example, my use of the term in this disciplinary sense as well as within a Kantian reading of Beckett's aesthetic development in "Beckett's Critique of Kant," *Beckett/Philosophy*, edited by Matthew Feldman and Karim Mamdani (St. Klimrnt Ohridski: Sofia University Press, 2012). The last sentence states "It is perhaps time for a 'Copernican Revolution' in Beckett Studies, one whereby we can move beyond the ideology of negativity that has restricted our ability to appreciate some of the more reconstructive aspects of Beckett's remarkable oeuvre" (220).

16. S.E. Gontarski, ed., Special Issue: Transnational Beckett, *JOBS*, Volume 16, Numbers 1 and 2, "Introduction: Viva Sam Beckett, or Flogging the Avant-Garde," 1. The same reservations about Beckett in the marketplace are evident in his "Foreword" to Dilks' study.

17. Ernest Hemmings was the director of the Beckett Fringe Festival in Las Vegas which ran from 2003 to 2008. In his posting announcing the end of this quixotic quest, Hemmings denounced Bush era politics as one of the deciding factors. My colleague and co-editor, Nick Pawliuk, arranged an interview with him in November 2009, which, alas, did not take place, Mr. Hemmings having been held up with other engagements. Future correspondence failed to establish a new rendezvous. Mr. Hemmings' Godot-like failure to show perhaps confirms in its own way the importance of being "Ernest."

18. Gontarski, "Viva, Sam Beckett," 10.

19. Linda Hutcheon, *A Theory of Adaptation* (London: Routledge, 2006), xi.
20. Andrew Gibson, *Samuel Beckett* (London: Reaktion Books, 2010), 156–57.
21. Fredric Jameson, *Postmodernism, Or, The Cultural Logic of Late Capitalism* (Durham: Duke University Press, 2001), 8.
22. Special thanks to Professor Werner Huber who sent me the Beckett stamp (of approval?) and who over the years has forwarded me a whole miscellany of Beckett and popular culture items.

Fail Better!
Samuel Beckett's Secrets of Business and Branding Success

Stephen Brown

Nick Pawliuk: After what perhaps seems like too many years of thinking and reading about Samuel Beckett, I was given Stephen Brown's essay "Fail Better! Samuel Beckett's Secrets of Business and Branding Success" (2006) by my wife who stumbled upon it on the Internet (actually, neither of us can remember who found what anymore). Here was a delight: the essay was completely surprising. It is clever, informative, and laugh out loud funny, the latter a trait largely missing from my experience with Beckett studies outside of the pubs. Brown is in great Irish company when he can turn a phrase like "vocabulary constabulary": Wilde and Joyce lovers take note.

But it is not just his impressive knowledge and concise, illuminating use of marketing examples. Stephen Brown's essay brings a non-specialist's eye to what has been neglected though always taken as a given in Beckett studies: that Beckett is important in the larger culture, though not perhaps for what many Beckett scholars might think. Beckett represents something more indefinable and marketable, best exemplified by the Apple "Think Different" campaign. Of course, Beckett scholars are familiar with this poster, but Brown's essay was the impetus needed at the beginning of this project to think differently about Beckett in a more sustained way for my input into this collection, to see that there was something going on with the myriad of Beckett and popular culture references my wife and I had collected over the years.

Thus, I contacted Professor Brown and asked if we could reprint his essay since it had largely gone unnoticed by those outside the business community. He was gracious and obliging, and as funny in his emails as in his writing, and for all that, I thank him. (Anyone new to his work should check out his website and reviews of his own books, sfxbrown.com.) His longer book length project entitled Fail Better! Stumbling to Success in Sales & Marketing *is well worth buying—even if he doesn't think so. In fact, his account of experiencing Harry Potter World in Florida in a separate essay is largely responsible for us now wanting to go there also.*

His essay is important as it anticipates how integral marketing is to Beckett himself—Brown even wittily calling him a "business exemplar" in an email—and to our study itself. He anticipates how important not only parody is through his stylistic creativity, but also marketing to Beckett himself, since brought to light by Stephen J. Dilks' in Samuel Beckett in the Literary Marketplace *(2011). Although Brown's essay might be a "wee bit tongue-in-cheek" as he himself said in an email to me, it is nevertheless crucial to a much needed reappraisal and understanding of Beckett's influence and the need to reintegrate it into the common domain.*

Fifty years ago, the U.S. premiere of *Waiting for Godot* opened at the Coconut Grove Playhouse, Miami. Starring Tom Ewell and Bert Lahr, the loveable cowardly lion in MGM's *Wizard of Oz*, it was ambitiously billed as "the laugh sensation of two continents."[1] Now, theatrical PR is a law unto itself, as everyone knows, but the Coconut Grove billing must rank among the greatest overstatements in the history of the boards. Beckett's nihilistic play was neither a comedy, though it contained wonderfully comedic elements, nor the laugh sensation of a single continent, let alone two. Rather it was a play where, as one early commentator memorably observed, "nothing happens, twice."

Nothing happened at the Miami box office either. It was a disastrous failure and went dark after two weeks. *Waiting* almost closed in London too, where the first performances were greeted with derision, catcalls and wholesale audience walkouts. Indeed, Beckett's masterpiece nearly didn't make its Parisian debut at all and only got mounted thanks to a government grant for foreign playwrights writing in French. Its extremely low staging costs—four actors, one boy, and a spartan set—also helped swing things in its favor, as did the scandalized reaction of early reviewers (which always draws a crowd).

En Attendant Godot, of course, is now regarded as one of the greatest artistic achievements of the twentieth century. It is a staple of the theatrical repertoire. Its characters, setting and tragicomic ethos are part of popular culture. It is one of those plays that everyone is familiar with, even if they haven't attended a performance. It is a seminal statement, the autograph work in fact, of the so-called "Theatre of the Absurd." It turned Samuel Beckett into a superstar and all but earned him the Nobel Prize for Literature in 1969.

Yet *Waiting* was within a whisker of ignominious failure, as the Coconut Grove debacle bears witness. Samuel Beckett himself had failed in everything he'd attempted prior to *Godot*. A brilliant scholar-cum-sportsman, he spurned the family business, thought better of a career in advertising, and abandoned an academic sinecure at Trinity College, Dublin, for a penurious existence in inter-war Paris, that famously bohemian destination where the lost generation went to find themselves. He joined the James Joyce set, penned occasional poems, novels, translations and works of literary criticism, all of which were roundly ignored. He received more rejection slips than pay slips during this period of professional purgatory. If it weren't for handouts from his father, a successful Dublin quantity surveyor, and the succor of his brother, who took over the family firm after his father's sudden death, Sam couldn't have afforded to fail for so long. He was almost fifty years old when he became an overnight sensation, much to his astonishment and not a little dismay.

Fifty years on from that unanticipated breakthrough, Samuel Barclay Beckett embodies the contemporary business condition. The peerless playwright's attitudes, achievements and aesthetic imperatives are directly relevant to today's creativity-driven, hyper-competitive, multi-mediated Entertainment Economy. This is a warp-speed world of fads, fashions and, as often as not, calamitous failure. This is a world, as the roller-coaster ride of Apple Computers reminds us, where thinking different is the order of the day. Although some readers may doubt whether anything can be learned from an angst-ridden 'fifties scribbler, much less an Irish management drop-out—he considered accounting at one stage too—Apple's "think different" injunction should give us pause. Perhaps it's time to think differently about thinking differently and give due consideration to Beckett's "fail better" ethic. *Waiting for Godot*, lest we forget, was first published in the same year as Peter Drucker's *Practice of Management*. We still look to Drucker. It's time we looked at the seven sizzling secrets of Samuel Beckett's success.

Wailing for Tenacity

The most obvious Beckett lesson, the one that'll be especially familiar to practicing managers and the majority of serial entrepreneurs, concerns *tenacity*. It is impossible to overstate the importance of perseverance. Hanging on in there in the face of repeated failure, abject failure, heart-wrenching failure is the trait that distinguishes biters and bitten in today's bare-knuckle bear-pit. Although management gurus constantly chant the mantra of success—how to attain it, how to sustain it, how to unearth it, how to unleash it—the sad reality is that the vast majority of business ventures end in failure.

Most product launches fail, most innovations implode, most mergers meltdown, most CEOs misfire, most R&D founders, most advertising campaigns crater, most long-range forecasts flub, except those that predict periodic gales of "creative destruction."[2] History shows that in business life there is no such thing as untrammeled success, only organizations, brands, leaders and suchlike that have staved off failure for longest.

History also shows that those who accept failure, learn from failure, and absolutely refuse to be beaten by failure are those who win through in the end. Walt Disney, for example, was repeatedly disparaged by the Hollywood establishment, royally ripped off by perfidious partners and sank every single cent he had into an expensive experimental short, *Steamboat Willie*. Fortunately, the steamboat floated and Walt never looked back.

Then there's Tide. The world's premier soap powder was once the ugly duckling of the detergent market. Its development caused all sorts of intractable technological headaches. The P&G product police tried to kill it off on numberless occasions. However, a ferociously fanatical Proctoid, Dick Byerly, resolutely refused to let it die. He formed a surreptitious skunk works,[3] decades before skunk works got the Tom Peters seal of approval, and eventually won the day in 1947, when the brand was launched to unparalleled consumer acceptance. Not only did Tide clean up, it wiped the floor with the competition. It does so to this day.

Take James Dyson. He spent twelve years developing his proprietary bag-less vacuum cleaner. He was ignored by venture capitalists; laughed at by the industry; and down on his uppers more than once. Today his polychromatic brand bestrides the vacuum cleaner business. Look-alike products are being manufactured by once-disdainful competitors, all of whom have embraced Dyson's bag-less revolution. He has ground their faces into the dirt and hoovered them up for good measure.

And then, of course, there's Johnson & Johnson. It suffices to record that the corporate credo of New Brunswick's baby-powder to Tylenol powerhouse is "failure is our most important product." This involves trying lots of new things, keeping those that work, discarding those that don't and, at all times, encouraging employees to take the initiative, to experiment incessantly, to fail better brilliantly.

Waiting for Brevity

Tenacity may have been the principal personality trait of the indomitable Irishman, but his aesthetic trademark was *brevity*. Beckett's complete corpus can be contained in a single volume. In a sixty-year career, he only wrote three full-length plays, six substantive novels and an (admittedly large) number of occasional theatrical pieces. His works were not only short, by and large, but they got shorter and shorter through time. He constantly pared and pruned his playlets. His stagings were spare, his cast lists short, his language compressed to the point of collapse. He reveled in silence, both onstage and off. Sam rarely discussed his works, refused to give interviews, avoided first nights like the plague and famously absented himself from the Nobel Prize giving ceremony. He was the minimalist's minimalist.

Minimalism has its place, to be sure, but many might maintain that the marketplace isn't it. Maximalism, rather, is the trait that marketing types are renowned for. We live, do we not, in a world of superabundant similitude, where countless identikit products compete in every conceivable product category—cars, computers, consultants, cell phones, cellulite removal creams, et cetera—and where each offering has to shout ever-louder in order to be heard. We live, do we not, in a world of bullhorn brands, where every organization is customer oriented, where marketing strategies are sourced from the same standard textbooks, and where those with the biggest bullhorns win. We live, do we not, in a world of shrill shilling, piercing pitching and cacophonous commercials, where there is no reward for silence.

Or do we? Sometimes the best way of selling a product or service is by not selling. Not only does not-selling sell well, but in today's Babel of bellowing brands it imbues *sotto voce* offerings with an irresistible air of authenticity, exclusivity and desirability. Godiva chocolates, for instance, make much of their lo-profile luxuriousness and rely on word-of-mouth to sell their melt-in-the-mouth indulgences. Muji is the modern master of minimalist magniloquence, its stores are a monument to the art of restraint, an aesthetic of asceticism. Aldi's absolute refusal to advertise is a wonderful advertisement for its lo-cost, no-frills, won't-be-beaten-on-price grocery retailing operation, perhaps the most profitable in Europe. Hermès bespoke handbags fly so far below the radar that there's a waiting list for the waiting list, which gets ever-longer as unavailability increases consumer demand. Armani, likewise, is living proof that silence says chic. The look is low-key. The range is narrow. The cut is singular. The fabrics are unique. The color palette is muted. The retail stores are few. The ancillaries are limited. The diffusion lines are confined. The concessions are controlled. The pre-eminent promotional tactic is celebrity endorsement. The brand whispers class, elegance, restraint. Less is always more where Armani is concerned. Understatement is the order of the day. Every day.

Waiting for Contingency

In 1939, Samuel Beckett was strolling back to his Parisian apartment in the company of friends. He got into an altercation with a pushy panhandler, who stabbed the penniless poet, almost killing him. Some time later, Beckett asked about his assailant's motive, only to be informed that there was no reason for the crime. He was attacked by chance. He had avoided death by sheer good fortune. This incident profoundly influenced Beckett's outlook and an air of *contingency* pervades his published work. Luck looms large in Beckett's cosmology. Lucky is one of his most memorable characters.

Luck, admittedly, is something that rarely features on the B-school agenda. Management scientists live in a luckless universe, near enough. Predictability is presumed. Unforeseeables are foreseen. Robust models and rigorous frameworks are par for the course. Despite the underpinning precepts of probability theory and contingency approaches to management understanding—to say nothing of resource-based theories of the firm—the overwhelming ethos is one of analysis, planning, and control. Chance, kismet and suchlike are all-but ruled out of court.

Set against this, however, business history reveals that happy accident is extremely important. Most managers will confirm that serendipity played a significant part in their careers, their creations, their accomplishments. So much so, that when it comes to business success, a scintilla of good fortune is worth shovelfuls of strategic planning. Happenstance, for instance, gave us Velcro, Kevlar, Corn Flakes, Band Aids, Post-it Notes, and Nike's waffle sole, to say nothing of Teflon, penicillin, dynamite, artificial dyes and polyurethane. McDonald's fast food empire was founded by chance, when milkshake shaker supremo Ray Kroc paid a visit to the San Bernadino roadside stand that ordered eight of his machines. Wal-Mart's much-admired greeters were first introduced in Crowley, Louisiana, simply because the store manager was plagued with shoplifters. American Express Travelers Checks resulted from an executive's unfortunate experiences on holiday in Europe, when no one would cash his letters of credit. Pfizer was searching for an angina alleviant, when it stumbled over Viagra's ithyphallic side-effects, much to the delight of middle-aged men worldwide. Ikea, incredibly, discovered the flat-pack furniture concept when an employee, Gillis Lundgren, couldn't fit a bulky table into the trunk of his car, so he promptly cut off its legs for convenience.

Steven Spielberg, similarly, has had close encounters of the serendipitous kind, specifically with *Close Encounters*. Despite his earlier success with *Jaws*, *Close Encounters* was expected to flatline at the box office. Cost overruns, production delays, and incessant interruptions from a nearly bankrupt studio led many industry insiders to fear the worst. Then, of all things, a series of massive power outages occurred on the east coast. These publicized the power-outage-inducing aliens in *Close Encounters*, the movie went on to earn a record $281 million at the box office, and Columbia Studios was judiciously snatched from the jaws of bankruptcy. As the old showbiz saying has it, "God made the heavens but luck makes the stars."

Waiting for Ambiguity

Serendipity is one thing, *ambiguity* is something else entirely. Ambiguity, in fact, would be Beckett's middle name, if it weren't already Barclay. Beckett's brilliance lies not simply in his ability to challenge and undermine theatrical convention—nothing happens, twice—but in his refusal to explain what his plays mean. When actors asked for guidance, or critics queried the creator, Sam resorted to stony silence and repeated some variant of "I only know what's on the page" or "let meanings fall where they may." However, because his works were so empty, so allusive, so seemingly symbolic (Who is Godot?; Does he exist?; Is she coming or not?), a veritable swarm of commentators, interpreters and dissertation-writing drones promptly descended on the plays, thereby keeping them permanently in the public eye. Beckett may not have invented buzz marketing, but he certainly benefited from it.

Ambiguity, yet again, is viewed with suspicion in contemporary corporate circles. Since the days of Sam Beckett himself, managers have been urged to eschew ambivalence. In the 1950s, Rosser Reeves made a case for the Unique Selling Proposition, and relentlessly hammered it home, a bit like his legendary Anacin adverts. In the 1970s, Al Ries and Jack Trout positioned themselves as the gurus of positioning, where brands aim to occupy a clear-cut niche in consumer cognition, everything from safety (Volvo) and freedom (Marlboro) to fortitude (Guinness) and sexuality (Gucci). The one-word-one-brand tradition is still going strong, though it now trades under terms like identity, essence, DNA, spirit, promise, personality, mission, vision, value, soul, mindshare and many more.

Ambiguity, nevertheless, is not to be sneezed at. To the contrary, when meanings are unclear, consumer intrigue increases, involvement intensifies, and commitment accumulates. Consider, for example, the latter-day emergence of polymorphic marketing, where brands embrace several strategic options that were once considered antithetical. Target, the burgeoning housewares outlet, retails exclusive products to a mass market. Southwest Airlines offers outstanding customer service *and* rock bottom prices, as does JetBlue.

Pixar studios produce movies, such as *Toy Story*, *Monsters Inc.* and *Finding Nemo*, which appeal to children and adults simultaneously. The Body Shop is back on top thanks to "masstige," cheap and cheerful cosmetics with middle- to up-market attributes. Red Bull soda combines hedonism and health, energy and enervation, the injurious and the innocuous. Prada's recently-launched perfume is predicated on a plurality of personalized appeals ("I am the first and the last. I am the honored one and the scorned one. I am the wife and the virgin"). Madonna, meanwhile, adopts and abandons every image imaginable, from sexually ambiguous virago to Kabala-espousing supermom. She embodies brand guru Wally Olins' sagacious words, "great brands are like amoebae or plasticine. They can be shaped, twisted and turned in all sorts of ways yet still remain recognizable."[4]

Waiting for Memory

The plays, poems and prose of Samuel Beckett are nothing if not paradoxical. They are also monuments to the power, pain and persistence of *memory*. From his first "proper" publication on Proust's philosophy of remembrance to the minimalist late-period works like *Worstward Ho* or *Stirrings Still*, Beckett's vision is sepia in tone, nostalgic in content. Sure, his yen for yesteryear is far from rose-tinted—*Krapp's Last Tape* is a painful reminder of the pains of reminiscence—but the recyclings, refrains, returns and constant repetitions that punctuate his corpus are timeless testaments to the grip of the past.

It almost goes without saying that western capitalism is not renowned for looking backward. New and improved, onward and upward, washes whiter than white, even more for your money et cetera are the leitmotifs of executive suites worldwide. Recent years, nevertheless, have witnessed a retro revolution, where old is the new "new," the past is ever-present, and future shock has been superseded by yestershock. Retro is all around. Retro autos (like the P.T. Cruiser and BMW Mini Cooper), retro radios (shellac outside, digital inside), retro sneakers (P.F. Flyers, Chuck Taylor All Stars), retro video games (from *Pacman* to *Doom 3*), retro rock music (The Strokes, The Darkness, etc.), retro house-furnishings (courtesy of Restoration Hardware, Ralph Lauren et al), retro movies (remakes, comic book rip-offs, sequels of prequels of *Star Wars*), retro television (*The Muppets* are back, Kermit akimbo), retro communities (Disney's celebrated Celebration), retro celebrities (Donald Trump returns, comb-over intacto), retro commercials (Britney Spears coos "Come Alive" for Pepsi) and countless others, are all the retro rage.

Retro, moreover, isn't just an American thing. In Italy, management training programs based on gladiatorial contests are going from strength to strength. In France, old-time dance halls, *guingelles*, have made a dramatic comeback. In Germany, a wave of nostalgia—*ostalgie*—is carrying consumers back to the good old bad old days when east was awful and west was best. In Britain, the fabulously successful website FriendsReunited is putting mid-life-stricken multitudes in touch with former school-chums and aging teenage heartthrobs. In Ireland, the *Titanic* is resurfacing once more, in a retroscape dedicated to the greatest new product failure in history. In Australia, the outback is back in again, on account of ancient mineral deposits that are economically viable once more. In New Zealand, tourism has been transformed by *Lord of the Rings*, the blockbusting movies of the '60s bestseller, set in a mythical medieval landscape, albeit based on Tolkien's painful memories of the First World War.

Retro's a go-go, no doubt about it, but many wonder why it's happening and what it all means. For some, retro is all down to demographics, as ageing, affluent baby boomers buy their Cadillac Escalades while recollecting that it's been a long time since they rock 'n' rolled to Led Zeppelin. For others, Valhalla's call is neither here nor there, since retro products seem new to younger generations of consumers, who regard ersatz nostalgia as the next big thing. Regardless of the reasons, the key point is that retrospection is indicative of exhaustion, enervation, expiry, the end. When every idea, approach, advert, strategy, tactic, marketing plan and suchlike has been tried several times over, there's nothing left to do but recycle the old, to keep on going and going, even when there's no place to go to that hasn't been gone to many times before. Or, as pessimism's poster boy, Sam Beckett, put it at the climax of his harrowing novel, *The Unnamable*, "You must go on. I can't go on. I'll go on."

Waiting for Narrativity

The crucial issue Beckett faced, the esthetic dilemma that drove him to the depths of despair, involved *narrativity*. Beckett was writing at the tail end of Modernism, when every conceivable literary experiment had been tried by Virginia Woolf, T.S. Eliot, Ezra Pound and, not least, James Joyce. Beckett fell in with, worked alongside and was deeply influenced by his fellow Irishman, the seditious scourge of the vocabulary constabulary. Joyce, however, couldn't be surpassed, so Beckett became different. He reinvented the nature of narrative, novelistic and theatrical alike. He abandoned established narrative conventions—plot, character, action, resolution even—and replaced them with abstraction, evasion, austerity, enigma, abrogation, equivocation. With nothing, near enough.

Modernist writers famously questioned, usurped and ripped apart the premises of narrative. But not so contemporary management consultants. Storytelling is the latest corporate craze. Organizational parables, homilies, legends, yarns, fables and so forth are being exhumed from the archives, recounted around short-course campfires and painstakingly recorded in company chapbooks, chronicles, circulars, CSR reports etc. Great American management novels are crash landing in airport bookstores nationwide. Fairy stories for VPs are being spun by cheese movers, squirrel wranglers, and giant hairball spitters-cum-pitchers. Boardrooms are besieged by quick buck makers claiming that lessons can be learned from the published works of Shakespeare, Milton, Machiavelli, Marcel Proust, Theodore Dreiser and, heaven help us, Samuel Beckett...

The essential point, of course, is not that narratives are nugatory. On the contrary, it is widely accepted that storytelling is a primal human activity. Philosophers, psychologists, anthropologists and theologians agree that, for good or ill, we live our lives as narratives. The salient point, rather, is that the repertoire of 21st-century management narratives is drawn from a very narrow range of possibilities. Most are variants of the quest, or rags-to-riches, or indeed cobbled together from compendia of sci-fi/fairy-tale/fantasy-adventure/murder-mystery/war-story clichés.

Yet, as every road warrior, cubicle conscript, and first class cabin shogun can attest, fairy tales rarely come true in business life. The good guys don't always win in the end, nor are the heroes rewarded, nor are the culprits caught red-handed. Nor, for that matter, are the stories as straightforward as corporate tale-tellers, yarn-spinners and dream-weavers imply. Great brand stories, for instance, are invariably multi-stories, stories piled upon stories *Arabian Knights-*, *Canterbury Tales-*, *Cloud Atlas*-style. Harry Potter is a $4 billion brand story, a rags-to-riches tale par excellence. Nevertheless, there's much more to the Harry Potter brand story than "impoverished author makes good." There's the story of the barnstorming bookselling, there's the story of the billion dollar movie franchise, there's the story of the gratuitous tie-in merchandise, there's the story of the anti-witchcraft critics, there's the story of the over-enthusiastic consumers, there's the story of the on-going, non-stop publicity campaign, there's the story of the inexplicable causes of Pottermania, there's the unresolved story of what'll happen next now that the seven-book brand is reaching its climax. Each of these stories draws sustenance from, contributes to, and occasionally contradicts, the other brand stories. The inevitable narrative upshot is a self-replenishing goblet of fiery fighting fairy tales.

It thus seems that once-upon-a-time to happily-ever-after is insufficient nowadays. The narratological issues that exercised the Joyces, Woolfs and Becketts of this world have yet to be addressed by today's top-dollar chronicle cobblers. They're long overdue. We're still waiting for the *Waiting for* of corporate storytelling.

Waiting for Author-Ity

Although he isn't exactly everyone's idea of a better business spokesperson, Samuel Beckett's corporate credo cannot fail to strike a chord with 21st century managers. Some of his precepts are widely shared and much discussed (tenacity, narrativity), some are commonplace but rarely commented on (contingency, memory), and some run counter to conventional wisdom yet contain a grain of truth notwithstanding (ambiguity, brevity). However, there is one strand of Beckettism that is utterly antithetical to common knowledge. And that strand is *author-ity*.

Amiable though he could be, Samuel Beckett brooked no opposition. He refused to alter, adapt or amend his work. His plays were staged to his exact, indeed exacting, specifications. He took legal steps to prevent unauthorized or otherwise illegitimate performances. He resisted all forms of censorship and abridgement, as well as anything that smacked of editorial control. In private, admittedly, he was always prepared to compromise—give and take is almost unavoidable in the theatre—but in public he was a perfectionist, an absolutist, an authoritarian through-and-through. He refused, in effect, to listen to his customers, be they actors, audiences, producers, directors, commentators or critics. Especially not critics.

This anti-customer orientation is unconventional, to say the least. Customer focus is one of the foundation stones of contemporary business life. *The* foundation stone, in point of fact. Every CEO worth his or her salt is a courtier of King Customer. Every management guru readily acknowledges the divine right of consumers and pays extravagant tribute to their suzerainty. Every marketing strategist subscribes to customer sovereignty, while seeking ever more ostentatious means of currying consumer favor. These days, satisfaction is insufficient. Delight is de rigueur. Enchantment is even better. Only euphoria will do. Ecstasy is next in line, enrapture thereafter, with ravissement to follow. The orgasmatron, presumably, awaits.

The problem here is not customer satisfaction grade inflation, or the fact that today's superlatives "have lost most of their charm," as Beckett once observed. The problem is that it is possible to become far too customer focused and to fall into the trap of assuming that customers know best. Sometimes it is better to step back from total customer orientation and recognize that, far from being always right, the customer is often wrong. Dead wrong. Innumerable innovative products, services, advertising campaigns, etc., have been roundly rejected by consumers prior to their triumphant release, everything from CNN and Chrysler's Minivan to the Sony Walkman and Boeing's 747. It is a mistake, what's more, to uncritically accept customer input or listen too attentively to the murmurings of the market. Consumers may be opinionated—many are—but they aren't omniscient.

More pertinently perhaps, and irrespective of the received wisdom that suggests otherwise, it is perfectly possible to be successful in business without being customer oriented. Ikea's reluctance to coddle customers is legendary—riots and fistfights in the vicinity of its retail stores are a regular occurrence—but Ikea's bottom line is second to none in its sector. Ryanair, the top dog of European low-cost airlines, is renowned for its maltreatment of paying customers—CEO Michael O'Leary boasts about it—yet Ryanair is one of the most profitable airlines in the western world. Bill Gates, furthermore, can be decidedly cavalier when it comes to customer care. The FCC, no less, formally ruled that Microsoft "harmed consumers in ways that are immediate and easily discernible."[5] However, when it comes to what really matters on Wall Street, Microsoft can't be beaten. Belittled, yes; beaten, never.

Now, none of this means that customers are irrelevant. Business can't do business without customers. And that's that. What it *does* mean is that undue customer obsession is unhealthy. Customers have their place, a very important place. But that place is not on a pedestal. Servility can cause as many problems as hostility. Although customer satisfaction is vital, customer dis-satisfaction is important as well. If they're not somewhat dissatisfied—by marketers who intimate that their existing stuff needs to be replaced or that they suffer from some easily eradicated malady—then consumers won't be motivated to put things right by buying what we're selling. There's more to marketing than selling solutions. The problems we have solutions for have to be sold as well. Marketing involves dissatisfying and satisfying simultaneously.

Waiting for Celticity

It follows, then, that instead of continuing to pander to customers, it's time to become more Beckett-like in our dealings with them. Rather than strive to be ever-more consumer centric, it is better to become congenitally concept centric. That is, to situate the brand, the product, the service, the offer, the message, the experience, the something we're selling at the center of the corporate universe. That's what Bill Gates does. Microsoft comes first. That's what Ryanair does. Fares come first. That's what Ikea does. First come first served. (Eventually.) That's what all great brands do. That's how great businesses are built. Business doesn't come to those who wait on customers. It comes to those who make customers wait, providing the waiting is managed properly.

In this regard, it is entirely appropriate that when *Waiting for Godot* was remounted in New York, six months after the Miami debacle, it was advertised, not as the "laugh sensation of two continents" but as a very difficult work, one that is off-putting, offensive and unlikely to appeal to the general public. It was a play for the cognoscenti, the discerning few, the tiniest proportion of the Big Apple's inhabitants, seven thousand at most. Almost inevitably, the theatre was besieged. *Godot* ran for months. Beckett never looked back. Thinking different triumphed.

In this regard, it is equally appropriate that Apple's celebrated "think different" advertising campaign, the one that cemented the brand's remarkable comeback, featured not only Einstein, Picasso and Gandhi, but one Samuel Barclay Beckett. Clearly, it takes one to know one. No one fails better than Apple. If ever a brand embodied the seven secrets of Sam's success, it is the one that aspired to, and continues to aspire to, the singularly ambiguous Beckettian state, "insanely great."

There is, then, an overarching takeaway from Samuel Beckett's business philosophy. Namely, that the individual components of the Nobel prizewinner's conceptual cosmology—tenacity, brevity, contingency, ambiguity, memory, narrativity, author-ity—together comprise a characteristically Celtic worldview which is antithetical to the essentially Anglo-Saxon ethos that dominates contemporary management thought. Whereas the Saxon perspective foregrounds facts, figures, order, rigor, and incredible attention to detail (all laudable and necessary traits), Celticity relies on imaginative leaps, compelling storytelling, irreverent iconoclasm, eloquent silences, indomitable obduracy, wellsprings of memory, and the crock of good fortune at the end of chimerical commercial rainbows. Both are needed in business.

Samuel Beckett, admittedly, was a reluctant Celt, as he was everything else. Nevertheless, he epitomizes the irrepressibly irreverent spirit of today's post–Saxon Entertainment Economy. If nothing else, in fact, his fifty year old theatrical masterpiece reminds us that "habit is a great deadener." It is time, is it not, to break our Saxon habits and resurrect the inner Celt. It is time, is it not, to be like Beckett. It is time, is it not, to "Try again. Fail again. Fail better."[6]

Notes

1. James Knowlson, *Damned to Fame: The Life of Samuel Beckett* (London: Bloomsbury, 1996), 420. *Editor's note: In standardizing references for this paper, I changed citation styles and abbreviated Professor Brown's extensive APA referencing.*
2. J.A. Schumpeter, *Capitalism, Socialism and Democracy* (London: Routledge, 1994).
3. *Editor's note: An informal working group, sometimes secretive or isolated from the larger company.*
4. Wally Olins, *On Brand* (London: Thames & Hudson, 2003), 18.
5. J. Heilemann, *Pride Before the Fall: The Trials of Bill Gates and the End of the Microsoft Era* (New York: Perennial, 2001), 194.
6. Samuel Beckett, *Worstward Ho* (London: Calder Publications, 1983), 20.

The Strange Case of Detective Fiction

P.J. Murphy

Images of Beckett abound throughout popular culture and detective fiction is a particularly rich field for the investigation of the various ways in which a number of critical perspectives on Beckett's work have been developed within popular culture. For such popular culture adaptations can entail much more than merely commercial commodification and kitsch, much more than simply pedestrian instances of cultural littering and name-dropping. Major examples of the adaptation of Beckett's work within the genre of detective fiction by Bartholomew Gill, Charles Willeford, and Bill James offer challenging and creative ways in which the binary of so-called "high" culture critique versus a so-called "low" culture degradation might be dismantled. In *The Elsewhere Community*, Hugh Kenner examines Western culture's insatiable hunger for stimulation encountered in an exotic elsewhere and makes the point throughout his study that "high and low culture aren't in opposition; the more you know of either, the more you enjoy the other" and concludes that there is no distinction between so-called high and low culture: "There's no high culture because there's no other culture that needs to be set aside as low."[1] Kenner's anecdote about meeting Samuel Beckett for the first time in Paris in 1958 in preparation for his ground breaking critical study also neatly draws together the abolition of such pseudo-cultural divides and wittily anticipates the linkages with detective fiction which we will be focusing on. Kenner relates how he jumped the queue of those waiting with written requests to see Beckett: on the plane over from Montreal he read a French detective novel which featured the use of a "pneumatique" in which your sealed message was put in a brass cylinder and dropped down a pneumatic tube which sped it across Paris (through the famous sewers) to the post office nearest its recipient where it was then hand delivered by a bicycle courier to the addressee. Kenner says the ploy worked like a charm and within a few hours he was in touch with Beckett, thereby stealing a march on his rivals for Beckett's attention.[2]

The various adaptations of Beckett's work in the detective fiction under consideration in this chapter reveal a threefold pattern: such depictions often afford complementary views of the prevalent academic views of Beckett, thus sometimes pointing, albeit indirectly, to the need to challenge such stereotypical readings, wherever they might be situated; popular culture irreverence can also supply through parody a much needed comic corrective often lacking in "serious" academic studies; indeed, popular culture recyclings can in some instances even produce innovative works which afford new critical insights. Bartholomew Gill's *The Death of a Joyce Scholar* (1989) is a campus "whodunit" which reflects in a clever and amusing way a number of stereotypical as well as ambiguous responses to Beckett. Charles Willeford's *The Burnt Orange Heresy* (1971) is a brilliant parody of the formulations of "nothingness" in the avant-garde, with pointed references to Beckett and his *Proust*. Bill James's *Astride a Grave* (1991) is a comic rewriting of the famous phrase from *Waiting for Godot*, and *Roses, Roses* (1993), his masterpiece in the detective fiction genre, incorporates Beckett's *Endgame* into its very structure. Beckett is indeed alive and well in detective fiction and the critical perspectives afforded in these works could be applied to other areas in which there is a dialogical engagement with Beckett's works in popular culture.

Before engaging these particular works, a few supplementary introductory remarks on Beckett as a reader and writer of detective fiction will serve to reinforce Kenner's important point about the inherent falsity of the "high/low" binary while at the same time acknowledging that different literary traditions with different expectations are at play in terms of a consideration of Beckett *and* popular culture vis-à-vis Beckett *in* popular culture. James Knowlson makes the point several times in the authorized biography that Beckett "devoured" detective fiction as a diversionary respite from his own work at times when it was particularly strenuous, and that he was especially fond of Agatha Christie's puzzles and French "série noir" thrillers.[3] Nat Gould, a writer of equestrian detective stories à la Dick Francis, was much admired by Beckett as a stylist,[4] but when he is brought into the discussion of how to read Joyce's *Work in Progress* in Beckett's essay, "Dante... Bruno. Vico.. Joyce" (1929), it is to underline the extensive literary gap between a writer of popular detective fiction and Joyce the masterful modernist innovator: "it is as inadequate to speak of 'reading' *Work in Progress* as it would be extravagant to speak of 'apprehending' the work of the late Nat Gould."[5]

As a reader of detective fiction, Beckett moved freely (like many of us) between the "puzzle" traditions and the more hard-boiled noir thrillers. The reference to Beckett in Robin Winks's distinction between such traditions is particularly suggestive: "The classical puzzle, while not wholly gone, has been displaced in large measure by the novel of police procedure [...], by a kind of gritty *Waiting for Godot*; by the psychological thriller in which the question is not 'whodunit' but 'whydunit'; and by the spy thriller."[6] Seeing the foremost mystery play of our time as a sort of "police procedural"—"gritty" or otherwise—does draw attention to the basic underlying principle of "detecting" texts from *Oedipus* onwards. It was certainly no surprise to learn that Beckett was reputedly one of the very earliest readers of Robbe-Grillet's first novel, *The Erasers*, to recognize many of the Oedipal parallels built into this adaptation of the classic detective story.[7] No surprise since Beckett had already carried out similar adaptations in his own writing: for example, Beckett's first published novel *Murphy* (1938), has always struck me in some respects as a re-writing of Dashiell Hammett's *The Maltese Falcon* (1930). There are indeed many parallels in terms of characters, subplot shenanigans, mise-en-scène, and—above all—the fruitless gyrations around an empty or missing center—whether it be Murphy and his "mind" or the missing Maltese Falcon.[8] Sam Spade, in the end, is caught up in what *Murphy* terms "the ethical yoyo," whereas Murphy the nihilist is, fittingly enough, blown up. Cooper in *Murphy* is a prototype of future detective figures in Beckett's own writing; Camier is a detective and carries with him on his ill-fated quest with Mercier his notebook in which he details his various clients; most famously Moran in *Molloy II* is a detective or secret agent working for the mysterious Youdi who communicates with him via Moran's handler Gaber—a novel which transforms the bourgeois "cozy" into a "noir" nightmare as it is famously "midnight" and "not midnight," as the ending of the work ambiguously suspends itself.

Beckett's adaptations of the detective genre would fit neatly in the category of what Patricia Merivale has dubbed the metaphysical detective story, namely, "a text that parodies or subverts traditional detective story conventions" and in which "the detective hero himself becomes ... the murderer he has been seeking"[9]; in short, postmodern mysteries enveloped by various ambiguities and with a pointed absence of closure. To pursue further this line of enquiry would be illuminating for a Beckett *and* popular culture critique; but the primary focus in the present discussion is on Beckett *in* popular culture, on how writers of detective fiction in the more traditional and conventional sense have adapted Beckett to *their* needs: whereas Beckett took the detective genre "up market," more conventional practitioners will in very interesting and critically challenging ways bring Beckett "down market" (the up/down binary here *not* to be identified with the sense of cultural superiority embedded in the high/low pairing).

In Bartholomew Gill's *The Death of a Joyce Scholar* (1989)—to cut a long story short—the Beckett scholar "dunit." Doctoral candidate David Holderness, depicted as an ersatz "Beckett clone without Beckett's depth, wit, or sympathy for the human condition,"[10] knocks off his professor at Trinity College, Dublin, one Kevin Coyle, a veritable second-coming of James Joyce as postmodernist critic, who has blocked submission of his dissertation. Of particular interest to the present discussion is how Gill's detective story is larded with stereotypical assumptions about the relative merits of the work of Joyce and Beckett. For example, Professor Fergus Flood, a colleague of the above named principals, launches at the drop of hat into a mini-lecture on Beckett and the so-called "novel of incompetence":

> By incompetence Beckett does not mean novels written by incompetent authors. He means that, unlike Joyce, he cannot assume the possibility of communication among human beings, much less between human beings and the collective unconscious [75].

The good professor then expounds on the well-worn thematic that "for Beckett words don't work," along with the oft-echoed corollary, "But if the whole point of communication is to confirm life and existence, then we must try, if only to know we live. With words that are inexact and ultimately unavailing" (75). Asked if he wants to hear anymore, the poor plod who is accompanying Chief Superintendent Peter McGarr for this "interview" hastily retorts, "Not today Professor. I think we catch on—Beckett's novels are worse than his plays. Now I know why he won a Nobel Prize" (75). The popular culture irreverence here redeems the academic banter (shades of Lynch and Stephen Dedalus in *Portrait*). The point, however, is that this mini-lecture is essentially a composite of leading ideas in mainstream criticism, indeed a fair to middling brow version of same. This is hardly surprising given that Bartholomew Gill is a pseudonym for Mark McGarrity, well-known American author of Irish crime novels, who completed an MLitt thesis at Trinity College, Dublin entitled "Language and the Narrative Voice of Samuel Beckett," and David Holderness's dissertation on Beckett even bears the same title as McGarrity's senior thesis at Brown, "Less and Less, Yes: A Study of Style and Narrative Voice in the Novels of Samuel Beckett" (221). In short, the popular culture genre of the detective story dramatizes, circa 1989, the year of Beckett's death, the "life and death" issues inherent in the Joyce-Beckett question, which, however vexed, is regarded as central to a host of important issues concerning the potentialities and limitations of contemporary fiction and the unsettling transitions between modernism and postmodernism.

The most striking feature of Gill's handling of this critical debate is its conflicted and contradictory nature in terms of its evaluation of the Beckett project itself and of Beckett's status as a writer in competition with Joyce. Beckett is, of course, taken for granted by the academic contingent in the novel as a celebrity author "genius" of a particularly Irish type, post–Joyce. But whereas Joyce's work has been "assimilated" and somehow come to terms with in so far as Kevin Coyle the Trinity College Professor is regarded as an authoritative spokesman—critic of his vision (albeit updated with Derridean "grammatology"—his great study published posthumously is entitled *Phon/Antiphon*), the Beckett critic David Holderness is throughout the book designated as a "fake" Beckett surrogate and his readings dismissed as mere "Beckett drivel." There is, of course, a patent irony at play here in so far as Bartholomew Gill as Mark McGarrity was a Beckett scholar himself at Trinity College and hence his negative presentation of the Beckett critic in this novel might in some ways be regarded as being self-reflexively critical of himself and the views of Beckett as forwarded by mainstream academic studies. The problem is that this critical stance, whilst arguably implicit at times, is never developed to the level of a subversive parody of such stereotypical views as foregrounded by Professor Flood's potted lectures on the subject as cited above.

The closest the novel comes to such a critical perspective is found towards its conclusion when McGarr at the Shelbourne Hotel launch of Kevin Coyle's book is engaged in an exchange with one Diarmuid Cox, who is at the Institute for Advanced Studies and is a friend of McGarr's wife. The discussion is essentially a reprise of the views on Beckett expounded earlier by Fergus Flood, and since McGarr has been through this once, he does manage to hold his own—and wittily at that—in this second go-round. Here's an excerpt from their dialogue—Cox speaking first and McGarr responding in turn:

"But if the thrust of literature, as we've known it since the Renaissance, has been the attempt—"

"—to define oneself as an individual in one's own term, then using the words of others makes it impossible. The second problem is that we think—"

"*Conceive*, Cox corrected, of the person as being an essential—"Blank slate."

"Meant." Cox's gaze was now stony. "And finally, modern philosophers tell us that—"

"—words don't work."

Cox nodded. "The naming process is too general, and essentially flawed. The only way to name a thing truly specifically is to negate everything else in the universe, which is absurd."

"But we are forced to try, since, poor fools that they are—"

McGarr waited for Cox to carry on.

"—words are all we have. But try minimally we must," Cox added, if only to have the last word, it seemed to McGarr. "Since the entire process of confirming our existence and therefore being human is just a nasty little joke that is being played upon each of us individually, Beckett calls it the *risus puris*, 'The laugh down the snout at that which is—silence please—*cruel*'" [193–4].

This is handled very cleverly, as a sort of academic vaudeville banter along the lines of *Waiting for Godot* Act II, which in this instance is further confirmation of Vivian Mercier's bons mots about how "nothing happens—*twice*." So McGarr has indeed learned at least to mimic the Beckett intellectual game, at least to cocktail party standards; but his mocking echolalia here never really approaches the dialogical in the Bakhtinian sense of challenging and contesting the status quo with alternative readings. The satirical potential here never advances beyond the recognition that all of the above expressed views—and which McGarr is obviously party to, especially so since he hasn't actually read Beckett—sound like prime candidates for *Private Eye's* "Pseuds Corner." Any implicit critique of the party line in Beckett studies—and the above views are a more or less fair summary of some of the guiding tenets of Beckett studies through the sixties to the late eighties when Gill wrote *The Death of a Joyce Scholar*—is subsumed by the complicity of all parties in subscribing to the rhetoric of the "art of failure" school of Beckett criticism, which has so far dominated discussion of his works. And the "pre-scribed" nature of so many judgements about Beckett is neatly caught in Gill's rendition of McGarr's "shared dialogue" with Cox. David Holderness's views are not fundamentally different from those expressed above by Gill's academic mouthpieces Flood and Cox: it is, after all, clear that Holderness's work is deemed highly respectable and meets the standards for a PhD at Trinity College. The only motivation of substance given for the Joyce scholar "killing" the Beckett scholar's career is formulated within a litany of stereotypical literary judgements:

> Analogies are often inaccurate or obtuse, but Kinch's approach to literature and life was indeed Joycean. It was inclusive and encyclopaedic and sometimes even rough and banal, though studiously so. Like Beckett's, David's is exclusive, elegant, and nearly minimalist in viewpoint. Each considered the other's a dead end [198].

In short, the visions of the two writers are presented as diametrically opposed, which is still today an all too common formulation of the Joyce-Beckett question.

Gill's literary fable about two of the most important writers of the twentieth-century as recast by the popular culture genre of the detective story does, nevertheless, possess some critical value. The genre writing does call attention, however inadvertently, to the inadequacy of the so-called "standard" interpretations of the academic world. The novel verges on a parody of such views but veers away from such prospects since it has no alternative reading of the Joyce-Beckett relationship to draw upon. Hence its would-be resolution of this critical "impasse" reads as a sort of low brow escapism. The novel is premised upon a clever doubling of art and life: Kevin Coyle is murdered on Bloomsday and his body is found at Prospect Cemetery in Glashevin and echoes of the Childs murder in *Ulysses* dutifully trotted out along with attempts to superimpose parallels to Beckett's stabbing in Paris. But such analogies do not develop in any significant way and are caught up in the convoluted hi-jinks (and sexual "low-jinks") of the often daft as a brush subplot. The eighteen chapters of *The Death of a Joyce Scholar* only vaguely echo *Ulysses'* configuration, of course, but the last chapters are more pointedly brought into conjunction. In Gill's ending, Ru'tie Brennahan is having a torrid affair with her fellow member of McGarr's Dublin Murder Squad, Hughie Ward. Her invocation of Molly Bloom's "he said I was a flower of the mountain…" combines a pastoral romance of her Kerry roots with a more hard core harlequin romance of her relationship with Ward. So: the literary impasse of Joyce—Beckett relations is side-tracked in favor of an escapist "low brow" resolution of a novel which in its more "fair to middling" brow moments did afford an interesting mirroring in popular culture format of various "high brow" literary questions.

Of course, McGarr as Beckett commentator knows not of what he speaks; his witticisms are really psittacisms—mechanical repetitions of words or phrases parrot—fashion (he barely crawls through *Ulysses* with the help of various "trots" by novel's end, and of Beckett's work, particularly the prose, he seems to have no first-hand knowledge at all). And the same applies to the would-be literary experts—the various professors: all they spout is a version of the Joyce-Beckett party-line circa 1989. Hence the unintended irony of the book's epigraph from Bishop Berkley, "We Irishmen think otherwise": no, when it comes to Joyce-Beckett relations, these stage—Irishmen in Gill's novel think well within the box of stereotypical approaches to this question. It is only with my own *Beckett's Dedalus: Dialogical Engagements with Joyce in Beckett's Fiction* (2009), some twenty years later, that there is a comprehensive re-thinking of this issue that foregrounds how the Joyce-Beckett question entails a telling number of complementary as well as contestatory aspects. The two perceived academic rivals—the Joyce scholar and the Beckett scholar—did in fact have much more in common than they could have imagined in 1989; we now know that Beckett's relationship with Joyce is much more complex and critically challenging once we have moved beyond such stereotypical assumptions. Consequently, *The Death of a Joyce Scholar* never effectively attains a critical perspective on its subject matter, popular culture irreverence petering out in the face of standardized readings, however simplified and distorted, of mainstream academic views.

Such is most definitely not the case in Charles Willeford's brilliantly noirish crime novel, *The Burnt Orange Heresy* (1971), which takes as its central satirical focus the concept of "nothingness" as found in avant-garde art of the 1920s and in subsequent literary as well as artistic developments, in which references to Samuel Beckett figure prominently and decisively. Willeford is probably best known for his *Miami Blues* detective series featuring Hoke Mosley (my favorite is *New Hope for the Dead*, a forerunner of the mania for "cold cases" in contemporary crime fiction and TV dramas). Willeford's dark vision of a psychotic American culture in his crime novels is brought to bear in his satirical debunking of the world of high art with its pretentious ideological and class distinctions. Indeed, the work as a whole is premised upon the linked ideas of hoaxes, frauds, and forgeries of the artistic variety. This is announced immediately in the novel's title and in its dedication, "For the late, great Jacques Debierue, c. 1886–1970, *Memoria in aeterna*." Jacques Debierue is, of course, a literary figment masquerading as an historical figure in Willeford's novel. He is referred to as the father of modern art and the most famous artist in the world, the mythical originator of Nihilistic Surrealism who wedded in the 1920s in Paris the schools of Dada and Surrealism. The novel's epigraph from Gorgias underlines the nihilistic aspects of existence and the concomitant problems of expression:

> Nothing exists.
> If anything exists, it is incomprehensible.
> If anything was comprehensible,
> It would be incommunicable.

As we will see in some detail, Jacques Debierue and his art indeed only exist as "nothings." The most famous variant of Gorgias's nihilistic syllogism in modern literature is, of course, Samuel Beckett's invocation of an "art of failure" in his "Three Dialogues with Georges Duthuit" (1949), in which the ostensible subject matter is various modern painters. Here is Beckett's famous formulation which has served as the mainspring for countless interpretations of his work (and which I would argue has engendered the foremost example of the intentional fallacy in twentieth-century literature): "The expression that there is nothing to express, nothing with which to express, nothing from which to express, no power to express, no desire to express, together with the obligation to express."[11] It is, for example, the epigraph for Michael Robinson's 1971 study (the same year Willeford's novel was published) of Beckett, *The Long Sonata of the Dead*, the introduction to which is entitled "The Poetics of Failure."[12] The publisher was Grove Press, Beckett's American publisher, and hence Robinson's study had an in-built aura of being in a sense "authorized." Grove Press's marketing of Beckett as the artist of failure is caught very neatly in Willeford's exposition of how Debierue's studied indifference in promoting his works worked brilliantly in fact in the promotion of his works and was indeed the keystone of a highly successful marketing campaign.

The three sentences from Gorgias[13] are deployed in sequence as the titles for the three parts of Willeford's novel; there are also three explicit references to Beckett by name, one in each section of *The Burnt Orange Heresy*, though Beckett's influence is felt throughout and is particularly foregrounded in part two. The first reference occurs in the midst of the narrator James Figueras's explanation to his girlfriend Berenice about Debierue's "first and only one man show" (43) and his most famous (and only known) painting, which consisted of a gilded frame that "enclosed a fissure or crack in the gray plaster wall" (44) and why it was entitled *No. One*:

> The fact that he used the English *No. One*. instead of *Nombre Une* may or may not have influenced Samuel Beckett to write in French instead of English, as the literary critic Leon Mindlin has claimed [43].

Figueras is an art critic and has been "commissioned" by one Joseph Cassidy, famous criminal lawyer and well-known collector, to steal a Debierue for him, the plot turning on the fact that Cassidy has arranged for Debierue to have his studio in the Florida boondocks where he can work on a new project, his Paris studio having been razed by fire and all his works lost. The pay off for Figueras is that he can get an exclusive interview with the most reclusive of all modern artists and hence be able to proceed towards his goal of being one of the happy few in America to make his living as an art critic. As his girlfriend Berenice prophetically announces, art is a life and death matter for him; while she seems to be genuinely in love with him, Figueras is very clear about where his priorities lie: after all, he maintains, a woman is only a woman, whereas 2,500 words is an article.

In Part 2, "If anything exists, it is incomprehensible," Figueras breaks into Debierue's studio, having dropped him off for his nightly sojourn to the local drive-in theatre ("The Bowery Boys Meet Frankenstein," with three color cartoons to boot), the perfect follow up to his favorite TV dinner, washed down with glasses of orange juice from concentrate. The anal-minded élitist Figueras's difficulties in coming to terms with the pop culture contexts relished by the "world's greatest artist" are, however, nothing compared to what he finds in the studio. For he does indeed discover that "nothing exists" in terms of Debierue as painter—all the canvasses are pristine and he is indeed perplexed about how to make this "comprehensible." And at the center of this *mise-en-abîme* is the second direct linkage to Beckett; Figueras reflects: "I fought down my impulse to steal the autographed copy of Beckett's *Proust*, the only book in the small library that I coveted" (98–9), so instead of the hoped for epiphany of "the miraculous in visual art" (97), the only reference point of substance is an autographed copy of *Proust*, thereby re-enforcing the connection with Beckett and suggesting further analogies between Debierue and Beckett's views about "nothing to express" in his "Three Dialogues'" discussion of his friend Dutch painter Bram Van Velde. Figueras is "bewildered" and "nauseated" by what he encounters: "I had expected something, but not Nothing" (97). Figueras, faced with this impasse, is still ever the critic and says, "I had to work it out" (and he is, of course, being true as well to his name: "figura," figuring it out). And here is his explanation, cum rationalization, one which salvages an heroic status of sorts for Debierue and which is cast in particularly Beckettian terms: "*Waiting*, the incredibly patient waiting for an idea to materialize, for a single idea that could be transferred onto the ready canvas—but no ideas ever come to him. Never" (100). Forget the Bowery Boys and Frankenstein: this is more a case of Henry James's "The Aspern Papers" meets "The Beast in the Jungle"—and the result is a double-negative: there are no paintings—Debierue has never painted a single painting in his whole life—and there is no great revelation—Debierue can only wait fruitlessly, endlessly for his Godot-moment of inspiration that would overcome "his dread of failure" (101). Part 2 ends with Figueras's anguished reflections on Debierue's "lost visions" as "scalding tears" run down his cheeks. Shades of Beckett's *Watt* in which the eponymous hero breaks into Erskine's room and discovers a painting, "and at the thought that it was perhaps this, a circle and a centre not its centre in search of a centre and its circle respectively, in boundless space, in endless time, then Watt's eyes filled with tears."[14]

Watt's inability to make sense of "nothings" and "somethings" leads him to the mental hospital where he meets a fellow inmate Sam who will record his story. Figueras's own "lost vision" leads him into a murderous art-induced psychosis: he carries on with his "confession" and in short order details how he stole blank canvases from Debierue, torched the studio and then forged the Debierue he owes Cassidy (a deal is still a deal)—the monstrosity that is entitled "The Burnt Orange Heresy" and which gives its title to the novel (a case, for sure, of double *and* nothing) and then to top it off he kills his girlfriend Berenice in a particularly gruesome scene so that she can't blow the whistle on his forgery, what she terms his "awful" painting.[15] There are then two endings, as it were, to this literary and artistic parable. In the first, Figueras has succeeded in his mission: he writes a scholarly article on

Debierue of the Borgesian sort (a review of an "imaginary" work) and goes on then to forge the painting which he has just "figured" out, which he has pictured in his mind. It is at this juncture in Part 3 that the third and final *direct* reference to Beckett occurs. Figueras ends his Encyclopaedia article on Debierue with a negative, with a final "No" and, praising himself, wonders why "does every contemporary work of art have to end with an affirmative? Joyce with his coda of yesses in *Ulysses*, Beckett, with the 'I will go on' of his trilogy" (120).

Here is the moral to the first ending: Willeford's diabolically clever satire shows how Figueras's art psychosis is linked to his culture at large and his glib endorsement of the negative without recognition of its dialogical engagements with various affirmatives reveals how mad he really is. Beckett is not figured as a Debierue type, as the final revelations cited above make clear: no, the real parody in this shaggy dog story of avant-garde art is the criticism directed at the art establishment. That is, there is a debunking of a superficial endorsement of the various "nothings" which supposedly govern discussions of modern art. This has most certainly been the case in the history of Beckett studies in which all too often an ideology of negativity has set the agenda, the guiding assumptions for so many critics, and many of these critical readings stem from the "nothing to express" litany of "Three Dialogues" which Willeford, via his epigraph from Gorgias and the figure of Debierue, so hilariously sends up.

And the second ending? It reminds us that there is still an ethical let alone legal dimension to all this cheap talk about art. Figueras will never discuss his role in the "apotheosis" (144) of Debierue, but he is compelled to confess the murder of Berenice: "The man who achieves success in America must pay for it" (144). And as he turns himself in at the police station for what he euphemistically calls "a crime of passion," he unfolds his handkerchief and lo and behold out rolls Berenice's finger. Case closed.

Bill James's adaptations of Beckett works, in particular *Waiting for Godot* in *Astride a Grave* (1991) and *Endgame* in *Roses, Roses* (1993), take the popular culture reception of Beckett to a new level in which an initial parodic doubling-effect issues forth in the creation of new works in which Beckett has played a collaborative role as a sort of ghost writer. In *Astride a Grave* the comic and the parodic elements dominate, whereas in *Roses, Roses* there is another significant strategic move taken whereby Beckett's *Endgame* is incorporated into the very structure of the novel and a new level of emotional complexity attained, qualities which add a new dimension to the scintillating satire of the Harpur and Iles series in which the police and criminal worlds are engaged in the intricate dialogical engagements of a dance to the music of crime.

Waiting for Godot is the most iconic of twentieth-century plays, and as such there are, of course, a host of passing references to the play in a host of popular culture venues and genres, and detective fiction is no exception. For example: there is the name-dropping of the play's title and author's name in a merely incidental manner in such postmodernist pastiches as Jasper Fforde's Thursday Next series, or—more pointedly—Kinky Friedman's references to the Godot Bar and his invocation of mock epiphanies at the end of his chapters, such as "Godot has arrived."[16] Indeed, so extensive is the referencing of the play that the most revealing examples, ironically enough, of its deployment as cultural allusion emphasize its *absence*, namely, various ways in which Godot references do not materialize. For example: in Stewart MacBride's *Broken Skin* (2007), the central character DS Logan McRae notes as he enters an Arts Centre in Aberdeen: "According to the posters up outside in the huge, columned portico, there was supposed to be a series of Samuel Beckett plays on this week, but *Waiting for Godot* had a big CANCELLED sticker across it"[17]—which is appropriate enough since in this particular novel there is no time to stand about and waste words when a serial rapist-murderer is on the loose. Another clever and memorable reference coupling the presence *and* absence of *Waiting for Godot*, so to speak, is found in William Peter Blatty's *Legion* (1983), a supernatural police procedural in which Lt. Kinderman, the homicide detective from *The Exorcist*, describes his stakeout modus operandi: he always has a paperback book in his pocket as a prop, but this can be counter productive in so far as he has been so caught up in his reading, for example of *Claudius the God*, that he has let his subject escape; this situation is rectified by replacing Graves's novel with another in his pocket library: "He looked at the title. It was *Waiting for Godot*. He sighed with relief and turned to Act Two," in which, of course, in Vivian Mercier's witticism "nothing happens, *twice*," and since it is a case of déja vu there is no danger (at least for Kinderman) of being engrossed in its "story."[18] An even more dramatic example of inclusion/exclusion, of being present at your own absence so to speak, is afforded by the *Service of All the Dead*, a TV dramatization of the fourth novel in Colin Dexter's immensely popular Inspector Morse mysteries. In the TV series starring John Thaw, Morse in *Service of All the Dead* holds up a copy of *Waiting for Godot* about half-way through and gives a mini-lecture to his sidekick Lewis in which he commends the play as a true modern classic which Lewis should most definitely read. And at the dénouement the play is invoked again as the key to the whole convoluted plot about a tramp playing a key role in unravelling the mystery. So imagine my dismay, when after having watched this episode—and, it seemed to me then, everything does come to those who only sit and watch—here, after all, was another Beckett and detective fiction wind-fall—I eagerly sought out a copy of the novel and discovered that there is *not one* reference to Beckett's play in the novel.[19] In short, so well known is Beckett's play, so much is it now a part of general cultural knowledge, that the screen-writer felt that it could be profitably and safely added to what was already an incredibly popular TV series! An example of adapting *Waiting for Godot* in a more thorough going manner comparable to Bill James's treatment of the play in *Astride a Grave* is Minette Walters' very first crime novel, *The Ice House* (1992), in which the image of a tramp in incongruous "bright pink trousers" winds its way throughout the story and turns out to be the key to the novel's mystery. Even though *Waiting for Godot* is never explicitly mentioned, the association with things Beckettian is made directly at the novel's climax as the tramp is figured to be "like something out of a Samuel Beckett play," not to mention the very last line of the novel in which the "wronged" heroine calls on her lover to make this a happy ending: "Well what the hell are you waiting for then?"[20]

Bill James's use of *Godot* materials in *Astride a Grave* proceeds from appropriation, through parody, to adaptation. The latter is evident in the very title of James's novel: in Beckett's play the actual phrasing is "astride of a grave," the small change here foreshadowing more significant alterations. In the opening chapter the literary provenance of the title is immediately established during Chief Superintendent Colin Harpur's attendance at one of his wife's literary club meetings:

> It was a session on the making of dialogue. A gymnasium owner in the group had gone first and cited something about all of us being born in a gleam by a woman standing astride a grave, which he stated had a multiplicity of overtones and came from the well-known play, *Waiting for Godot* by Samuel Beckett. Harpur had heard of both and was ready to agree with the gym owner that the line might be "seminal." Now and then Harpur had to deal with graves—mostly shallow, hastily made, ineffective—though he never encountered a woman astriding one.[21]

"Seminal," indeed: here are the quintessential elements of Bill James's world of Harpur and Iles. Namely: the dialogical engagement between "posh" and "popular culture" references; in this instance, Harpur's own example of an opening bit of dialogue is "Make my day, punk," to which his wife wearily replies, "As bloody ever; low-browing for effect." Furthermore, the most striking feature for readers of Bill James is how dialogue operates in his fictional world, a realm in which discourse seems to be a hybrid product of Oscar Wilde type witticisms and outlandish criminal effronteries à la Jonathan Wilde. That is, his characters seem to read each other's minds as if their words and thoughts were transparently projected for all to see. In the above instance, the dialogue also will be developed in broader ironic terms by the third person narrator's manipulation of how the title of the work is actually embodied in the novel's plot.

Harpur may have never "encountered a woman astriding one," but the central character in this particular installment of the Harpur and Iles series—and one of James's great comic creations—Panicking Ralph Ember, certainly does and the dialogical engagement with famous lines from *Godot* is indeed truly "seminal." In Chapter 8, Ralph ends up having sex atop a grave (a shallow one) with the wife of the man he killed and buried there (one Caring Oliver who was part of a robbery gang with Ralph and whose inordinate greed at divvying-up time necessitated his elimination). Ralph, however, like all of James's characters, is astutely aware that there are various protocols and standards that should be observed (by *all* classes, so-called law-abiding or criminal) and the series as a whole might be rightly regarded as a comedy of manners: "Was it seemly to have someone astride a grave—her husband's grave?"(50). The grotesque pastoral coupling in the lonely woods does have its up and down moments as Patsy, who is "short on looks," exhorts Ralph to "do the whole thing slowly." Poetically, she opines, "The leaves make such fascinating patterns against the sky. I could lie here for ever and ever and ever"; more realistically, Ralph's silent "dialogue" takes on very briefly a Beckettian flavored echo: "He did not like that thought, and for a second felt unable to go on" (52). Of course, he must go on—the "petit mort" and the "grand mort" indeed neatly coupled in a "seminal" fashion.

There is another version of an encounter astride a grave in Chapter 29, near the ending of the novel. In this "second act," the earlier pastoral interlude has turned into tragic farce. Other members of the robbery gang have kidnapped Ralph and forced him to take them where the loot is buried and this leads back to the plot site where Ralph buried Caring and had it off with his wife. Ralph, who has a knack of escaping very tricky situations à la Patricia Highsmith's Ripley—once he has overcome his panic-attacks—takes action and, in this reprise, comes to the point very quickly: Ralph whacks one of his kidnappers on the shins and he consequently "staggered and slid on the soft mud, toppling leftwards but still upright, fighting for balance, his legs momentarily astride the grave" (179). Later in the dénouement, Ralph needs to be rescued deus ex machina-style by Harpur and the police contingent and the convoluted plot is brought to a neat conclusion. In the concluding remarks with Chief Lane, who has asked about Megan's literary club, Harpur retorts that his wife thinks he believes "Rimbaud wrote scripts for Sylvester Stallone" (201). Predictably neither speaker gets her point; but to give Harpur his due, as his boss Desmond Iles (manic and demonic enforcer of "justice" even if it is often of his own devising) wryly observes: "Colin straddles so many worlds" (203).

In *Roses, Roses* (1993) Bill James also straddles various literary worlds, but it is his further adaptation and indeed incorporation of Beckett's *Endgame* which is primarily responsible for producing what, in my estimation, is his masterpiece in the crime writing genre. Bill James, a pseudonym for James Tucker, is a very prolific author of several crime series, the most famous being the Iles and Harpur franchise and we have already highlighted some of its specific stylistic aspects in our discussion of *Astride a Grave*, particularly the uncanny prescience whereby characters seem able to read each other's minds. This can generate some very penetrating satirical insights about varieties of criminal experience (by *both* sides in this dialogical encounter). But there is also the danger that the whole exercise becomes too much of a series of set pieces, a series of merely amusing encounters of a static and superficial nature, lacking in any emotional depth. *Roses, Roses*, the tenth novel in the Harpur and Iles series (which now numbers over twenty), is, however, very different from other works in the sequence, as is announced in the novel's very first sentence, which describes the murder of Harpur's wife Megan of literary club fame, and it is pretty nasty, brutish, and short : "When she was killed by three chest knife blows in a station car park, Megan Harpur had been on her way home to tell her husband she was leaving him for another man."[22] The other man is "Tambo" (so nicknamed since he once played Tamburlaine), another copper, in fact Iles' predecessor, and since he is "on the take" from a very powerful criminal organization Megan is collateral damage as they get to their man through her. Such is the basic plot of the novel; but the power of the story is generated by a doubling-pattern whereby the emotional context is further enhanced by certain formal aspects of the novel's structure. Namely, with some minor variations, the chapters alternate between the present—the aftermath of Megan's murder, her funeral, and the police investigation of her death—and the past, focusing primarily on a sequential reconstruction of her last day in London at one of her trysts with Tambo, so that at the very end of the novel we return full circle to her stabbing in the station car park. It is hence Megan's story and not the prescribed lines and ritualized actions of Harpur and Iles and company that holds center stage; indeed, the stalking of Megan by her would be killer on the final journey home from London is clearly a sort of endgame, the final stage of a human game of chess, and no escape is possible.

And this final movement of *Roses, Roses* depends heavily on Beckett's *Endgame*, one of Megan's favorite plays, which she has recently seen in the West End with Tambo. Again, the full power of this literary analogy as resolution to the story is dependent upon its dialogical engagement with another cluster of more traditional literary imagery from which the novel has taken its title. At Megan's funeral a couple of the men from her literary club read poems, only one of which as readers we are privy to: Megan's daughter Jill begins to weep as she listens to the first lines of Mathew Arnold's "Requiescat":

> Strew on her roses, roses,
> And never a spray of yew.

Megan's other daughter, the older Hazel, offers a more critical review later, scorning the paltry tribute to her mother consisting of "a scrap of was it Arnold and some lines of an Edna St. Vincent Millay" (75). The Millay poem is never identified, but the choice of author is fittingly enough poetic justice of sorts (albeit of the ironic variety) by one of her fellow literary club members since Millay personified the romantic bravado and rebellion of the Liberated Woman of the 1920s, something Megan Harpur could only offer a pale mimicry of in the 1990s. Certainly, she never "Flung roses, roses, riotously with the throng," to borrow Ernest Dowson's famous phrase. Megan's own final thoughts on the application and adaptation of the Arnoldian hail and farewell are down-to-earth—literally so, while retaining a residual trace of the grand poetic defiance: as she lies dying in the station car park, she thinks, "All it needed was a few flowers. Strew on the oil leaks, roses" (102). Metaphor, meet metonymy, and welcome to the "rag and boneshop of the heart." This counter movement to the other end of the literary spectrum is underscored by the Beckett references in the novel's final scenes (the three such Beckett references neatly paralleling the three references to the novel's highly poeticized title). In Chapter 37, Megan says of what will turn out to be her last meeting with Tambo: "This was still a freedom ride, a love jaunt and a mind mission: they would see *Endgame* today, that frightening parable, with people in dustbins" (159). When they reach the theatre, Tambo wants to change seats, recognizing that they are being stalked there, as their own affair reaches its own endgame:

> Tambo's anxieties even reduced her pleasure in *Endgame*, usually a favourite play of hers. Tonight it seemed to her wilfully bleak and negative: the cruel absurdity of people in dustbins, the bare set, the poverty-stricken language. To her surprise she found herself craving costume, colour, escape. God, was that what she was or had become—an escapist? [164].

And there is no escape possible at this juncture: in the final chapter 44 (consisting of a very minimal paragraph of less than a hundred words—Beckett would have been pleased), Megan's next to last thought as her murderer closes in for the kill is fully Beckettian: "Crazily, a line from *Endgame* on that earlier trip rushed to her mind: *This is what we called making an exit—*" (204). Fully Beckett, but no longer solely Beckett's line: James has adapted it and incorporated it in his own work, and this collaboration has given a new perspective on Beckett's play and allowed James to reach a highpoint in his writing career.

Beckett is alive and well in various reincarnations in popular culture, and detective fiction is a particularly rich area in which to investigate this cultural phenomenon. Beckett's presence is in many cases employed as merely a fashionable turn in celebrity name-dropping: the appropriation of Beckett's own name being the main focus in some instances. One of my favorite examples of this is Hilary Norman's detective Sam Becket (yes, only one "t") in *Mind Games* (1999) who is black and Jewish (the latter by adoption).[23] Another example is Meg Gardiner's Jo Beckett in *The Dirty Secrets Club* (2008), whose occupation is termed a "dead shrinker," a forensic psychologist who profiles victims' lives to help solve their deaths.[24] Beckett's name is everywhere employed as a talismanic invocation of the genius-celebrity. Another example of such name-dropping that proceeds beyond mere cultural littering is provided by the novels of Dallas Murphy: his first novel *Lover Man* (1987) begins as a sort of reprise of Beckett's *Murphy*, with the central character, Artie Deemer, declaring, "More than most anything else, I liked to do nothing"[25] (except sit back and listen to jazz); in his second novel *Apparent Wind* (1991) the protagonist Doom Loomis describes the eccentric order in which he read Beckett's novels while in prison[26]; and in *Lush Life* the main character, Artie Deemer again, describes how he often signs himself in as "Samuel Beckett" when required to do so before being granted access to certain buildings etc.[27] Other belle lettristic allusions à la Dallas Murphy are found in Denise Mina's *The Last Breath* (2007) in which two women subversively exchange the witticism of being "fair to middling women."[28] A more concentrated cluster of Beckett allusions is offered in John Barker's *Poet in the Gutter* (1995) in which Sam Turner, of the so-named Detective Agency, tells a character named Celia that "I liked the ginger biscuits with tea because we dunked them and it reminded me of my childhood."[29] So here we get references to Beckett's *Murphy* crossed with echoes of Proust upon whom Beckett wrote an early critical study. Now, how many readers of this genre book are likely to recognize such intertextual play? Not many surely, but that is hardly the point. These Beckett references aren't going slumming in the ghetto of popular culture crime fiction: "high" and so-called "low" share a very porous border (for example, Barker's novel's title is taken from a Bob Dylan song). It is, of course, still an issue of class and education; nevertheless, allusions such as those we have discussed in this chapter can be employed to contest these differentiations. For example: a character in William Marshall's *Whisper*

(1988) speaks Beckettese: "I'm alone. I'm alone all the time now,—waiting, waiting for Godot [...] See? Education."[30] Using references to Beckett's now classic play as a touchstone for education and class—and indeed for a mass audience, remembering how, for example, *Godot* was superimposed upon the Inspector Morse episode cited earlier—is revealing: Beckett has "arrived" in modern culture and can be invoked in so-called "higher" or "lower" realms, as the case may be.

There is an amusing instance of this in a later Bill James novel *Easy Streets* (2004) in which our old friend Panicking Ralph offers this assessment of "quality drama" that "brings unmatchable revelations to the human state": "Think of that *Mousetrap* going on for years, decades in London. Then *Waiting for Godot* or *Les Mis*. These are insights."[31] Indeed, of the "howler" variety by a *nouveau riche* half-baked criminal—the delightfully inane conjunction of *Waiting for Godot* with long-running "bestsellers" tellingly makes James' satirical point. We have, however, gained a number of genuinely valuable insights through our investigation into "The Strange Case of Beckett and Detective Fiction": namely, how in Bartholomew Gill's *The Death of a Joyce Scholar* mainstream academic criticism can be implicitly subjected to a revisionist critique by means of its recasting within a popular culture genre; how Charles Willeford's *The Burnt Orange Heresy* affords a satirical subversion of the avant-garde's love affair with "nothingness"; and, finally, how in Bill James' two novels under discussion here there is a complex adaptation process afoot whereby Beckett's works are recycled in new works that testify to the creative and transformative powers within popular culture.

Notes

1. Hugh Kenner, *The Elsewhere Community* (Concord, Ontario: House of Anansi Press, 1998), 106.
2. *Ibid.*, 10
3. James Knowlson, *Damned to Fame: The Life of Samuel Beckett* (London: Bloomsbury, 1996), 553.
4. *Ibid.*, 63.
5. Samuel Beckett, "Dante...Bruno. Vico.... Joyce.," in *Disjecta*, ed. R. Cohn (New York: Grove Press, 1984), 28.
6. Robin W. Winks, ed., *Detective Fiction: A Collection of Critical Essays* (Woodstock, VT: A Foul Play Press Book, 1988), 8. The careful reader will detect that neither Beckett's name nor *Waiting for Godot* appears in the index in support of Winks' judgement in his "Introduction."
7. Vivian Mercier, *A Reader's Guide to the New Novel: From Queneau to Pinget* (New York: Farrar, Straus and Giroux, 1971), 190.
8. Samuel Beckett, *Murphy* (New York: Grove Press, 1957), 112. There are indeed many parallels worthy of further exploration between *Murphy* and *The Maltese Falcon*, beginning with the mise-en-scène of Sam Spade's room with its wall-bed (a Murphy

bed), padded rocking chair, and telephone (Dashiell Hammett, *Five Complete Novels* [New York: Chatham River Press, 1986], 334).

  9. Patricia Merivale and Susan Sweney, eds., *Detecting Texts: The Metaphysical Detective Story from Poe to Postmodernism* (Philadelphia: University of Pennsylvania Press, 1999), 2. It is later pointed out that there is potentially a "reciprocity" between these two different types of detective fiction, that a dialogical engagement "between literary and popular detective genres is a thought-provoking development that deserves further study" (I56).

  10. Bartholomew Gill, *The Death of a Joyce Scholar* (New York: Avon Books, 1990), 71.

  11. Samuel Beckett, "Three Dialogues," in *Disjecta*, ed. R. Cohn, 139. In *Beckett's Books: A Cultural History of Samuel Beckett's "Interwar Notes"* (New York: Continuum, 2006), Matthew Feldman notes that in a 21 April 1958 letter to A.J. Leventhal Beckett cites three propositions of Gorgias of Leontini and that this was a reprise of the citation which he had made 25 years earlier in his "Philosophy Notes" (76).

  12. Michael Robinson, *The Long Sonata of the Dead: A Study of Samuel Beckett* (New York: Grove Press, 1971).

  13. Charles Willeford, *The Burnt Orange Heresy* (New York: Vintage Crime / Black Lizard, 1990), 2, 56, 105. All future references are from this edition.

  14. Samuel Beckett, *Watt* (New York: Grove Press, 1953), 129.

  15. The forgery carried out here may be in part a nod of homage to John D. MacDonald's *Bright Orange for the Shroud* (New York: Fawcett Gold Medal, 1991; first published in 1965). In this novel Travis McGee "forges," as it were, the crime scene and a "bright orange dressing gown plays a key role in the deception" (181). In his obituary for John D. McDonald, Willeford mentions that he has "read most, if not all, of his 72 books," in *Writing and Other Blood Sports* (Tucson, AZ: Dennis McMillan Publications, 2000), 165. Throughout this collection of various critical writings, Samuel Beckett receives prominent mention: for example, in "Notes on Beat Writing" he is identified as a beat poet, 107; Willeford also mentions in passing that in one of his English classes at the University of Miami he gave an impromptu half-hour lecture on hats in Beckett (25); the most substantial and suggestive references come in his 1964 Master's Thesis, entitled *New Forms of Ugly: The Immobilized Hero in Modern Fiction*, in which Willeford insists on calling the immobilized hero "The Burnt Orange Heresy" (224).

  16. Kinky Friedman, *Musical Chairs* (New York: William Morrow and Co., 1991), 35. One of the several examples of the "Godot has arrived" formulaic is found in *Frequent Flyer* (New York: William Morrow and Co., 1989), 74.

  17. Stuart McBride, *Broken Skin* (London: Harper Collins, 2007), 154.

  18. Wlliam Peter Blatty, *Legion* (New York: Pocket Books, 1983), 26. Needless to say, the *Godot* allusion did not appear in the film version of *Legion* (2010). Vivian Mercier comments on the fact that nothing he has written on Beckett has attracted as much attention as this "one phrase in an *Irish Times* review of the Faber first printing of *Waiting for Godot*." See his *Beckett/Beckett* (New York: Oxford University Press, 1977), xii.

  19. The lack of a Beckett reference in the novel is perhaps not so surprising in that Colin Dexter has not made any references to Beckett in any of his other works. A prime case in point is the thirteenth and final instalment in the series, *The Remorseful Day* (1999), in which Dexter's fondness for epigraphs reaches epidemic proportions. One might say that Morse was dispatched by an excessive consumption of such allusions as well as his favorite malt whiskey.

  20. Minette Walters, *The Ice House* (London: Pan Books, 1992), 109, 192, 219 and 264 for the "bright pink trousers" motif. The reference to the proceedings resembling a Beckett play occurs at the end of Chapter 22, 266.

  21. Bill James, *Astride a Grave* (London: Pan Books), 7. All future references are from this edition.

22. Bill James, *Roses, Roses* (London: MacMillan, 1993), 1. All future references are from this edition.

23. Hilary Norman, *Mind Games* (London: Piatkus Publishers, 1999). Note in this regard her standard declaration: "As always in my novels, all characters and situations are fictitious."

24. Meg Gardiner, *The Dirty Secrets Club* (London: Hodder and Stoughton, 2008), 26.

25. Dallas Murphy, *Lover Man* (New York: Pocket Books, 1987), 9.

26. Dallas Murphy, *Apparent Wind* (New York: Pocket Books, 1991), 103: "He read *Murphy, Malone Dies, The Unnameable* [sic], and *Watt* in that order."

27. Dallas Murphy, *Lush Life* (New York: Pocket Books, 1992), 260.

28. Denise Mina, *The Last Breath* (London: Bantam Books, 2007), 49.

29. John Barker, *Poet in the Gutter* (London: Indigo Books, 2000), 44.

30. William Marshall, *Whisper* (New York: Viking Press, 1988), 175.

31. Bill James, *Easy Streets* (New York: W.W.Norton, 2004), 79.

Far Out Worlds
Sci-Fi and Speculative Fiction

Nick Pawliuk

"This article is about the Irish writer. For the *Scott Bakula* character, see *Sam Beckett*."
(Wikipedia, Samuel Beckett, September 13, 2010)[1]

The epigraph above from Wikipedia, probably now the most accessed source of information on the planet, indicates the power of popular culture and how boundaries between what has been termed high and low culture are problematic. Samuel Beckett has had a profound influence on all aspects of our culture as this volume indicates, and science fiction and related genres have a long history of association with Beckett. Sci-Fi and speculative fiction provide an interesting example as they show the appeal of his vision. Starting from classic works such as Jules Verne's *20,000 Thousand Leagues Under the Sea*, through Stanislaw Lem and Philip K. Dick, to Paul Auster's *In the Country of Last Things* and *Lulu on the Bridge*, Beckett has an affinity for a certain mental and physical landscape that is attractive to other writers. Indeed, an interesting description of this world is "depersonalized" and "degeographized,"[2] making the affinity that much more appealing as Beckett can become a blank slate of sorts. Beckett's influence on writers ranges from name dropping to complex doubling, where one must be familiar with both of the writers' worlds to see some of the "respectful" ethos of parody that is employed. In the space between Verne and Auster, we have the full range of reference from cliché and name-dropping, to hilarious politicized parody. Through Beckett we can see how our culture integrates disparate—sometimes challenging—parts to form a new vision that relies on a complex series of doublings.

Much work has gone into tracking down references, inspirations and sources for Beckett's work, and frequently they are of the high culture variety, Caspar David Friedrich's painting as the inspiration for *Waiting for Godot* comes to mind. However, Beckett uses lighter fare, more popular texts, and transforms them into his vision as well, even seminal science fiction texts. One of these is Jules Verne's *20,000 Leagues Under the Sea* (*20,000 Leagues*). Friedrich makes sense, but Verne? There appears to be an aura around Beckett of an unassailable high culture aficionado. Of course he was, but he also liked dipping his toe into low culture: whether it be mystery novels or rugby. Or going down to the local for a pint, or a Jameson. And this is what pop culture can allow us: a new way to see Beckett. It may originally seem incongruous that Beckett uses a seminal science fiction text as compared to, say, an author like William Gibson who has the Rue Jules Verne in *Neuromancer*. This makes sense. However, Gibson has a long association with Beckett, even possibly *looking* like him,[3] and until we recognize the Beckett who partakes of popular culture, *is* part of popular culture, he will continue to be the "sand in [the] scrambled eggs" as William Gibson calls him, a challenging figure.[4] This is why we need to recognize the positive Beckett which is what popular culture can assist us with, so we can fully digest him and not have to be spoon fed baby pabulum all the time. There are alternatives, and when we see how Beckett integrates Verne into a series of seamless references and allusions, these can shed new light on his texts.

At first glance, there appears little in such a strange narrative of three people imprisoned on a submarine that would interest Beckett, but if we look at the number of similarities and allusions, we can see that Beckett is playing with Verne in subtle ways. The first coincidence is the date of the attack on the Cunard ship the *Scotia*, April 13, 1867, by a mysterious "monster."[5] This is 39 years before Beckett's birthday on April 13, 1906, and he had a friend named Nancy Cunard who published his award-winning poem "Whoroscope" in 1930. She later published many of Beckett's translations when he was desperately in need of money,[6] and Beckett returns to the name as a reference in *Waiting for Godot* during Lucky's "think."

Just as the name "Cunard" might be more than coincidental, the name "Nemo" reoccurs in *Dream*, and it is significant. In *Dream*, Nemo is a perplexing incidental character. John Pilling in his companion text to *Dream* indicates that, like the Swiss clown Grock, Nemo is a type of "demiurge," a creator or controller of the fictional universe,[7] but we do not find out much about him. The protagonist, Belacqua, never talks to him, but the novel revolves around him, somehow, as he continually reappears. Nemo is, as Pilling indicates, a "compound" of literary characters from Homer, Dickens, Verne, and even Burton.[8] The Nemo of Verne, however, is a strong attraction for Beckett as Nemo possesses several appealing characteristics. First, Nemo has characteristics that are reminiscent of how Beckett will later be seen. For instance, Nemo is "a man who has broken with humanity" and in doing so does "not therefore obey any of its rules."[9] Nemo's phrase here could be a good description of much of Beckett's writing from his turn to French onwards, in particular his plays, where *Waiting for Godot* breaks many traditional rules of drama. Also, Nemo and Beckett share a love of what James Knowlson describes as "spartan simplicity."[10] Second, Nemo has rejected society due to imperialistic injustice, but in this rejection he ultimately becomes an oppressor himself, incarcerating the three protagonists, with the language of imprisonment proliferating: "floating prison," "dungeon," "iron cage," and "iron-plated cell," to name a few.[11] Beckett later uses imprisonment as a central metaphor and focus in his writing, whether it is by one's own body or mind, or by external forces. It is not until the end of the novel that the characters are liberated, and throughout the Canadian Ned Land repeatedly reminds us of their lack of freedom.

Beckett returns to the theme of freedom and the sea, even using a watery metaphor to describe his writing process: "fathoms deep." And this connection of the sea is recurrent in his writing: "The sea too, I am conversant with the sea too, it belongs to the same family, I have even gone to the bottom more than once, under various names."[12] There is a layering of ideas here that seems to be a reference to many works. First, Beckett's own "The Calmative" has its narrator "fathom deep in the grey of dawn, if it was dawn,"[13] while in the following story "The End," the narrator is on his "knees prying out the plug with [his] knife" to let the sea water into his boat, only to end up "crushed" in a "mighty systole" of sea, sky, mountains and islands, and "scattered to the uttermost confines of space."[14] So here are two further narrators who have taken Beckett to the bottom of the sea, just as Nemo did in *Dream* decades earlier. Why the bottom of the sea? Verne here can give us an answer:

> Here we have perfect tranquility, for the sea does not belong to despots. On the surface, they can still exercise their iniquitous laws, fight, devour each other, and indulge in all their earthly horrors. But thirty feet below its surface their power ceases, their influence fades, and their dominion vanishes! Ah, monsieur, to live in the bosom of the sea! Only there can independence be found! There I recognize no master! There I am free![15]

Verne gives Beckett a metaphor here for what his writing gives him when Beckett's narrator can move "with no limit to his movements in all directions."[16] This is a virtual rewriting of Nemo's motto "Mobilis in Mobili," or "mobile within the mobile element."[17]

The pattern Beckett sets out here can be useful in looking at Beckett's reception in science fiction and related genres. Beckett is a disproportionately popular figure given the challenging nature of his work. He seems to be everywhere, even in genres far removed from Beckett's own: popular horror fiction. For example, in book two of *Dean Koontz's Frankenstein, City of Night*, there is a criminal gun dealer named Godot. The whole novel cycle revolves around failure and how Victor Frankenstein tries to keep building a New Race of genetically engineered clones to replace the imperfect humans. Victor repeatedly fails, but he keeps trying, essentially failing better each time. The references to the gun dealing Godot are little more than a tip of the hat to Beckett, with lines like "I expected we'd have to wait for you, Mr. Godot, not the other way around. I hope we're not late," and, "'Mr. Godot,' Michael said, 'it's been comfortable doing business with you, knowing we're dealing with real human beings.'"[18] Aside from the larger theme of failure, the references to Beckett here amount to a bit more than the usual name dropping as they will elicit a smile from the knowing reader—at least Godot has finally arrived. In contrast to the quick name drop or brief allusion to further a theme, references to Beckett are popping up in more unusual places. For instance, in *The Widow's Guide to Sex and Dating* (Henry Holt and Co., 2014) Carole Radziwill copies a personal note Beckett had written in her own note to meet Ralph Fiennes because "I knew Ralph would get the reference. He's very intelligent, you know. That note and the subsequent meeting at the bookstore was [sic] loosely detailed toward the end of the book. I'm afraid that is all I will say. Wink."[19] I guess we need to read this to find out more. Although a seemingly trivial reference, the exclusivity of Beckett as an academic exercise relates to how Beckett was marketed after the initial failure of *Godot* in Miami. The play was suddenly not the laugh sensation on two continents, but now a must see for the exclusive intellectual audience to try to gain *an audience* for *Godot* in New York. And it worked, both popularly and academically. The success of the marketing campaign can be seen with even a quick perusal of a text such as the survey *On Contemporary Literature* (1964, 1969, edited by Richard Kostelanetz), a handy "pocket" book of literary criticism. Of the fifty-eight (!) authors and genres included, Beckett is the only author to have four separate essays on him and his work, with only Nabokov having more than the two another half dozen authors have. Clearly, Beckett has gripped the popular and academic imagination early on.[20]

It is this excitement that allows for the possibility of a text like Edwin Schlossberg's *Einstein and Beckett: A Record of an Imaginary Discussion with Albert Einstein and Samuel Beckett* (1973, Link Books), a connection that anticipates Apple's advertising campaign which also connects the two "geniuses" together.[21] As John Unterecker writes in his foreword to the book, "The project, as imagined Einstein notes, is that of man's becoming aware of the harmony of nature and the possibility of understanding that harmony

[...] and, as imagined Beckett adds is—by the very nature of man's mind—doomed to an enriching failure" (viii). Schlossberg imagines a dialogue between himself, Einstein and Beckett, recording it in a form that reflects the complicated and fictional nature of it, with copious footnotes offset creatively on the page. For instance, he records Beckett as saying, "The use of characters is difficult to avoid. I did away with it to some extent in *Krapp's Last Tape*, but not enough. *The Unnamable* is better—*Texts for Nothing* really has no characters, except it does, but it is the combination of the reader and myself" (33). What is interesting is how Beckett is *imagined*, a created Beckett based upon his texts and the reception they have, but it is not a real dialogue as we know Beckett did not engage much with his critics on textual exegesis. At the end of the text, Schlossberg has Beckett wanting "to write a text that would physically fall apart as it was read" (116) and records that "The process of writing this discussion seemed to have structurally paralleled the development of the thoughts that were discussed. It probably could not have been any other way" (117). Schlossberg is very creative and engaged in an interesting academic exercise, but one wonders if it *could* have been another way.

Stanislaw Lem in *A Perfect Vacuum* (1971, English translation 1979, 1978, Harvest/HBJ) "found brave new worlds for parody in this collection of perfect yet imaginary reviews of nonexistent books" (dust cover blurb), and shows us another way to engage with Beckett. The book begins with a review essay of the collection by Lem entitled "A Perfect Vacuum" where he concludes by arguing that "*A Perfect Vacuum* [the complete book] turns out to be a tale of what is desired but is not to be had. It is a book of ungranted wishes" (8). And it is this tongue-in-cheek assessment of the text that is missing from Schlossberg. Lem's Beckettian parody is a "review" written of Solange Marriot's first book entitled "Rien du tout, ou la conséquence" purportedly published by Editions du Midi, Paris, a thinly veiled reference to Beckett's French publisher. This is a dense parody of the standard view of Beckett as the author of negativity. Here, the review of "Nothing, or the Consequence" (English title) is hilariously similar not only to Beckett's own reviews but also to the popular excitement of a writer writing about nothing, as evidenced by the presence of a text like Schlossberg's and the number of essays on Beckett in Kostelanetz' volume. Lem gives us a review of the "first novel ever to have reached the limit of what writing can do" (69), and gives the reader, as Linda Hutcheon argues, a "smirk, the knowing smile" (61) on his or her face in the parody of the uproar around Beckett and his play about nothing happening twice. The review shows how the popular academic excitement around writing about nothing, through the actual *act of writing*, is absurd and comical. For example, Lem writes that the merger of non-being with being in language forces the language to "suicidally disown itself" and that its author should be some "mathematician, but one only who with his mathematics proved—and cursed—literature" (79).[22] Beckett is the perfect subject for Lem because he complements Lem's repeated thematic concerns of the unknowability of the Other. As Fredric Jameson argues in relation to *Solaris*, Lem's ultimate message is "that in imagining ourselves to be attempting contact with the radically Other, we are in reality merely looking in a mirror and 'searching for an ideal image of our own world.'"[23] *Solaris* is thus similar to "Rien du tout, ou la conséquence" as it too is "negative proof of our thesis about writing: for here there is no writing, no message." Ironically, by focusing on negativity in his "review," Lem actually *anticipates* much of the later work and focus in Beckett criticism of the coming decades which makes the smirk all the more broad for the reader.

As Lem, the "master of terminal pessimism" (*A Perfect Vacuum* dust jacket blurb), can so clearly parody Beckett, Philip K. Dick's works are more often associated with Beckett in a vaguely generalized way. For example, Harlan Ellison's dust jacket blurb for Dick's *The Simulacra* (1964, ACE Books, New York [price $1.50!]): "If there is such a thing as 'black science fiction,' Philip K. Dick is its Pirandello, its Becket [sic] and its Pinter. No other creative intellect qualifies." Later "creative intellects" as diverse as Jean Baudrillard (*Simulations*, 1983) and Neil Postman (particularly in *Amusing Ourselves to Death: Public Discourse in the Age of Show Business*, 1985) would in fact also qualify, neatly combining to foreground Dick's major themes of what is real-human in our postmodernist world and how does one take a moral stand on such "amusements." While there are some common affinities between Beckett and Dick's works, there is only one text in which Dick seems to be directly referencing and adapting Beckett, and that is in *The Simulacra* with its detailed echoing of *Waiting for Godot*.

The Beckettian references focus on two minor (but significant) figures, namely, Al and Ian, two vaudevillean-type performers like Didi and Gogo who play the jug and offer up versions of classical music in an attempt to win a talent competition to play before "Nicole" (the simulacrum of the title), who rules the White House. Their appearance occurs dead center in Dick's novel, which depicts a weird post-apocalyptic 21st century that is organized around concepts of matriarchy. It is in this regard a vision diametrically opposed to *Godot*'s patriarchy. Here is the key Beckettian passage as appropriated and adapted closely by Dick, in which the unifying concept is "to be is to be perceived," much like Vladimir's worries. In his mind, Ian imagines Nicole's knowledge of them:

> *She knows of our existence.* In that case we really do exist. Like a child that has to have its mother watching what it does, we're brought into being, validated consensually by Nicole's gaze.
> And when she takes her eye off us, he thought, then what? What happens to us afterward? Do we disintegrate, sink back into oblivion. Back, he thought, into random, unformed atoms. Where we come from, the world of non-being. The world we've been in all our lives, up until now [125–126].

Al also has doubts, even if they are not of such a philosophical nature:

> She may ask us for an encore. She may even request a particular favorite. I've researched it, and it seems she sometimes asks to hear Schumann's "The Happy Farmer." Got that in mind? We'd better work "The Happy Farmer" up, just in case. He blew a few toots in his jug, thoughtfully [126].

Then Ian interrupts with a Beckettian refrain of "I can't do it" and "I can't go on. It means too much to me. Something will go wrong; we won't please her and they'll boot us out. And we'll never be able to forget" (126).

They are just dupes in a political intrigue to overthrow Nicole's regime and end up with their memories erased. The "I can't go on, I will go on" impasse of the last words of *The Unnamable* are echoed here, but the final stage directions-injunction of *Waiting for Godot*, "they do not move," is indeed superseded: the couple is in fact transported to Mars, where in some way or another so many of Dick's scenarios play out. The general theme throughout *The Simulacra* is that everybody is "waiting. For something that hasn't happened yet..." (237). And this affords a rationale for why Dick decided at the very center of his novel about "waiting" to employ a series of identifiable allusions to Beckett's postmodernist mystery play.

Whenever something becomes so over-used in popular culture it appears to be omnipresent, there is an inevitable backlash. For an example of how this backlash can be manifested, one can look at the best-selling Irish teen lit series featuring Artemis Fowl, juvenile criminal genius who mediates between the human and fairy worlds. The series takes a Beckettian twist of sorts in the sixth book, *The Time Paradox* (2008), in which Eoin Colfer presents young Artemis upon his return from one of his world-saving adventures with his new brothers, "two year-old twin boys, Beckett and Myles." Myles brings to mind one of the many pseudonyms of Brian O'Nolan (Flann O'Brien), namely, Myles na Gopaleen, and Artemis has a lot in common with him, both being "natural born scientists" and child geniuses. Interestingly enough, Beckett, on the other hand, is depicted as an "unruly" child and a "dirty" one to boot, who determinedly resists toilet training. When Artemis points out that Beckett should be wearing a diaper, the following exchange takes place between the sibling rivals:

"Diaper," snorted Myles, who had potty trained himself at the age of fourteen months, building a stepladder of encyclopaedias to reach the toilet seat.

"No diaper," pouted Beckett, slapping at a still buzzing fly trapped in his sticky blond curls. "Beckett hates diaper." [4]

Introduced in the "Prologue" and Chapter 1, the twins disappear from the rest of the novel, reappearing briefly in the last chapter where Beckett is dubbed "the whirlwind known as Beckett Fowl" (385).

There is no reference to the twins in the next volume, *The Atlantis Complex* (2010). In its opening paragraphs, there is, however, an extensive and revealing comment on James Stephens' *The Crock of Gold* (1912) which Artemis Fowl I reads to his young son Artemis and which "told the story of a greedy bucko who captured a leprechaun in a vain effort to steal the creature's gold" (3). Here is the real clue to the Irish literary background of the Artemis Fowl series: Stephens' fairy-tale world is the decisive factor, not the works of either O'Brien or Beckett. Colfer's introduction of the twins Myles and Beckett would seem to be an Irish in-joke as it updates the modern Irish literary tradition. These allusions would not, of course, be recognized as such by its teenage audience (Irish or otherwise), no matter how appreciative they might be of some of Colfer's more outrageous puns designed for their entertainment. The Artemis Fowl series might be best characterized as "sci-pi," in so far as it deals with Artemis' battles against pixie power of the paranoid variety.

The twins do appear in the eighth and final volume of the series, *The Last Guardian* (2012), and in this instance they are more integrated into the plot of the novel (both are "possessed" by alien figures from the fairy-world and released in the dénouement). Beckett's characterization remains the same: not willing to "follow the simplest instruction" and still adamantly "sick of underpants (80). So: in "kid lit" of the Irish popular culture variety, Beckett, unruly and excrementally challenged, doesn't quite seem to fit in with his Irish family. And this depiction does make for a refreshing change from the Beckett as genius-writer refrain of so much Beckett hagiography.

Finally, Paul Auster is a writer so familiar with Beckett that the "degeographized" worlds are linked together seamlessly, and his worlds are close to Beckett's. Auster has a long and well-known relationship to Beckett, from personally knowing Beckett to becoming a series editor for his work. As Linda Hutcheon argues in *A Theory of Parody*, parody can be "an act of emancipation for [an] author to transcend predecessors,"[24] and it is in this sense that we can see Paul Auster using Beckett. Auster has parodied Beckett's world and created an original, authentic world of his own, much as Beckett used Verne before him in creating his own vision. As Julie Campbell argues in

"Beckett and Paul Auster: Fathers and Sons and the Creativity of Misreading" via Bloom's *The Anxiety of Influence* and psychological theory from D.W Winnicott,[25] Auster recreates Beckett's works through his act of "misreading."

In the Country of Last Things and Auster's film *Lulu on the Bridge* are works that are heavily indebted to Beckett but have not had as much critical notice as, say, *The New York Trilogy*. *In the Country of Last Things* is a very close rewriting of some of Beckett's shorter pieces, in particular "Enough" (1965), while *Lulu on the Bridge* encompasses much of Beckettt's *Murphy* and other texts. The similarities and allusions are not merely superficial to keep readers intrigued: parodying Beckett in this manner is a method of bringing what could be termed Beckett's perceived "elitist aestheticism" into the everyday by a very talented author. Auster's parodies of Beckett, therefore, allow us to make "sense of the unintelligible" by transposing Beckett's challenging texts into a new context, placing "the contemporary under scrutiny."[26] Or, as Julie Campbell points out, "Auster is not only 'twisting' Beckett's work in a different direction but also filling in many of the gaps in Beckett's work, giving substance to what lacks substance" (302). Auster has said he intended to "open up the process, to expose the plumbing" of writing, and Beckett's appeal is thus evident as Beckett deconstructed traditional narrative. Deleted scenes from *Lulu on the Bridge* have been called "Auster's best attempt to date at exposing the "plumbing of cinema," the implications and complications of filmmaking."[27] By noticing these connections, we can see how Paul Auster, too, shares much of Beckett's world in creating his dystopia.

In "Enough," Beckett has a female narrator recounting her past relationship with a much older male teacher who taught her everything, as "All I know comes from him."[28] These two wander through the country for at least ten years, the old man crippled and bent, looking at the flowers they step upon. Ultimately, the old man stops, asks the woman to leave, which she does without looking back, and they are forever separated. For the woman, she reflects back that she learned everything from him but it was now her turn to create. She is then the author having emancipated herself and "transcended her predecessor." Auster also uses a female protagonist, Anna Blume,[29] in *In the Country of Last Things* who leaves her home country to come to the nameless port city to find her brother who had come earlier to report back on the changes happening to the city. The city is in a far more desperate plight than she could have known, and it quickly becomes evident she will not be able to find her brother, let alone return. She then begins "scavenging" lost or last items to sustain herself, meets up with some people who quickly become family, one of whom is a Sam Farr—surely not a coincidence—and then, after many devastating events, begins a letter which is the text we are reading as she and her companions are ready to attempt to leave the city. Like the female protagonist in Beckett's "Enough," Anna finally becomes an author too. Auster knows Beckett so well that his references to Beckett are not so much allusions but have become integral to his writing, and he will, like Beckett's female protagonist, use parody as a form of transcending his predecessor, whether in *The New York Trilogy* or *In the Country of Last Things*. Although not immediately evident apart from the obvious shared female narrator, Auster's use of "Enough" in *In the Country of Last Things* has many similar images and aesthetic views, where the female narrator must be birthed or resurrected into narrative.

Early in her letter in *In the Country of Last Things*, Anna asks: "Do you see what I am trying to say? In order to live, you must make yourself die." Here is Beckett. The opening of "The Calmative" is "I don't know when I died. It always seemed to me I died old, about ninety years old,"[30] and we can see that Auster and Beckett share a vision that one is birthed into narrative the same way one is expelled (dies) into narrative. Julie Campbell goes further and points out that "Auster can be seen to be 'giv[ing] birth' to his literary father through his creative misreading" (302). The act of storytelling is like taking a walk as Beckett told John Pilling regarding *Molloy*, or, as Anna says, "I put one foot in front of the other, and then the other foot in front of the first, and then hope I can do it again. Nothing more than that. You must understand how it is with me now. I move. I breathe what air is given me. I eat as little as I can. No matter what anyone says, the only thing that counts is staying on your feet" (2). This is another rewriting of the impasse of the Unnamable. Anna thinks that to a large degree she is just a transcriber, saying, "There is no way to explain it [the city consuming itself]. I can only record, I cannot pretend to understand" (22), much like in Beckett's "Text 5" where the quill notes the "dictation" from the voices. Again, Auster's use of Beckett is a complex interweaving because he knows Beckett so well. What these respective narrators are transcribing is the tortured process of turning life into art, whether it be in Beckett's purgatorial zone of creativity or Auster's apocalyptic city of creativity. For both of these authors, though, it is a tortured process, using imagery of imprisonment for which they feel they are on trial. In "Enough," the narrator and the old man walk upon the flowers, the beautiful, and the narrator will turn these into art: "The art of combining is not my fault. It's a curse from above. For the rest I would suggest not guilty" (187). Anna is likewise incarcerated, this time in the larger city, and also possesses the same necessity to create, writing "I don't believe there is any way this letter can reach you" (183), yet she will not give up writing it. She is compelled.

The references to Beckett are so numerous and, at times, subtle, that it is hard to distinguish that *something* comes from this particular work of Beckett so much as this *something* is part of a larger aesthetic that can also be found in Beckett. The repeated echoes in Auster are too similar to be coincidence, and we begin to see the complex layering of allusion and doubling. Being birthed into narrative, Anna must go on even when she does not want to, nor feel the ability to. Here again is Beckett and the famous conclusion to the trilogy. Auster has Anna abandoned in this decaying, purgatorial existence where she must struggle for every step that she takes, and she must take them to stay alive. However, she forms attachments, and it is these artificial families that keep her alive. In the Director's Commentary for the film *Smoke*, Auster comments on the importance of these bonds:

> What is this story about? It's about people who are fragmented, unattached, without any grounding in family life. And it's, I think, in some sense, a story of how people who are adrift in the world sometimes manage to form artificial families, families of affection that are not linked by blood, but just by circumstances and mutual sympathy. And it is about family in that sense and it's also about lost children and who takes care of these lost children.[31]

This is an important statement in understanding some of the continuing aesthetic that underlies Auster's work, but this could also be a good description of much of Beckett's work.

Using Paul Auster's other works can help understand his world of *In the Country of Last Things* and can also help us see further connections to Beckett's world, through both geography and image, and bridge the gap between the literary world and the more popular cinematic. During the late 90s, Auster was involved with the three films *Smoke*, *Blue in the Face*, and *Lulu on the Bridge*. *Lulu on the Bridge* (1998) is a complex film that works on top of the 1929 German silent film *Pandora's Box*, as well as having some cleverly disguised parodies of Beckett. The most obvious similarity is the female character Celia, played by Mira Sorvino. At the outset, she is a struggling actress working as a server in a restaurant in order to support herself. As the plot progresses, she meets up with the musician Izzy (Harvey Keitel) who had earlier been shot in the chest, and they begin a relationship centered around a box with a mysterious levitating, incandescent stone that brings them together through feelings of empathy, love, and giving. Izzy then manages to help Celia land the coveted role of Lulu in a movie remake of "Lulu on the Bridge" being filmed in Ireland. He is going to join her there, but he is kidnapped and she left to worry about him. Later, people after the stone confront her in Dublin, and she is forced to flee from them, ending in her jumping off the Ha'penny Bridge over the river Liffey.

Auster explains how this story manifested itself to him in the Director's commentary. He says that "I had the name 'Celia' which I liked, and then as often happens, an idea spins out from something you've already established."[32] "Celia," however, is also the name of a prostitute in Beckett's *Murphy*, and this is no coincidence. It is from here that Auster gets the name once we see the further similarities. Beckett's Celia is also connected to suicide as she benefits from "the old boy's" "felo de se" in the room above where she is living, allowing Murphy and her to take the cheaper room that would now be hard to "let."[33] Murphy also may commit suicide, killed in a gas explosion,[34] much like Mr. Kelly almost commits suicide upon waking, losing his kite and walking into the pond to retrieve it.[35] These may be trivial, but in *Dream of Fair to Middling Women*, Nemo commits suicide by jumping into the Liffey, just like Auster's Celia, with Nemo's obituary reading: "A finding of Felo-de-se from Natural Causes was found."[36] Auster did not just "have" the name Celia. He is far too familiar with Beckett's corpus for this to be a coincidence.

The other parodies are many and subtle. Auster as director uses strategies and images that are strikingly similar to Beckettian mise-en-scènes and images in his works. For instance, after Izzy is shot in the chest and we see him in a hospital bed, the lack of defined setting with a recognizable backdrop is very similar to any of the "degeographized" settings of Beckett that seem to represent a limbo or purgatorial-type setting, in particular *The Unnamable*. Also, when Izzy is first opening the mysterious box that has the stone in it, Auster has a cacophony of indistinguishable voices that represent the multicultural origins of the stone. Beckett frequently uses this device, for example in *Play* where the stage direction reads, "Voices faint, largely unintelligible."[37] These stage directions seem to be a condensed version of Auster's when Izzy unwraps the newspaper covering the stone: "The papers are written in different languages: Russian, Chinese, Hebrew, Arabic. Sound: all through this shot, a vague murmuring of different voices can be heard, male and female alike, each one speaking a different language. Nothing can be heard distinctly. Every now and then a word emerges from the confusion, but only for the smallest flicker of a second."[38] Again, Auster can be seen to be filling in the "gaps" of Beckett's minimalism. And when Izzy breaks out of his imprisonment, we have a scene where the camera stays on Izzy for a prolonged time as he struggles to get out of a high window to the outside. The image begins on the inside with a focus on Izzy breaking out of the window, then switches to the outside where we see that it takes him a few moments to completely wriggle out. Izzy is, here, being birthed, much as Beckett has his protagonist of "The Expelled" birth himself into narrative after the cabman allows him to sleep in his stable: "So I was obliged to leave by the window. It wasn't easy.

But what is easy? I went out head first, my hands were flat on the ground of the yard while my legs were still thrashing to get clear of the frame. I remember the tufts of grass on which I pulled with both hands, in my effort to extricate myself."[39] Auster has given us a visual representation of the Beckettian passage, focusing on the "legs ... thrashing to get clear of the frame."

Regardless, even if one wants to cavil at the depth of connections—does this name really come from Beckett? does this image really come from Beckett?[40]—it is the shared aesthetic vision that is realized in the last scene where the depth of Auster's indebtedness to Beckett is clear. Izzy is being rushed to the hospital in an ambulance, having been shot at the beginning, and he dies as the ambulance passes Celia Burns on the street. She makes the sign of the cross seeing the ambulance. It is in this deconstruction of traditional reader expectation of narrative structures where the authors share an aesthetic similarity. Consistently, from "Assumption" and *Dream of Fair to Middling Women* on, Beckett challenged authorial control and reader expectations. After Celia makes the sign of the cross,[41] we too are left trying to figure out what we have just seen: was it all a dream? There are no easy answers. Beckett is not easy, but he is necessary, and this is what Auster gives us.

When one encounters a notoriously difficult author in different mediums quite consistently, *something* is going on. As we have seen, trivial coincidences—similar dates, similar names—proliferate at times, but taken together, the trivial becomes significant: Nemo and Celia show how each author is rewriting, filling in the gaps of, his predecessor and finding his own authorial voice: helping us, the readers/viewers, with the difficult job of "digesting" them. In the talented hands of a writer like Stanislaw Lem, Beckett is also transformed into a critique against the ever changing fashions of academia, and one can see Beckett laughing at this too, having voluntarily left academia as he had nothing to say, but it certainly has a lot to say about him. Beckett's frequent interrogation of subject and object, the other, speaks to Lem, even if he too is referencing the early popularity of "Beckettmania" that creates the conditions for a *Beckett und Einstein* and will also influence Philip K. Dick. And finally, Beckett can be completely transformed and refashioned as Paul Auster shows, engaged on a similar quest for meaning and presence as Beckett. Beckett's aesthetic speaks to a contemporary world-view, and here Paul Auster's film works are important: they bridge the high culture/low culture worlds and bring Beckett's aesthetics into a new genre and to a new audience. Beckett's comedy and striking imagery reflect and embrace the absurdity of life, the desire to escape this life but the imperative to "go on." Here is someone who cannot be co-opted by the prevailing forces; here is someone who will resist even in the face of insurmountable odds; here is someone who will go on even if only to fail. Thus, Beckett truly is "Mobilis in Mobili"— "Mobile within the mobile element"—and is being continually updated and refashioned for audiences that will create new possibilities for meaning, and when we recognize this, through an Auster, Lem or even a *Red Dwarf*, we can finally fully digest the sand in the scrambled eggs.

Notes

1. Samuel Beckett. http://en.wikipedia.org/wiki/Samuel_Beckett. Accessed September 13, 2010.

2. David Leon Higdon, "Samuel Beckett in Outer Space," *Journal of Beckett Studies: Old Series* #11 and 12. Accessed online: http://www.english93fsu.edu/jobs/num1112/153_HIGDON.PDF 1.

3. William Gibson strikes a familiar Beckettian pose, replete with black hoody, in "The Last Word," a UBC Alumni publication, responding to the question "Which famous person (living or dead) do you think (or have you been told) you most resemble? 'I used to think I looked a bit like Samuel Beckett, but it's getting harder to see.'" (*Trek*, Alumni UBC, No. 34, 2012. 52) Gibson is, actually, accurate in his description (less so in the photo that is with the *Straight* article below), but one wonders if the resemblance is getting less because of the difference growing between his and Beckett's famous hairstyle!

4. In an interview with John Burns for *The Georgia Straight*, Gibson answers, "The author has to trust the reader. In some way it's a social obligation. And as the reader, you know when that social thing is being violated by the writer, and it's not a good thing. It's not good. There are extraordinary cases where that's what it's about. Beckett, right? That's what you go there for. The guy's going to put sand in your scrambled eggs. But I'm not going to do that." www.straight.com. *The Georgia Straight*, 8 August 2007. Web. 25 April 2015.

5. Jules Verne, *20,000 Leagues Under the Sea* (New York: Signet Classic, 2001), 16.

6. James Knowlson, *Damned to Fame: The Life of Samuel Beckett* (London: Bloomsbury, 1996) 111–112, 137.

7. John Pilling, *A Companion to Dream of Fair to Middling Women* (Tallahassee, FL: Journal of Beckett Studies Books), 33.

8. *Ibid.*, 34, 63. We can now add echoes in Disney/Pixar's *Finding Nemo*, another adventure under the sea that shows the enduring appeal for this character.

9. Verne, 70–71.

10. Knowlson, 388.

11. Verne, 53, 55, 58, and 67.

12. Beckett, "Text 5," 119.

13. Samuel Beckett, "The Calmative" in *The Complete Short Prose, 1929–1989* (New York: Grove Press, 1995), 76.

14. Samuel Beckett, "The End" in *The Complete Short Prose, 1929–1989* (New York: Grove Press, 1995), 99.

15. Verne, 77–78.

16. Samuel Beckett, "Text 5" in *The Complete Short Prose, 1929–1989* (New York: Grove Press, 1995), 119.

17. *Ibid.*, 60.

18. Dean Koontz and Ed Gorman, *Dean Koontz's Frankenstein Book Two: City of Night* (New York: Bantam Dell, 2005), 150, 152.

19. Marquina, Sierra. "Exclusive: Carole Radziwill of Real Housewives of New York

City Dated Ralph Fiennes, Romance Inspired New Novel." usmagazine.com. Wenner Media, 9, July 2014. Web. 28 April 2015.

20. Early and consistently: As Mikkel Bruun Zangenberg puts it, "In an exceedingly odd way, this general, cultural demise is played out in the work of Samuel Beckett." ("Imagination Dead Imagine: On Cantankerous Fantasy" 9). Retrieved from http://static.sdu.dk/mediafiles

21. And in anticipating Apple's use, the connection also shows the sliding status of the word itself over the following decades: Even the quirky intellectual Sheldon on *The Big Bang Theory* refuses to use the word "genius" in relation to Apple's employees as he doesn't want to contribute further to the word's "devaluation" (Season 3, Episode 14, 2010). The word and images it invokes have now become cliché and ripe for parody by Hollywood. Maybe fearing this outcome ("this general, cultural demise") is why the Beckett Estate squashed the connection?

22. Which Beckett does consistently throughout his oeuvre, showing how prescient Lem is: regarding the sixty sentences rearranged in twenty-four paragraphs of *Lessness* (1969), H. Porter Abbott indicates that "Beckett followed a calculus" in "Extratextual Intelligence," *New Literary History* Vol. 28, No. 4 (Autumn, 1997): 813.

23. Fredric Jameson, *Archaeologies of the Future: The Desire Called Utopia and Other Science Fictions* (London: Verso, 2005), 111.

24. Linda Hutcheon, *A Theory of Parody* (Chicago: University of Illinois Press, 2000), 96.

25. Julie Campbell, "Beckett and Paul Auster: Fathers and Sons and the Creativity of Misreading," in *Beckett at 100: Revolving It All* (Oxford: Oxford University Press, 2008), 301.

26. Hutcheon, 110, 108, 57.

27. Jesús Ángel González, "Words Versus Images: Paul Auster's Films from *Smoke* to *The Book of Illusion*," *Literature Film Quarterly* Vol. 37, Issue 1 (2009): 39.

28. Samuel Beckett, "Enough," in *Samuel Beckett: The Complete Short Prose: 1929–1989* (New York: Grove Press, 1995) 187. For the indeterminacy of the narrator's gender see Paul Lawley "'The Scene of My Disgrace': 'Enough' and 'Memory'" in *Samuel Beckett Today/Aujourd'hui* 7 (1998): 259.

29. As well as being an allusion to the Swiss Dadaist Kurt Schwitter's 1919 poem "An Anna Blume," Anna Blume echoes Joyce's Leopold Bloom, with Bloom a Jew in a city without Jews (*Ulysses* [New York: Penguin. 1992], 44), just as there are not supposed to be any Jews in the city of Auster's *In the Country of Last Things* (95).

30. Samuel Beckett, "The Calmative," in *Samuel Beckett: The Complete Short Prose: 1929–1989* (New York: Grove Press, 1995), 61.

31. Paul Auster, *Smoke*. Director commentary at: 18 min. (Miramax 1994).

32. *Lulu on the Bridge* Director commentary at 1:20:00 (LionsGate 1998).

33. Samuel Beckett, *Murphy* (New York: Grove Weidenfeld, 1957), 145–147.

34. Murphy's death could be either suicide or accident as C.J. Ackerley points out at length in *Demented Particulars: The Annotated* Murphy (Tallahassee: Journal of Beckett Studies Books, 1998), 205–6.

35. *Ibid.*, 253, 282.

36. Beckett, *Dream*, 183.

37. Samuel Beckett, *Collected Shorter Plays of Samuel Beckett* (London: Faber and Faber, 1984), 147.

38. Paul Auster, *Lulu on the Bridge* in *Three Films: Smoke, Blue in the Face, Lulu on the Bridge* (New York: Picador, 2003), 276.

39. Samuel Beckett, "The Expelled," in *The Complete Short Prose, 1929–1989* (New York: Grove Press, 1995), 59.

40. And there are many more, too many to list here, but much more work could be

done on this: for example, Celia disappears after 13 days of filming/13 chapters of *Murphy*; Gene Kelly singing in the rain/Mr. Kelly in *Murphy*.

41. Yes, at one point in "The Expelled," Beckett's narrator even comments on this action: some people are so sloppy in making the sign, they are crucifying "people all of a heap" (*CSP*, 52).

Through a Glass, Lightly and Darkly
Depictions on Prime Time Television

P.J. Murphy *and* Nick Pawliuk

When German television broadcast Beckett's television plays in prime time, works which did indeed think "outside the box" in terms of challenging the boundaries of the medium, there was a popular revolt of sorts as viewers across the country either turned off their sets or tuned in to other channels.[1] Ironically enough, popular culture depictions of Beckett on TV have often been highly successful, and not only as kitsch versions of "Beckett lite." Beckett on TV is a much more complex phenomenon: while comic depictions predominate (as in "light" comedy invocations of Beckett), there are also a number of telling instances of Beckettian dark comedy, as well as others in which both aspects are intertwined. Underlying this basic distinction between situational comedies and dramas (with genre depictions in detective fiction and science fiction occupying a middle ground) is the fluctuation between various so-called highbrow and lowbrow characterisations of Beckett. For example: in the immensely popular *Criminal Minds* (2005–) series, in episode one of season one, Gideon name-drops Beckett's mantra from *Worstward Ho*: "Try again. Fail again. Fail better," to which his side-kick Morgan counterpoints Yoda's words of wisdom from *Star Wars*: "Try not, do or do not."[2] Another example of this tongue-in-cheek debunking of pretentious allusions to Beckett is featured in one of the opening episodes of the first year of *Miami Vice* (1984–1990): Sonny and Tubbs are on stake-out and Sonny opines that this tedious exercise is too much like *Waiting for Godot*, to which his sidekick mockingly retorts that Sonny doesn't really know anything about Beckett. (Neither, of course, did most Miamians since the premiere of *Waiting for Godot*, "billed as the laugh sensation of two continents," was a big time flop there.)[3] A more complex satirical version of the high-low cultural divide is developed in the cartoon sit-com *The Critic* (1994–1995). Jay Sherman, the host of "Coming Attractions," gives up his job as TV film critic because he refuses to be "a shill for corporate America"; taking the high road (literally so), he begins a new career as a long-distance truck-driver (the episode is entitled, "Easy Rider," and one of his first jobs is to deliver politically correct school textbooks from New York to Miami). The Beckett references are a clever inversion of the anticipated stereotypes: the red-neck sheriff of *Smokey and the Bandit* fame and his partner are in a bar when they discover that Beckett's *Endgame* is on in the West End and, ecstatic over their unbelievable good luck, exeunt, madly seeking tickets for same. There are also a couple of nice touches at the ending of the episode: Jay returns to his job and re-embraces his professional role (à la *Godot*'s pronunciation) as a "crritic" and rushes off to the studio, only to be caught in a Manhattan traffic jam, wittily echoing *Godot*'s final "They do not move."

Beckett's name does indeed pop up all over TV land, such "identity theft" admittedly often indicative of a culture vulturing aimed at appropriating the high class status of Beckett as "genius-writer." Detective shows are a case in point for such name-droppings: for example, the romantic interest in *Castle* (2009–), one Lieutenant Beckett; a postcard of Beckett is caught sight of on *Cracker*'s (1993–1996)desk; a poster advertising a production of *Waiting for Godot* is on the wall of an apartment in the last year of *24* (year 8, hour 8–9); and how about John Woo's assassins in *Once a Thief* (1996–1998), alias Murphy and Camier for the well-informed Beckett reader—not to mention our earlier reference to an episode of *Morse* in which the sub-plot that explains all turns on the *addition* of *Waiting for Godot* references *not* present in the Colin Dexter novel it is based upon. There are also substantial and insightful adaptations of Beckett in a number of sit-coms, which in addition to playing for laughs also bring to bear a focus on more problematical and "darker" elements.

The most important example in this regard is, of course, *Seinfeld*, the most famous TV sit-com of all time in the estimation of many critics, a series reputedly "about nothing." Roseanne Barr's disparaging comment about *Seinfeld*, "they think they are doing Beckett,"[4] can, as we will see, be deconstructed in such a way as to reveal how *Seinfeld* is in fact useful as a popular culture counterpoint to the mania for "nothingness" which has played such an inordinate role in Beckett studies from its very beginnings. There is a complex blending of the light and dark aspects of comedy in *Seinfeld*, even if the two specific references to the "Samuel Beckett Comedy Club"[5] do focus on Beckett's name as a venue for stand-up comedy acts such as Jerry's. A more concentrated focus on the dark comedy of the Beckettian vision is evident in the early episodes of the eponymously titled *The John Larroquette Show*, most extensively in "A Dark and Stormy Night." On display is an admixture of Beckettian elements within the Bullwer-Lytton derived mock-stock-phrase for would-be serious writing (not to mention allusions to Charles M. Schultz's *Peanuts* cartoon). On the other hand, in "No, No, Godot," an episode of *Home Improvement*, the Beckettian back drop of a production of *Waiting for Godot* is played purely for laughs.

The most darkly envisioned TV depiction of Beckett is his reincarnation as a black American soldier, Private Samuel Beckett of the Graves Registration Unit, in the late 1980s drama *China Beach*, dealing with the Vietnam War. Episode Four of its first year is titled "Waiting for Beckett" and, as this Sam Beckett's job description indicates, is focussed mainly on issues of death and dying. A lighter treatment of such issues is on display in the thirteenth and final episode of the first year of *The Riches* (2007–2008), a series in which a family of "travellers" (gypsies) has appropriated the identity of a wealthy dead couple (the Riches). In the first year finale, "Waiting for Dogot," there is a farcical as well as dramatic byplay around "Dead Doug" (Riches), who, naturally enough, never materializes and for whom the other characters are supposedly waiting.

Science fiction depictions of Beckett on TV supply an interesting variation on the above patterns: in addition to the light-dark combinations, there are also visionary and romantic elements. Dr. Samuel Beckett in *Quantum Leap* (1989–1993) combines the name of the historical Irish author with characteristics of the great scientist as genius figure (neatly combining the Beckett and Einstein images of the short-lived Apple ad campaign, "Think Different"). In addition the basic plot device of the time travelling Beckett figure who appropriates the identity of others, there are two episodes in which the historical author figure is indeed the main subject in question. The discussion of the interplay between these different roles throws some interesting light on the cult of Beckett's name. A minor instance of such name appropriation occurs in *Stargate* where there is a science officer, one Dr. Beckett, a Scotsman (perhaps an echo of the "Scottie" of "Beam me up" fame). It is hardly a surprise that the most sophisticated and arguably most witty adaptation of Beckett references in sci-fi is found in a *Star Trek: The Next Generation* episode, "Captain's Holiday" (1990), which counterpoints Joycean references with a series of intertwined Beckettian ones. While by no means exhaustive, this brief survey of Beckettian references and allusions in TV land does show the extent and variety of Beckett depiction in this most influential of popular culture mediums. Dialogical engagement with Beckett's works and the image of Beckett in the popular imagination is more than mere name-dropping or kitsch commodification. In many cases, most notably *Seinfeld*, it could be argued that they actually afford a necessary qualification of some of the entrenched critical judgements which have proved so influential in mainstream academic criticism.

Roseanne Barr's comment aside, *Seinfeld* is not, of course, really "doing Beckett"; nevertheless, there are a number of interesting parallels between the two which can assist us in reassessing via popular culture the academic reception of Beckett's works. The "show about nothing" had its debut in 1989, the year of Beckett' s death, and ran for nine years, the finale focusing on the "New York Four" on a trip to Paris to celebrate the acceptance (however much belated) of the series *Jerry*. Of course, they never do make it to Paris and make an emergency landing in Latham, Massachusetts, and are caught up in their subsequent trial for violating a Good Samaritan law. So, in a sense, ending it began: the legacy of Beckett, poet of nothingness, poster boy for postmodernist experimentation, is engaged in some interesting ways in *Seinfeld*, the postmodernist sitcom par excellence about nothing. Such a comparison reveals that, ironically enough, *Seinfeld* criticism is much more attuned to a *critical* analysis of the "nothingness" theme than Beckett criticism. A case in point, a classic instance, is *Beckett and Nothing: Trying to Understand Beckett* (2010), edited by Daniela Caselli. In her "Introduction," Caselli cites a spoof article in *The Onion* (2006) with the title "Scholars discover 23 blank pages that may well be lost Samuel Beckett play," and then adds to the gloss that the parody "identifies and mocks what is now often taken to be the defining, almost clichéd characteristic of Beckett's work: its engagement with 'nothing.'"[6] "Almost clichéd"? How about: "yada, yada, yada," which is not that far from "nada, nada, nada." Caselli's premises for her collection effectively deconstruct themselves before even getting fully underway; certainly the case for "nothingness" is not strengthened by the twelve page "Foreword: Nothing New" in which Terry Eagleton's "Cook's tour of Western Philosophy" proffers profoundly ambiguous gyrations around the issue of a postmodernist self while concluding, with a pointed reference to *Waiting for Godot*, that "Ambiguity is curse as well as blessing": "It may retrieve us from the clutches of the autocrats, but only at the cost of plunging us into a state of chronic ontological anxiety. If Beckett is decisive about at least one thing, it is that this, in the end, is the only choice."[7] But is this in fact the "only choice"? Caselli would essentially concur, maintaining that "no critical tradition has been able to disengage from the problem of nothing in Beckett, and for good reasons, even if sometimes, as P.J. Murphy has argued, this happened at the expense of being able to trace 'alternative dimensions of his work of a more affirmative nature.'"[8] All this might be deemed fine, as far as it goes—or in *Seinfeldian*,

"Not that there is anything wrong with that"—but it is not the whole story. As Murphy has argued, there are other critical traditions in which somethings and nothings can be realigned so as to bring word-worlds into being in which, without glossing over the contingencies of a destabilised self, there also exist possibilities for engagement with new horizons of the ethical and political. We need in Beckett studies more of a focus on these affirmative possibilities, on *both* "somethings" and "nothingness." The decision in Beckett studies to give such predominance to the tradition of "nothingness" is a *choice*, and not the only one. Such an either/or proposition is fundamentally ideological, assuming that the "natural" way to read Beckett is via negativity and nothingness.

Here is where *Seinfeld* can actually, believe it or not, help us "do Beckett." William Irwin's *Seinfeld and Philosophy: A Book About Everything and Nothing* (2000), the first and still arguably the strongest entry in the Popular Culture and Philosophy series, explores the sit-com's "field of being" (a rough translation of the German "sein" and "feld"). The fundamental point in this regard is that the "nothings" of *Seinfeld* are indeed "something." *Seinfeld*'s comedy is *situational*: it deals with consciousness within a world, a highly mannered world at that. The primary determinant in terms of our responses to the characters is how they disrupt in comic fashion various forms of etiquette. Beckett's worlds of fiction also often pivot around a sophisticated verbal and physical comedy of mannerisms (*Murphy* is the example par excellence in Beckett's early works).[9] But Beckett's work is also characterised by a number of philosophical conundrums around the concept of a more absolute sense of nothing: most famously expressed in Beckett's own advice to any prospective reader of his works to begin with the propositions in *Murphy* of Democritus ("Nothing is more real than nothing") and Geulincx ("Where one is worth nothing, one should want nothing").[10] The problem is, however, that such programmatic pronouncements, along with the "nothing to express" litany of "Three Dialogues" (1949), are arguably among the most striking as well as influential examples of the intentional fallacy in modern literature. Such statements cry out for *critical* appraisal, and this is still what is missing in the full sense of the word in Beckett studies, the deluge of poststructuralist studies in the 1980s and 1990s serving in large part to obfuscate the possibilities for any serious investigation of other ways of approaching Beckett's oeuvre.

The philosophers in *Seinfeld and Philosophy* have, generally speaking, one thing in common in their views on nothing: namely, that it is a relative term designating that something is less important than something else. The first classic *Seinfeld* episode is also the most "Beckettian" of all: "The Chinese

Restaurant" (1991). Here are highlighted the elements of no plot, no central romance interest, no particularly likeable characters, nor—perhaps—any meaningful transactions of any sort, only waiting for a table that never materialises, until the cast has left the stage. NBC executives vowed after this episode that never again would there be such a "no show" about "no—thing." Of course, such caveats were more or less ignored as the series developed its own distinctive "branding" through further variations on just this type of "nothing." As Jerry said when George first proposed a series about nothing, "I think you've got something there." And in the controversial conclusion to the series, the *critical* perspectives on the characters and "their little enclosed playground" (as Newman terms their narcissism) are further developed when the principals are brought to book: doing "nothing" is revealed as a "something" as the "New York Four" are sentenced to two years in jail for dereliction of civic duty. A stand-up comic is not necessarily a "stand-up guy." Why can't Beckett's works be viewed in similar fashion as *critical* evaluations of various world views instead of being too easily accepted as endorsements of such views? We need to curb our enthusiasm for fashionable clichés, whether in critical theory or popular culture; we need to go beyond Larry David's witty reiterations of "I can't go on, I will go on" in *Curb Your Enthusiasm* when he encounters another ludicrous impasse in this sequel of sorts to *Seinfeld* in which "nothing," again, happens twice.

China Beach was a critically acclaimed, albeit poorly rated, dramatic series which ran for four seasons (1988–1991), focusing on the U.S. Army's 510th Evacuation Hospital and the roles of various characters as they dealt with casualties of the Vietnam War. This is no M.A.S.H.-type mixture of the comic with pathos. The often macabre story-telling was also known for its innovative techniques, a veritable "mash-up" at times: cartoon sequences, for example, interspliced with documentary realism. At the heart of the series is a double-edged Beckettian presence. Front and center is one Private Samuel Beckett of the Graves Registration Unit who "undertakes" (literally so) the last rites for fallen combatants. In episode four of the first season, "Waiting for Beckett," we are introduced to this enigmatic character who, because of his duties, is distanced from the other military personnel and is most often characterised as being "strange," or in an irrefutable tautology, namely, "Beckett is Beckett." And from this new TV version of Beckett the standard retort in various paraphrases is: "My men. I got to take care of them." He sleeps in the morgue with them and it is as if he is privy (as in *Waiting for Godot*) to "all the dead voices." Death is the all pervasive theme and this Sam Beckett is dead tired as he sees and hears that death, "it's all around us." *China Beach*'s homage to Beckett emphasizes almost exclusively the morbid, at times pathological, sensitivity to death. A weeping Beckett in one scene is depicted on a bridge, looking into the darkness, suspended between the worlds of the living and the dead. The most iconic Beckettian scene is when Private Beckett's friends try to entice him into learning to surf; he takes off his big heavy military boots, which are then prominently displayed *Godot*-style on a set of portable steps on the beach and feature in several extended close-up shots.

The boot image on the beach strikingly recurs as two lines of dozens of empty boots on tables as Beckett eulogizes all the dead, all the "names," and he remembers them all, because he has "the gift of the words" ("Hello Goodbye Part I" season 4, episode 16). The scenery and lighting become much brighter, however, as his character develops away from the flat stereotypes of the nihilist Beckett, author of negativity. This Beckett does not turn his future wife's brother in to the South Vietnamese Army even though the brother is VC and had almost killed him; instead, he helps rebuild Mai's family's hut after the Tet offensive, pays off a debt so she can still work at the base, and ultimately gets married to her and has an immediate family with her son. This Beckett is indeed a "saint" in 'Nam ("Escape" season 4, episode 4). That Private Beckett is reminiscent of Samuel Beckett the author goes beyond the similarity of names. Both held marginalized jobs during the war effort: Sam Beckett in the GRU at the Red Cross hospital that is China Beach, just as the author worked as a driver at the St. Lô hospital in France after World War II. The show tells us that "The boots are all that are left" and "we musn't forget" as "the boots belong to us" ("Hello Goodbye Part I").

The Beckettian presence in *China Beach* is more than just the complex depiction of Private Sam Beckett: the central character on the series is Nurse Colleen McMurphy. The series ended before all of her various issues, including "reintegration" into American society, were worked out. Colleen McMurphy (a double, or even triple dose of Irishness embedded in her names) is another variant on the "Americanisation" of Beckett as found in Ken Kesey's *One Flew Over the Cuckoo's Nest* with its anti-authority hero Randall McMurphy. The in-depth orchestration of Beckettian elements in *China Beach* does warrant further attention.

The Riches adopts a less heavy-handed approach to Beckettian materials. The series ran for a season and a half (2007–2008); a critical as well as a ratings success, it dealt with a family of crooks (Irish travellers or gypsies) who assumed the identity of an upper-middle class family (the Riches) who have died in an automobile accident. Hence the premise is designed to engage in social satire of various sorts, such as social status itself as a con game, the gypsy code of values versus that of straight society, and so on. What is of interest to us is how the series also engages in literary satire and how this adds another dimension to the "high" / "low" material and cultural divide. This is most evident in the thirteenth and final episode of year one: "Waiting for Dogot."

The labyrinthine twists and turns of the scam perpetrated by Wayne Mallory when a friend of the dead Doug Riches shows up need not concern us. The main point is that Wayne and his wife Dahlia conspire to convince the friend that Doug has "gone dark" in a witness protection program. So: the mise-en-scène is waiting for a dead guy to phone back and what those on stage do to while away the time. One of the more mundane activities they engage in is a game of Scrabble, which is indeed fitting in so far as "Doug," "Dog," and "Godot" are shuffled around in anagrammatic patterns. All is smoke and mirrors: as one of the characters opines, "I'm not myself," to which in Beckettian wit à la *Godot*, another retorts, "Who is?" Besides the playing around with the *Godot* plot, there are a number of other suggestive echoes of a Beckettian spectral presence. Namely: Wayne and Dahlia Mallory's children—the adolescent daughter Delilah is nicknamed "Di Di," and their youngest son, the cross-dressing Sam, speaks French and has an artistic sensibility, as evidenced in his wall paintings depicting his family's criminal history as imposters caught between two worlds. No "Godot" arrives to sort out the plot, there is no *deus ex machina*: instead, Dahlia's cousin from the clan, the villainous Dale, makes an appearance and plans to cut himself in on the Riches scenario. The series ended in the middle of its second year, primarily due to the TV writers' strike. Since then lead actor Eddie Izzard has attempted to finish the story by securing the financing for a movie "sequel," thus far without success, suggesting yet another variation on Beckett's last words in *Three Novels*: "I can't go on, I will go on, perhaps."

The John Larroquette Show (1993–1996) provides a very interesting counterpoint to *Seinfeld* at the height of its powers in the 90s and to Roseanne Barr's disparaging statement regarding the cast of *Seinfeld* thinking that they are "doing Beckett." Larroquette plays John Hemingway, a recovering 20 year alcoholic, 36 hours sober at the series outset, who, with his MA in English literature, takes on the job as a manger of a second rate—possibly third—bus station in St. Louis. Four of the last six managers were murdered, with the other two committing suicide, the last of whose chalk outline is still on the office floor. This is not *Seinfeld* or *Roseanne*. On the office door of the previous manager was the sign "Abandon All Hope"—this might be the entrance to Hell Dante envisioned, arguably Beckett's favorite author. The show reveals its early true nature, however, in the hanging of a sign that John Hemingway takes pleasure in—a sign that is actually John Larroquette's from his youth. The sign reads "This is a dark ride"—liberated from a carnival in Larroquette's youth and still hanging over his desk in his office today. Mahalia, the all-knowing station assistant, comments on it and John Hemingway retorts, "There should be one hanging at the end of the birth canal." Shades of Vladimir's comment in *Waiting for Godot* when he says, "Astride of a grave and a difficult birth. Down in the hole, lingeringly, the grave-digger puts on the forceps. We have time to grow old" (II. 90–91).

The John Larroquette Show is indeed very Beckettian at times, and nowhere more so than at the end of season one in the episode "A Dark and Stormy Night." John Hemingway has all the angst of a failed academic, a failed husband (he initially refuses to believe his marriage is over), and perhaps even a failed drunk (it was the one thing he was good at), but in this episode he is confronted with his own death and chooses life. Hemingway's bus station inhabitants are taken hostage by a man angered that his mother died and was buried as a "nothing" in an unmarked grave due to a Kafkaesque bureaucratic blunder and lost papers erasing her identity. Hemingway offers to stand in for the hostages, but when he is almost killed, he chooses life and wants to live. Fortunately, the gunman suffers a heart attack at the crucial moment: "Oh good, he's having a heart attack," Mahalia says to relieve the tension. Hemingway then saves him by, we surmise, performing CPR. Hemingway then wants to know what it—life, death—is all about.

The show then cuts to the final scene in Hemingway's rented apartment. There is much Beckett here, the anguish, the angst, the existential question, the rain, the artist's garret even. The influential musician David Crosby, who plays Chester, Hemingway's recently deceased AA sponsor, is there as a ghost and he tries to comfort Hemingway and answer his questions about why should one live if this is all there is: pain, suffering, and saving a life so the person might be able to inflict more suffering on others. Crosby/Chester's answer is simple: have a donut. Enjoy life. Life is for the living. And here, because there is a God (made clear through Chester's presence as he is not a figment of John's imagination) there is a knock on the door and Carly, a prostitute/love interest à la Celia in Beckett's *Murphy*, shows up with donuts and an answer to all Hemingway's questions: sex. Even Didi and Gogo didn't have it this easy.

The scene that ends season one is dark—too dark for a 90s Prime-Time sitcom, so the series underwent a dramatic "reset" for season two rather than be cancelled. Naturally, Beckett's influential "darkness" is minimized, immediately noticeable as John Hemingway gets a larger, brighter, ideal apartment in episode one, with the rest of the tone, scenes and social situations much more light and lighthearted. However, Beckett is still present, if only in spirit, as a spectral presence, in a highly stylized poster in the key location in Hemingway's apartment, visible in almost every scene there—beside the entry door. The poster is the classic image of Beckett as a floating head, part of his carefully crafted authorial presence. Larroquette's personality and talent, with Don Reo's effective writing, not only embrace the stereotypes of Beckett and transform them for a popular audience, but also engage with some of Beckett's more subtle themes and present them in a contemporary, and humorous, context. They are "doing Beckett," even if it was only for one season.

Tim Allen's *Home Improvement* (1991–1999) exploits a much more common depiction of Beckett. The fourth season episode "No, No, Godot" goes much further than the usual name-dropping or brief allusion. *Waiting for Godot* is woven into the main script as both a destination and ordeal. Tim the Tool Man Taylor, played by Tim Allen, would much rather be at a Detroit Red Wings hockey game but must sell the tickets because hockey tickets are much easier to resell than community theater tickets. He tries to scalp them with his *Tool Time* co-host and friend Al, his straight man, while Jill, Tim's wife and Eileen, Al's girlfriend, are at the theater waiting for them. Al is enthused about the play, in fact preferring to be there than possibly being late because of selling the hockey tickets, as he played the "definitive" Pozzo in his high school production. When Tim finally does get a buyer for the tickets, the buyer is an undercover police officer and Al trades lines from *Waiting for Godot* with him, to Tim's dismay and disgust, even commenting that maybe they wouldn't be going to jail if Al had not "pulled out his Pozzo" back there. Meanwhile, Jill and Eileen think they have been stood up, waiting for their partners.

Jill vents her frustration throughout the play, being overheard and loudly hushed by different members of the audience, even Pozzo on stage at one point. It is in her frustration, and Tim's at having to go to *Godot*, that we get the most popular stereotypes of Beckett: pretentious, academic, intellectual, inscrutable, and for the elite. Even when Tim finally arrives the comedy continues. The show ends with Tim waking up to audience applause, confusing intermission for the play's end, and we see his anguish when he learns there is another act where nothing will happen, no one will arrive: "You serious! I've got to sit through more of this crap?" Tim is the voice of all those long suffering husbands who have had to sit through a production of a Beckett play.

Quantum Leap (1989–1993) deals through science fiction with much comic fare, but also delved into serious historical issues that still remain favorites to some of the cast, two of many being feminism, and racism and desegregation. With the recent DVD release of the show and its supplementary material, we can see behind the scenes, in particular how Scott Bakula, who plays the protagonist Dr. Sam (Samuel) Beckett, still doesn't fully understand the show and thinks he probably cannot fully explain it. The Wikipedia entry directly recognizes the confusion the show can cause with its caveat: "For the Irish writer, see Samuel Beckett."

Dr. Sam Beckett has six Ph.D.s, was named the "next Einstein," has developed a "parallel hybrid computer" named Ziggy, and developed a time travel machine that he enters, but the "time travel experiment … went a little kaka." He has a close friend named Admiral Albert (Al) Calavicci (close to the Hal of Kubrick) who appears to him as a neurologic hologram. Sam has become stuck, bouncing around time: as he entered the time machine, God, they think, took control. We learn much later that Sam has been unconsciously controlling his leaping the whole time. Sam appears to everyone as the character he enters except to himself in a mirror. Even Al sees him in his new guise, which causes him to go into therapy when Sam leaps into an attractive woman in season two. Ziggy, a type of artificial intelligence computer with an ego, calculates why Sam is where he is and what he needs to do or fix before he is able to jump through time again, with Sam always hoping it will be the jump back to the present, to home. Sam at first is distraught when he voices his fear that he could be "bouncing around in time forever," but Al comforts him saying, "No, nobody lives forever."

This series had a rocky start and did not get really popular until the fans clamored for it after its first season was cut short. In season two, Donald P. Bellasario wrote episode one entitled "Honeymoon Express," and this is where the Beckett references become subtle and detailed at a very significant place in the show's history:

> Sam: "I have something to tell you. My name isn't Tom Macbride."
> Diane: "Oh, then what is it?"
> Sam: "B … Beckett. It's … uh…. *Sam* Beckett"
> Diane: "The playwright?"
> Sam: "I don't think so."
> Diane: "Then who?"
> Sam: "Well, primarily I'm … uh … a quantum physicist."

Sam's life as the honeymooning Tom Macbride is threatened—he will be stabbed in the heart by the ex-husband of Diane just like Samuel Beckett was stabbed in the chest on a Paris street before World War II. Diane's ex-husband is a former French resistance psychopath who has earlier in the day killed his psychiatrist in New York who had diagnosed him as "regretfully … quite mad." The French resistance fighters were betrayed to the Nazis by a French woman who had a German lover, with all of them being killed by the Gestapo except Diane's ex-husband, Roget. The casual viewer of the show is probably not aware that Beckett, the writer, himself participated in the French resistance, with his cell being discovered too, and his fleeing from Paris to hide out for the remainder of the war, some of which influences happenings in *Waiting for Godot*.

Bellasario wants us to connect his show with the Nobel Prize winning Beckett, and this is made clear near the end of the series. In a very ideologically charged episode on the women's liberation movement in which Sam leaps into a housewife who must engage with her changing family and her daughter's politics, Sam makes the family breakfast, "Griddle cakes à la Beckett." His/Her husband, George, says to Sam, "à la what?" Sam responds, "Beckett." The daughter, Suzie, clarifies, "Beckett, dad. He's the famous playwright, Samuel Beckett." Sam explains, to cover his mistake at almost revealing his "true" identity, "Actually, I was thinking of Ma Beckett, the famous cook." So here the scene comes back to the standard name-dropping, but by the end of the series, the name-dropping functions differently. It is to remind us, the audience, that throughout the series the name Sam Beckett has always performed two roles, the "famous playwright" and the "quantum physicist." Both are engaged throughout at all times in the minds of the audience, even if we don't know consciously that we are engaged in such an act. Thus Beckett functions as a presence that is always there, even when the references are not directly to his work.

Beckettian elements in television programs occur across genres and almost defy cataloguing. There is everything from simple references by name-dropping to more clever ones such as in *The Simpsons* episode "In the Name of the Grandfather" (2009). Here Grampa Simpson guilts Homer into accompanying him to complete an item on his bucket list, which turns out to be having a last drink at Tom O'Flanagan's pub—in Ireland. With the scene introducing the pub, Irish stereotypes abound in the musical number. Most patrons are dancing and singing, but seated at a table from left to right are Joyce, Beckett, Shaw and Wilde. Many empty glasses are on the table and the sedentary Joyce and Wilde are throwing darts while singing. Beckett is all in black with his shock of grey hair: the usual image portrayed. What is different here is that even though his image is stereotypical, the "Irish" nature of drinking and singing is discordant with the popular stereotypes of the cultured author. Not so in the popular American series *House* which makes the usual references to *Waiting for Godot*. Here Gregory House suffers unending agony with a painful physical condition. The references are likewise dark: that *Waiting for Godot* could have been titled *Waiting for House*, but the prospect was too bleak; and that waiting for results from the Atlanta center for disease control is like *Waiting for Godot*. Beckett is also used in more complex ways, particularly evident in the clever parody of both *Waiting for Godot* and *Endgame* in the *Red Dwarf* (1988–) episode "Waiting for God." The protagonist Lester is a representation of a Godot-figure as "God" to a Hamm look-a-like who is dying on the spaceship, which stands in for the set of *Endgame*. The difference here, though, is that even though this "Godot" arrives, he is, of course, not Godot, just the "working class git" Lester.

A much more detailed use is found in *Star Trek: The Next Generation*'s "Captain's Holiday" (1990). Captain Jean-Luc Picard is the future embodiment of the "genius"-type that Beckett popularly represents. He is a figure who can do anything, even negotiating a virtually impossible peace accord, and reads Joyce's *Ulysses* for relaxation on his "enforced" holiday, a little "light reading."[11] The Beckett references are subtle and encrypted. Although the female archaeologist Vash's mentor was a Professor Estragon who had researched a crystal from the future for half his life, he never found it. In the search for the crystal, Vash and Picard become a Didi and Gogo substitute, even with some of their comic behavior. The set also takes on *Waiting for Godot* elements. They are bathed in moonlight on a rocky, barren set:

> Vash: "We're a lot alike. It's probably why we get along so well"
> Picard: "You call this getting along?"
> Vash: "Fine. We don't get along; we're not getting along."
> Picard: "I didn't say that."

This conversation could be taken right from Didi and Gogo and their banter. The difference in "Captain's Holiday" is that Picard, of course, finds the crystal and apparently solves the problems; but not for everyone: Sovak, the antagonist and competitor for the crystal, is left digging an endless hole for the crystal he will never find. Even Picard pities him. The scene of Vash and Picard ends, however, with a nod to the cyclical nature of *Waiting for Godot* via time travel. As the crystal is from the future and people there want it, Picard tells Vash that he and she might be "doing this all over again" as the agents from the future might "try again" to get it. "Uh-huh," Vash answers back in a parody of Molly Bloom's "yes," similarly sexualized. Here, the Beckettian and Joycean elements are so seamlessly integrated in a subtle parody that they are probably not consciously recognized by the average viewer.

Canadian TV has a unique history given its geographic proximity to the powerful American media and, paradoxically, its striving to be "Hollywood North" for economic benefits. To counter this media behemoth, made in Canada media was promoted through a national content-based requirement, abbreviated as CanCon. This requirement promoted much "homegrown" media in all its forms and the broadcasting of specific quotas. More recently, however, with the evolving media landscape and larger corporations controlling more independents, this content requirement has dropped, but in the 90s there were still many television programs that did not see a larger global audience. For instance, a Toronto-based drama called *The City* did a whole hour-long episode entitled "Out of the Box" (2000), which was an adaptation of Beckett's *Endgame*, with an armored car robber and a hostage in a closed warehouse. But another Canadian produced show that did have a somewhat larger impact was John Woo's *Once a Thief* (1996–98), based on a 1991 movie of the same name and trying to tag along with Woo's incredible Hollywood success. The show is about a "shadowy, nefarious" government agency that works outside the law and has recruited two thieves on the run from a Hong Kong crime family. The show had a poor reception, even taking a hiatus a third of the way through the first season. In some ways, it was possibly too complex as it is very postmodern, breaking down the fourth wall, using pastiche, parody, and editing to keep the humor light, the gun play privileged and the audience guessing and entertained.

Two producers and frequent writers seem to be primarily responsible for much of the Beckettian elements: Phil Bedard and Larry Lalonde. Wikipedia includes the brief mention that "Episode 19's subplot, featuring the organization's assassins Camier and Murphy, is a parody of the Samuel Beckett play *Waiting for Godot*."[12] This brief allusion to Beckett does not recognize extensive engagement throughout the series. For instance, Murphy and Camier, a parody of the main characters of *Mercier and Camier*, Beckett's first French novel, are used repeatedly throughout the series, have distinctive aquiline features like Beckett himself, and speak in the cultured airs of European elegance, which ironically contrasts with their careers as assassins, or "the cleaners" who tidy up the messes of the "shadowy agency" they work for. They enjoy the finer things in life while dealing with the worst things in life. As well, they are reminiscent of many of Beckett's duos, like Didi and Gogo, as are the two male protagonists of the show, Mac and Vic. The series features minor, unnamed characters called "Moran," for instance, many of whom are now possibly lost as the DVD release didn't include a character list. Only someone with a thorough knowledge of Beckett's work would know some of these references, and more work needs to be done on Bedard and Lalonde's partnership. For instance:

The Director: "Where's Love?"
Crohn: "I talked to Knott, who talked to Hamm, who talked to Mr. and Mrs. Tough, who talked to Boss Croker. None of them knew. So I tried Estragon, who put me on to Vladimir, who, who knew Lady Alba, who knows Otto who knows…"
Dir: "Is there a happy ending to this story?"
Crohn: "Yes, there is, but it's a long story and it must be told."

The assistant to Nicholas Love is one Bingo Belacqua, and here is the key to unraveling many of these names to a non-Beckett scholar. Bedard and Lalonde know very thoroughly Beckett's canon, in particular *More Pricks Than Kicks*, not one of Beckett's most popular works. And it is not just name-dropping either. Nicholas Love is a parody of the "homespun Poet" in Beckett's "A Wet Night" with possible elements of James Joyce. For instance, the episode, entitled "Drive, She Said" (but here the French title might be more telling, "Tout en Poème"), opens with Love performing the same shaving ritual, employing virtually the same implements, with which Joyce's *Ulysses* opens, even with Love sharing a tower, though here a military guard tower stands in for Joyce's Martello Tower. Clearly, more work needs to be done on this series than one line in Wikipedia (actually, this episode is not even annotated). The show has a lot of fun with its literary allusions[13]; unfortunately, not much of the audience did, with the show having incredibly poor ratings and barely making it to the end of a season, with the final episode aptly entitled "Endgame." In this series, Beckett is not just comic fodder, not a stereotype to be ridiculed and held up as an example of the pretentious art world. The series, through much postmodern film techniques and parody, is engaging and transforming the author for a mass audience—here, unfortunately though, they were not buying it.

What is happening with all these references to a "high" brow, notoriously difficult author in a "low" brow medium? First, popular culture reworkings of Beckett's difficult and trying aesthetic can help us envision new ways of looking at him outside ossified, negative academic representations, too often focusing on his exclusiveness and negative aesthetic. We can see that there is still life in Beckett; his image does confer an immediate identity in popular culture. If one can indeed "think different," like Apple wants us to, we can see why Beckett is popular: he is an unassailable figure in contemporary culture: one who never sold out or succumbed to commercialism, one who stood above and alone as an artist with true integrity, one who recognized how difficult life could be or was. And these are all traits that appeal to people faced with the exact opposite in their daily life, in which all our popular culture is recycled and sold back to us. John Hemingway at the beginning of the Beckettian "A Dark and Stormy Night," upon hearing Melanie's "Look What They Done to My Song" used as a Quaker Oats commercial advertisement soundtrack, says, "Unless you laugh, you might as well blow your brains out." This representation of Beckett and all we think he might stand for—even down to baby naming—might be why the name Beckett has so much cultural importance and exchange value. And all these Becketts stand for *somethings*, not *nothings*.

Notes

1. Eckart Voights-Virchow maintains that while two million Germans did watch *Nacht und Träume* in June 1983 it "most likely remained a marginal experience for two contrasting reasons: (a) Beckett's liminal aesthetics, and (b) the cultural liminality of any single unit in the fragmented, channel-hopping TV flow" ("Face Values: Beckett Inc., The Camera Plays and Cultural Liminity," *JOBS* Vol. 10 Nos. 1 and 2: 122.)

2. Another popular culture variation is Homer Simpson's advice to his kids: "You tried your best, and you failed miserably. The lesson is, never try" (*The Simpsons*, "Burns' Heir," 7:56). All these proverbial sayings are, of course, variations on the Aesopian moral: "If at first you don't succeed, try, try again."

3. If at first you don't succeed with a popular appeal, try again with an up-market appeal to the cognoscenti—which indeed is what occurred when *Waiting for Godot* tried again—successfully—in New York.

4. This quotation can be found extensively online. See, for instance, *The Guardian* online article entitled "Life After Seinfeld," http://www.theguardian.com/tv-and-radio/2012/apr/30/after-seinfeld-jerry-sitcom.

5. The reference is apocryphal, but there is indeed a Samuel Beckett Theater in New York, not to mention Sports Bars et al.

6. Daniela Caselli, ed., *Beckett and Nothing: Trying to Understand Beckett* (Manchester: Manchester University Press, 2010), 6.

7. *Ibid.*, xxvi.

8. *Ibid.*, 8.

9. See in this regard David P. Pierson's "A Show about Nothing: *Seinfeld* and the Modern Comedy of Manners," *Journal of Popular Culture* Vol. 34, Issue 1 (Summer 2000): 49–64.

10. There is only one explicit reference to Beckett in *Seinfeld and Philosophy: A Book About Everything and Nothing*, William Irwin, ed. (Chicago: Open Court), 2000. Kelly Dean Jolley in "Wittgenstein and *Seinfeld* on the Commonplace" points out the fundamental flaw in the Costanza Maneuver in which George does the opposite of his normal behavior: "Opposing these inclinations would bring George back to square one, since an opposite's opposite is simply what you started with. Worse yet, George would have to apply the principle over and over again, without end, in a pointless regression barely more absurd than his own life. Like something out of Beckett, no?" (124).

11. In an absurd parody of the famous Marilyn Monroe picture where she is reading the same text, Picard is likewise sexualized via a sunbathing outfit.

12. http://en.wikipedia.org/wiki/Once_a_Thief_(TV_series).

13. For example, in "It Happened One Night," the exotic dancer performing to her voicing of Molly Bloom's soliloquy from James Joyce's *Ulysses* first plays a game of "guess who" with the protagonist Mac and gives him the two hints that she likes "Irish literature" and "quantum mechanics," a playful reference to *Quantum Leap*.

Screenings for Beckett in Modern Film
Ghostly Presences and Popular Culture Manifestations

Cameron Reid

It is necessary to speak of the ghost, indeed to the ghost and with it.[1]

A comical 2½-minute video-short (commissioned by the Irish Film Board in 2001) depicts James Joyce and Samuel Beckett out for a round of golf in Zurich, 1922. The short, entitled "Pitch 'n' Putt with Joyce 'n' Beckett,"[2] takes full advantage of the familiar public image of Samuel Beckett, the mysterious Beckett: enigmatic, remote, dressed in black. The actor playing Beckett sits on a park bench, staring out to sea. At one point, he reaches into his pocket, pulls out a golf ball, looks at it, then transfers it to another pocket. (The scene recalls the movement of *sucking stones*, from pocket to pocket, in Beckett's *Molloy*).[3]

As Beckett looks off into the distance (or maybe the void?), a cursing, dissatisfied James Joyce rages (i.e., about golf clubs, his shot, little yellow pencils, chocolate bars, etc.). Joyce does all the talking in the short:

(*To himself*): "Pitch 'n' putt? It's bitch and slut."
(*To a shop girl, selling clubs*): "Do you think I'm fucking blind? Giving me a five [iron], and I the cock of the land. You are no more than nothing."
(*To Beckett*): "You're very fucking quiet."

Unresponsive to Joyce's rantings, Beckett sits *quiet*—in fact, "very fucking quiet"—in his dark trench coat and trademark black turtleneck. His gaze, unbroken, remains fixed on a distant sea: he is present, but absent.

Being Perceived, Avoiding Detection

> Beckett was more effective than any other twentieth-century writer in the strategic control and dissemination of a personal aesthetic and an authorial persona.[4]

Surely, there is something contrived about this persona—one so tightly controlled by a litigious Beckett Estate, if not by Beckett himself, during his life. He cuts the figure of a detached, inscrutable man; of one who ostensibly eschewed celebrity, but used press agents and professional photographers to disseminate precisely that image (of one who hates to be seen, who resists publicity, who hides).[5]

His plays, too—so well known, but so guarded, with licenses granted to those who maintain the strictest adherence to Beckett's stage directions, mise en scène, dialogue, lighting cues: *no additions, no omissions, no alterations*. Following Beckett himself, who in his life demanded fidelity be paid to even the most niggling details of his work, Edward Beckett (Beckett's nephew and current executor of the Estate) has maintained a near-obsessive control over professional performances of Beckett's plays. Australian theatre director Neil Armfield was once deemed adversary to Beckett's fixed intent for his proposed alterations to a Sydney production of *Waiting for Godot*: "In coming here with its narrow prescriptions, its *dead controlling hand*, its list of 'not alloweds,' the Beckett Estate seems to me to be the enemy of art."[6]

Renowned video director Mark Romanek, who directed the original "man in black," Johnny Cash, in Cash's last video, "Hurt," might well concur. For his part, Romanek recreated images from the first Paris staging of Beckett's *Waiting for Godot* in his video for k.d. lang's "Constant Cravings." Romanek shot the video in black-and-white and married scenes from the play with images of a delighted Parisian audience watching the performance. Offstage, lang sings into an old reel-to-reel tape recorder (a key prop from Beckett's *Krapp's Last Tape*). Romanek's vividly imagined, even impressionistic, rendering of that first performance (with its bright lights, exuberant energy, and marionette-like dances) may have hinted at what he (Romanek) would have done with his proposed feature film of *Waiting for Godot*—a proposal, of course, shot down by the Estate.[7]

The specter of Beckett, furthered by the "dead controlling hand" of the Beckett Estate, haunts both the uses and productions of his work: not merely as residual energy, but as active energy—one that resists, from beyond the grave, any stab at alteration, renovation, or adjustment to the work. Ironically, the seeming paranoia over how Beckett and his work are seen or perceived (*if* they're even seen at all) is dramatized in the author's own, brief foray into cinema.

Beckett made one film in his life, called "*Film*" (1965)—an experimental, silent short, some 20 minutes in length, with an aging and bloated Buster Keaton in the lead. *Film* follows the erratic movements of its main character, named "O" (not named as such within the film, but by Beckett himself in his cryptic 6-page outline/script for the film). "O" (short for *Object*) is at odds with the world. "O" sees *things*, and he sometimes runs into them (or around them, alongside them): e.g., walls, objects in the street, bystanders, a staircase, a room, house-pets, paintings, photographs. He *sees* these things, but to the extent he crosses paths with them, they *see* him too. Their sightlines converge, collide, bottleneck, thus hooking "O" into their perceptual field. "O" is marked or identified by their gaze. He is exposed.

This basic problem drives the narrative. That is, "O" wants to avoid being seen—or at least deliberately control *how* he's seen; he resists detection, and so his life becomes the ceaseless battle (depicted with Vaudevillian flair) to avoid being perceived, or, more to the point, avoid becoming an *object* (of perception). That desire to become imperceptible reads as a basic resistance to himself (so named "O")—i.e., a resistance to becoming "Object," or a resistance to being.

But again, the things he sees keep seeing him, and "O" doesn't like it. For instance, the people he passes in the street look at him, disapprovingly; the animals in his apartment watch him; the mirror reflects his face; even the religious portraiture on the surrounding walls keep an attentive, judgmental eye on him. Moreover, the camera—named in the outline "E" (or the "Eye")—sees him. In all these ways, "O" is made the object of perception, and he tries repeatedly to shield himself from the prying, inquisitive eyes of the outside world. Given Beckett's notorious attempts to tightly control and restrict access to both his literary and public faces, with almost obsessive urgency, there is surely something telling about how his only direct contribution to cinema builds its entire narrative around this singular conceit.

At the end of the film, "O" looks squarely into the camera ("E"). For the first time we get a close-up of his grizzled face, and of his one eye (the other eye is covered by an eye-patch). "O" is finally seen, and thus sees himself. He is no longer able to hide. In the end, "O" buries his face in his hands: the horror.

So, to sum up, one character, "O," played by Keaton; two basic perceptions: that of "O" and that of "E." He sees *and* is seen.

At first blush, the film seems obscure, maybe a bit of a trifle—easily overlooked, easily forgotten. The filmmakers "had difficulty marketing the film. No one wanted it.... It became a lone, very lone, piece indeed. Which no one ever saw, and seeming very few wanted to see."[8] Beckett called it an "interesting failure."[9] Keaton seemed not to understand it, and denounced it. According to its director, Alan Schneider, "The critics, naturally, clobbered us or ignored us."[10] One critic wrote, "it strikes me as being far more a poor attempt by a genuine writer to move into a medium that he simply hadn't the flair or understanding of to make a success."[11] I would argue Beckett understood the medium all-too-well.

Philosopher Gilles Deleuze devoted a short essay to Beckett's one incursion into cinema, entitled, "The Greatest Irish Film." In that essay, Deleuze suggests that *Film* asks the basic question: Is it possible to escape perception? Or can we avoid being perceived? Not only perceived by others, but by ourselves? The philosophical roots of Beckett's film trace back to the 18th-century Irish philosopher Bishop Berkeley, and his famous dictum, "To be is to be perceived" (*"esse est percipi"*). *Film* speaks directly to this concept. In the story, "O" slides along walls, darts between buildings, runs away from people; he hides in his apartment, covers up mirrors, rips up pictures, denies the house pets (with their sidelong glances) a chance to look at him, either by putting them outside or throwing a towel over the cage or fishbowl. The camera, "E," seems complicit in "O's" attempt to avoid being seen by always tracking him from behind—i.e., just out of eyeshot.

In short, *Film* is all about perception, and about resisting perception, about hiding and keeping out of sight—an interesting topic for a film, given that the cinematic medium itself is so essentially engaged in the crafting and production of images, with particular attention paid to the face in close-up. Moreover, the film industry, as a whole, especially in its more commercial or sensationalistic aspect, could so readily accept the edict, "to be is to be perceived"; or rather, "to be (in this industry) is to be looked at," "to be seen'" "to be filmed or photographed"—endlessly, ceaselessly. Resisting perception, or even escaping detection, has always been the shadow side of the industry—as to try and do so (i.e., escape perception) seems incompatible with the perpetual imaging of the face, both on and off-screen. But it is the images out-of-sight or off-limits (e.g., the starlets without make-up, or who just "want to be alone," and the illicit affairs, the tell-all's, the behind-the-scenes exposés, divulging the sordid details of the hidden face, the hidden life), which render the unperceived perceptible, and in a way that propels Hollywood Babylon. For every face made-up and presented for public consumption, a face hidden (off-stage, behind the scenes) lies undetected. But the public "eats it up" when the hidden visage of some shamed celebrity comes shockingly into focus. It has, at least, the semblance of truth for dedicated readers of *People* magazine.

Nonetheless, Beckett's *Film* speaks to this question of perception, and does so, as Deleuze claims, by suggesting, "There is something intrinsically terrifying in the fact of being perceived, but what?" Indeed—what?

The Filmic Unconscious

Beckett, himself, and his work, enter cinema as ghostly or spectral images. His presence may be felt, but not clearly, not distinctly. Beckett is perceived, but just barely, as traces of the work and, on occasion, the author himself, emerge from the shadows—much like that disembodied head of his, so often depicted in his *non*-publicity photos[12]—and then, a moment later, draw back into the darkness. But for those attuned to the whispers of the spectral Beckett, the evocation goes unnoticed. And yet, by blinking in and out of existence that way, Beckett haunts the film, the scene, or the characters' lives; and, in so doing, his presence disturbs. Recall, for example, the iconic moment waiting in line at the movie theatre, in Woody Allen's *Annie Hall*:

> Man in Line: It's like Samuel Beckett, you know—I admire the technique but he doesn't.... He doesn't hit me on a gut level.
> Alvy (to Annie): I'd like to hit this guy on a gut level.
> (*Man in Line* continues his speech, all the while *Alvy* and *Annie* talk.)
> Annie: Stop it, Alvy!
> Alvy (wringing his hands): Well, he's spitting on my neck!

The scene is staged as a somewhat generic situation. Alvy asks: "What do you do when you get stuck on a movie line with a guy like this behind you?" Or rather, what do you do when someone's rambling, self-important pontifications get too hard to ignore? The name "Samuel Beckett" here is the semiotic marker of that egg-headed rambling. But there is something more, something about the way that Alvy, Allen's character, just wants the guy to shut up: "He's screaming his opinions in my ear." Alvy adds, "I'm-I'm gonna have a stroke." *Man in Line* talks in a way that recalls Berkeley's edict ("to be is to be perceived"). In this case, the man's pontifications, his very public pronouncements, allow him a stage. They mark his being. While Alvy thinks the man should be ashamed, *Man in Line* thinks differently: "Wait a minute, why can't I give my opinion? It's a free country!"

Alvy, however, doesn't want to have anything to do with this. He feels assaulted, violated: "Well, he's spitting on my neck ... when he talks." The man's pontifications draw him out, but—like "O" in Beckett's *Film*—Alvy resists; he resists being marked, or being put on the spot like this. He is forced to listen, to hear, but does not want to be implicated in/by this man's words.

Annie wants Alvy to ignore the man ("Well, stop listening to him"), but Alvy is repeatedly drawn in. He reacts again and again to the words, and to the name-dropping (Beckett, Fellini, Marshall McLuhan). Finally, he exclaims, "What I wouldn't give for a large sock with horse manure in it."

Beckett here is just a mention from behind, and an irritating one at that. He is glimpsed; he's in Alvy's blind spot, just over his shoulder. In the end, Alvy, like "O," meets the camera directly in an act of self-awareness, but one that culminates *not* in the look of horror (that crosses "O's" face), but in the fabulation of a strategically placed Marshall McLuhan, there to help Alvy make his case against *Man in Line*. Alvy concludes, "Boy, if life were only like this."

In all, some 200 or more contemporary films and documentaries reflect the presence, if only vaguely, of Beckett, looming in the background. Generally speaking, these films are often built around some Godot-like figure—one who is not always known, but for whom the characters typically *wait*. In fact, the phrase "Waiting for..." has become an enduring conceit, restlessly employed, in modern film (in shorts, documentaries, features). Why all this waiting? What are they waiting for? For nearly everything: *for Superman, ... for Guffman, ... for God, ... for Lightning, ... for Butterflies, ... for Santa, ... for Armageddon, ... for the Miracle ... for Mercy ... for Dracula, ... for Gaga, ... for Woody Allen, ... for The Light to Change, ... for The Snow to Fall, ... for Yesterday, ... for Tomorrow, ... for Better Times, ... for Daddy, ...* and even *for Beckett*, himself.

In story after story, the plots are similar—a waiting for something to happen, a waiting for something to change, a waiting to be seen or heard, a waiting to have "an audience with," a waiting for something better, a waiting for resolution, a waiting for redemption, a waiting for a chance, etc. Often the exact thing waited on/for seems, for most, to be out-of-reach, as in Christopher Guest's celebrated "mockumentary," *Waiting for Guffman*, which depicts the efforts of a cast of delusionals waiting for producer "Mort Guffman" to come to their town and see their show; a positive word from Guffman brings the potential for Broadway to these people—or so they think. Of course, Guffman never arrives. More dramatically, the documentary *Waiting for Superman* tells the story of disenfranchised families hoping for a chance to put their kids into better schools. The movie's poster depicts a destroyed school on a decaying educational landscape. A lone child—like a lone, leafless tree—sits at a desk, *waiting for* a good education, and hence the hope of a better life.

Acts of "waiting," as suggested, permeate modern cinema. Waiting has become an axiomatic—a given, even knee-jerk, conceit, ceaselessly put to work in stories built on the promise of something more, something unnamed (or *unnameable*). Dozens of feature films, shorts, and documentaries with simply the word "Waiting" in the title take part in this conceit. A couple of titles: *Waiting to Exhale, The Waiting City, Lady in Waiting, A Child Is Waiting, Waiting Alone, The Waiting Game, Still Waiting*. On and on. Consider, also, the Cuban film *The Waiting List*, about a group of desperate people waiting for a broken down bus to be fixed. While waiting, the group work together to create a just and egalitarian society (a Socialist utopia) inside the decrepit bus station where they have been forced to wait. They will work together; and through creative, self-reliant measures, they will endeavor to get the old Soviet bus running.

Moreover, films that have acts of waiting at their core are certainly not limited to the countless movies that actually employ the words "Waiting" or "Waiting for..." in their titles. For example, one might look to films like *Big Night* or Michael Moore's documentary *Roger and Me*. In both, the one "waited for"—i.e., jazz singer Louis Prima in *Big Night* and the Chairman of General Motors, Roger B. Smith, in *Roger and Me*—end up being veritable after-thoughts in the film. Louis Prima, like Godot, never arrives. The two brothers (Primo and Secondo) believed Prima *had* been summoned, but were deceived: he was never going to come. Yet the brothers pinned the hopes of their dying business on him. They prepared elaborate dishes, anticipated his arrival, celebrated the big night; they waited.

Michael Moore, in *Roger and Me*, is left waiting for an audience with the General Motors' Chairman; while waiting, Moore's documentary explores the burned out, apocalyptic landscape of his hometown, and does so in a way suggested by Vladimir in *Waiting for Godot*: "Let us make the most of it, before it is too late! Let us represent worthily for once the foul brood to which a cruel fate consigned us!"[13] But Moore's objectives are frustrated at every turn; he is continually blocked access to Roger B. Smith by GM's henchmen and by Smith himself. Spotted briefly at a shareholders' meeting, Smith refuses Moore's request to come to Flint and see the results of the layoffs at General Motors.

The locals in Moore's documentary hope for a resurgence of Flint's economy, of working conditions, of dignity, of respect from their corporate leaders, but the film details the crumbling of those aspirations. The people are destitute, screwed up, sad, deluded, and in some cases mentally ill. Crime rates are skyrocketing. The people are enslaved, haunted not only by the past (i.e., what they used to be) but by the promise—always the *promise*—of something more, something better: The American Dream? Jobs? Dignity? So they wait; there are few options but to do so. Repo-men have jobs, and the prison system is a growth industry.

Consider, likewise, the Irish film, *Adam & Paul* (2004). At the outset, the two titular characters wake up in an abandoned lot on the outskirts of Dublin, literally stuck to a mattress—a mattress (one assumes) urine-soaked. They don't know where they are, nor why they're even there to begin with:

> Adam: How the fuck did we end up out here?
> Paul: I don't know. I haven't been out here in years.

Traces of Beckett echo in and through the film, about a day in the life of two junkies out to feed their heroin addiction. The film is reluctant to actually identify who's who, and so the pair, always together, are collectively named 'Adam and Paul.' Godot, here, is reflected in the film as the unnamed dealer, referred to simply as "what's his name." He is sought, but never found:

> Adam: Come on.
> Paul: Where?
> Adam: To see if "what's his name" is around.
> Paul: Who?
> Adam: Fuckin'… "What's his name?" … Small fellow.

Emotionally and psychologically damaged, the drifters remain firmly lodged in the margins of Dublin society, clinging together both out of habit and necessity:

> Paul: I'm fucked [read: "sick, in pain, needing a fix"].
> Adam: Yeah.
> Paul: Do we have a plan?
> Adam: Into town … see who's around, what's going on … get some money … then score.

Every day is then the same. The wandering—sick, hurt, strung out, trying to score. The pair have random conflicts and encounters with others, those who seem to be stuck as well—waiting, existing. The film traces the fate of these junkies: their pathetic hopes, their fading optimism and aimless sojourns through the most neglected, demoralized neighborhoods of Dublin. The film, with its use of physical comedy, often brutally realized, mixed with the extreme vulnerability and weakness of its characters, becomes a kind of "tragicomedy"—a Beckettian fairytale. On their ceaseless search for a fix, they steal (or attempt to); they are battered by circumstances, and repeatedly diminished by those they encounter. The *Bulgarian* asks, "Why the fuck are you here?" Yet still, they show signs of empathy for the most vulnerable around them (a baby, a man with Down's Syndrome—whom they had wanted to rob). They are, in general, overwhelmed by life. They are damaged. They are hopeless, but not without hope.

Samuel Beckett's Ghost

The specter of Beckett is felt in even more remote corners of the film industry. Here, I would point to a somewhat curious Canadian documentary, *Waiting for Fidel*.[14]

In 1974, a film crew from the National Film Board of Canada (NFB) and a small band of seekers were invited to Cuba by Fidel Castro to interview the man and report on the revolution. The team, at the time, was headed-up by Joey Smallwood (Newfoundland's notorious ex-premier) and his friend of 25 years, media mogul Geoff Stirling. On the flight to Cuba, Smallwood first tells of his love for China ("perhaps the most exciting place on earth today")—a country that all at once "flabbergasted," "fascinated," and "entranced" him; but now he wants a taste of communism closer to home. He says: "right alongside us is Cuba. I thought I'd like to go down and see—you know, after all the talk there's been ... very little of it, if any, friendly." Smallwood hopes Castro will spell out what Cuba (or technically Castro himself) might want for the restoration of "perfectly normal relations" with the U.S.: "If he'll do that," Smallwood calculates, "we could be the ones to break the news to the world." His traveling companion, Geoff Stirling, shares a similar vision: "If we're going to do films and documentaries, they should be films and documentaries that have some positive aspect and overview." They should *change* hearts and minds. And the director/narrator of the film concludes, "If we could film Fidel, we'd have something rich and rare."

The team's aspirations extend beyond mere talk and into the realm of diplomacy; and with that, a not unconscious dialogue between the documentary itself—eventually titled *Waiting for Fidel*—and Beckett's *Waiting for Godot* unfolds.

Smallwood's reasons for wanting to meet Castro echo those of Vladimir and Estragon, in *Waiting for Godot*, for wanting to meet Godot. Vladimir says,

> Let us not waste our time in idle discourse! (*Pause. Vehemently.*) Let us do something, while we have the chance! It is not every day that we are needed. Not indeed that we personally are needed. Others would meet the case equally well, if not better. To all mankind they were addressed, those cries for help still ringing in our ears! But at this place, at this moment of time, all mankind is us, whether we like it or not. Let us make the most of it, before it is too late! Let us represent worthily for once the foul brood to which a cruel fate consigned us! What do you say? (*Estragon says nothing.*) ... In this immense confusion one thing alone is clear. We are waiting for Godot to come—.[15]

Similarly Smallwood, in desiring to be emissary to Cuba, "at this place, at this moment of time," assumes this role (with Vladimir-like zeal) to "represent worthily for once the *foul brood* [read: the U.S., Western Capitalism] to which a cruel fate consigned us." In the service of this singular moment, and despite mounting evidence that Castro-Godot will *not* be able to sit for an interview, Smallwood never loses hope of getting the Cuban leader on film: "I still have faith. I have faith in Fidel." He sees that faith manifest in the very name of that leader, drawing a link between *Fidel* and *fidelity*. Castro as virtue.

Early in the documentary, the director, unsure of their efforts in Cuba, asks Smallwood, "Do you think *he* [meaning Castro] really knows us?" In their favor, Smallwood had been assured by Castro, whom he had met in Newfoundland, that an interview was possible: "Come down [to Cuba]," he tells Smallwood, "and we will help in every way." Upon arrival, the offering of comfortable, even oddly luxurious, accommodations to the NFB crew suggested a meeting in the offing ("The Cubans certainly seemed to be expecting us"), while providing the perfect staging ground for the team's preparations: "So here apparently we will *wait*, sorting out our questions, waiting for Fidel to drive through the gates."

While waiting, they meet and talk with the Cuban people (who Smallwood naively asks, "[those] in favor of the revolution put up your hands"). The team investigates the country's working conditions and labor practices; they debate the merits and failings of Socialism, and the effects of the revolution on the mental health of the people. All the while, they *wait*. And wait— "simply wait."[16] And while waiting, tensions develop within the group: "we argue constantly about what is natural in human society." Similarly, in *Godot*: "We wait. We're bored. (*He throws up his hand.*) No, don't protest, we are bored to death, there's no denying it."[17]

The team begins to wonder if they are even on Castro's radar? Vladimir wonders the same and says to the *Boy*: "Tell him ... (*he hesitates*) ... tell him you saw us. (*Pause.*) You did see us, didn't you?" Smallwood, then, but *not* the rest of the NFB crew, snags an invite to a State function. Going to the dinner, Smallwood dons an ill-fitting, dark suit—the only suit he can find at the last minute ("I feel like a tramp," he says); he mugs for the camera and shuffles about, pretending to walk into the event where he'll plead his case to the elusive Castro: "All this is useless without you. We've got to have you. We got to have an interview, and we're going to build the whole thing around you." Castro agrees but is further delayed—just like in *Godot*. The *Boy* tells the tramps: "Mr. Godot told me to tell you he won't come this evening but surely tomorrow."[18]

Smallwood continually develops and rehearses his questions for Castro (about religion, the revolution, etc.), but we only hear those questions in voiceover. They will never be asked; the meeting will never happen (as in

Godot: "Nothing happens. Nobody comes; nobody goes. It's awful").[19] But the crew does not leave (again, just like in Beckett: "Let's go." "We can't." "Why not?" "We're waiting for Godot").[20]

The Beckettian overtones of Smallwood's quest become more and more apparent to all involved. At one point, for instance, the film loses sight of its historical objectives and turns, inexplicably, to the image of a single, yet foreboding tree set against the night sky. Through a prolonged close-up of that lone, largely leafless tree, we watch mindless, worker ants (the laborers, if you will, of this insect revolution) move up and down the tree, hard at work. The ants, for their part, work silently, walking away with the leaves in an endless procession—one morsel at a time. Of course, the leafless (or partially leaved) tree is itself an iconic image in *Waiting for Godot*. But for the dearth of rope, and the erections they'll get from hanging themselves, the tramps choose not to end it all. But suicide was, in fact, on the table—even if they remain a little fuzzy on the details. In *Godot*, the dialogue unfolds as follows:

> Vladimir: The tree, look at the tree. (Estragon looks at the tree.)
> Estragon: Was it not there yesterday?
> Vladimir: Yes of course it was there. Do you not remember? We nearly hanged ourselves from it. But you wouldn't. Do you not remember?
> Estragon: You dreamt it.[21]

Smallwood's team reflects on its own confusions and misperceptions, its own useless expenditures (e.g., of time, NFB resources, tax-payer dollars) for this ill-fated endeavor. Why should they go on? Had they hung themselves? In the end, the film's director tells Smallwood, as they prepare to leave Cuba: "'Waiting for Fidel.' That's the film we have right now." And *Waiting for Fidel* would stand as the documentary's title.

The Unnamed, "The Unnamable"

All these films and documentaries, in their way, certainly stage Beckettian themes, even if Beckett himself is little more than a ghost for these filmmakers, a filmic unconscious. Gus Van Sant's film *Gerry* (2002) reflects that same presence. As one writer puts it, Van Sant "[goes] all Samuel Beckett on us in [a] fascinating exercise in tedium,"[22] and then adds,

> The dialogue provides little explication, and we know only that the two Gerries are hiking towards "the thing." Eventually they abandon their journey and decide to head back, ultimately losing their way. There is a Samuel Beckett feel to the film, [with] the two men moving meaninglessly through their confined world, a "thing" drawing them in and leading them into destruction. The dialogue also

feels very Beckett to me—lighthearted and mundane, but somehow taking on new meaning in their unique and dark situation.... If you're a Beckett fan, you might actually love it.

So even without a direct mention of Beckett in the film: "If you're a Beckett fan, you might actually love it."

So, too, the movie *Bandslam*, throws a bone to the discerning and consciously attuned "Beckett fan." In this case, a group of teens put together a band to win a competition; the name of the band, "I can't go on, I'll go on"—a phrase from Beckett's *The Unnamable*—is first deemed "ridiculous" by members of the band: "Okay, well, what do you want to call us?" "'*I Can't Go On, I'll Go On*.'" "I can't a what a what?" "'*I Can't Go On, I'll Go On*.' It's evocative. It's memorable." "It's ridiculous! And it's not a name, all right?" So the proposed name, judged "not a name," for an as-yet unnamed band, derives from an unnamed source—ironically, Beckett's *The Unnamable*. Here again, we have Beckett's ghost—a semblance, largely silent and off to the side. But still "evocative," mystifying, and even to some in the film, bothersome.

Yet for director David Cronenberg, Beckett is not standing behind, but lies ahead, in the promise of filmmaking. Cronenberg seeks to realize, through a kind of groping in the dark, something uniquely Beckettian in his work: "I think I'm feeling my way toward a different kind of filmmaking, a kind of Samuel Beckett style, very ascetic and simple and direct."[23] Before a public exhibition of his life in film (in late 2013), Cronenberg further clarifies his stylistic aspirations as a filmmaker: "Very unblinking, and not too tricky or artful. An attempt to get at some basic, primordial understanding of the human condition." Recalling his movie *Film*, Beckett is here again cryptically identified as that "unblinking" *Eye*, gazing intently on some sort of "primordial, human condition."

In the end, Beckett himself is like the "Godot" of modern film. He is both mystery and ideal. He shadows film, as a consciousness, just off-stage, and does so until something manifests, and then one is made aware of his presence in various ways. He exasperates ("Well, he's spitting on my neck!"; "You're very fucking quiet"). He offends ("I'd like to hit this guy on a gut level!"; "It's ridiculous, and it's not a name!"). He's inexplicable ("I can't a what a what?"; "How the fuck did we end up out here?"). He's discovered ("There is a Samuel Beckett feel to the film"; "'*Waiting for Fidel*,' that's the film we have right now"). He's intuited or sensed ("I think I'm feeling my way toward a different kind of filmmaking, a kind of Samuel Beckett style, very ascetic and simple and direct"). He stirs ("It's evocative. It's memorable"). And what with all the "*waiting*" in film these days, a kind of Beckettian energy repeatedly chills the cinematic air—even if that energy only manifests in hidden or unconscious ways.

Beckett looms as part of the mise-en-scène of modern film. He's perceived, though in ethereal, non-descript ways. He's spoken but unspoken, unnamable. He remains the still, silent witness—just as he always would have wanted.

Notes

1. Jacques Derrida, *Specters of Marx: The State of the Debt, the Work of Mourning and the New International* (New York: Routledge, 1994), xviii.
2. YouTube video, 2:32, posted by John Hyland, June 16, 2006, http://www.youtube.com/watch?v=p856CfM64w8.
3. Samuel Beckett, *Three Novels: Molloy, Malone Dies, The Unnamable* (New York: Grove, 1991). A portion of the passage reads: "I took advantage of being at the seaside to lay in a store of sucking-stones. They were pebbles but I call them stones... I distributed them equally between my four pockets, and sucked them turn and turn about... Taking a stone from the right pocket of my greatcoat, and putting it in my mouth, I replaced it in the right pocket of my greatcoat by a stone from the right pocket of my trousers, which I replaced by a stone from the left pocket of my trousers, which I replaced by a stone from the left pocket of my greatcoat..." (69).
4. Stephen John Dilks, "Portraits of Beckett as a Famous Writer," *Journal of Modern Literature* 29, no. 4 (2006): 163.
5. Stephen John Dilks' recent book, *Samuel Beckett in the Literary Marketplace*, 2011, and his aforementioned essay "Portraits of Beckett as a Famous Writer," from which the following quotes are taken, provide insight into Beckett's strategic control of his public persona, and his "participation in the process of authorial image-making" (162). Commenting on one of the more well-known, spectral images of Beckett—that taken in 1973 during rehearsals for *Krapp's Last Tape* and *Not I*—Dilks writes, "the photograph isolates Beckett's head in a field of black, presenting him as a flesh-covered skull cut off from his body, from his background, from any context except that of his own head. [...] This representation is, however, complicated by the haute couture lighting, precise staging, and deliberate costuming. These features call attention to different kinds of artistic expertise, revealing the complex network of professional work that goes into the marketing of a specific authorial image. Just as importantly, it hints at Beckett's willingness to reveal his complicity in the construction of this image" (161–62).
6. Eric Prince, "A Tempest in a Billycan: *Godot* and *Endgame* in Sydney," *Journal of Beckett Studies* 11, no. 2 (2002): 98.
7. On this, the Beckett Estate follows Beckett's lead, who, in his life, "generally refused permissions for filmed versions of *Godot*...He rejected lucrative offers from Bert Lahr ... and by Tyrone Guthrie, the latter to be directed by Ingmar Bergman." C.J. Ackerley and S.E. Gontarski, *The Grove Companion to Samuel Beckett: A Reader's Guide to his Works, Life, and Thought* (New York: Grove, 2007), 622.
8. Alan Schneider, "Alan Schneider on Samuel Beckett's *Film*," *A Piece of Monologue.com*, last modified June 6, 2010, http://www.apieceofmonologue.com/2010/06/alan-schneider-samuel-beckett-film.html.
9. Maurice Harmon (ed.), *No Author Better Served: The Correspondence of Samuel Beckett and Alan Schneider* (Cambridge: Harvard University Press, 1998), 166.
10. Schneider.

11. Ted Sludds, "Film, Beckett, and Failure," *Film West* 21 (1995), accessed February 11, 2014, http://www.iol.ie/~galfilm/filmwest/21sludds.htm.

12. Recall Dilks' comment about Beckett's publicity photo (cited in note 6, above): "...the photograph isolates Beckett's head in a field of black, presenting him as a flesh-covered skull cut off from his body, from his background, from any context except that of his own head" (161).

13. Samuel Beckett, *Waiting for Godot: A Tragi-Comedy in Two Acts* (New York: Grove, 1982), 90.

14. Michael Rubbo, *Waiting for Fidel*. Montreal: NFB, 1974. Documentary.

15. Beckett, 90–1.

16. Ibid., 39.

17. Ibid., 92.

18. Ibid., 55.

19. Ibid., 43.

20. Ibid., 79.

21. Ibid., 66.

22. Izzy, "Gerry," *Ain't It Entertaining?* February 21, 2014, http://izzyisalwayswrite.wordpress.com/2012/06/.

23. Robert Everett-Green, "At 70, David Cronenberg Is Still Tough to Pin Down," *Globe and Mail.com*, last modified November 2, 2013, http://www.theglobeandmail.com/arts/film/david-cronenberg-is-tough-to-pin-down/article15212014/.

The Graphic Novel
Another "Stain upon the Silence"?

Nick Pawliuk

Most Beckett scholars are used to seeing parodic or satiric versions of *Waiting for Godot* represented in comic form. These are particularly prevalent on the internet, grace the pages of high culture magazines such as *The New Yorker*, and even end up in our Sunday funnies newspaper strips. Most people would get a chuckle, groan or a smirk from such renditions, but these are easily dismissed as so much more cultural excess. They are the equivalent of Sirs Patrick Stewart and Ian McKellen's New York escapades in their Beckettian bowlers that were Tweeted around the web in early 2014: Cute, but is there anything serious going on here? Actually, there is, and they can help us:

> "All my acting life, I have been drawn to the principles and practice of a "company," and working with familiar, trusted friends/colleagues," said Patrick Stewart, "whether in British repertory theatre, The Royal Shakespeare Company, *Star Trek* or *X-Men*. It's not that strangeness/newness isn't exciting—it is—but when there is a common language and experience, then the unpredictable can happen. So, Ian McKellen, Sean Mathias, Stephen Brimson Lewis, Sam Beckett, Harold Pinter—plus two yet-to-be cast actors—it feels good."[1]

Patrick Stewart's reflections on "company" indicate the appeal of Samuel Beckett to the genre of comics: Beckett's diction, themes, mise en-scènes and popular perception are similar to the language and themes of comics, so it should not be a surprise when we see him popping up in differing comic environments. Beckett is actually complementary to the genre of comics, and comics can even aid us in reading Beckett.

Some references to Beckett in popular culture, however, transcend the derivative or quick name-drop though they still fall into stereotypical representations. *Masterpiece Comics*, by R. Sikoryak, is a collection "where classics and cartoons collide!" including "Dante, Bronte, The Bard, Voltaire, Wilde and many more great authors in one giant comic book."[2] Although Samuel Beckett doesn't make the cover blurb, nor the image of these "great authors" as superheroes in action running towards us on the cover, he does manage to have a page and a few references inside, and this should not be surprising given that Sikoryak has engaged with Beckett before, notably on the infamous "Beckett/Bushmiller" correspondence that turned out to be a hilarious parody.[3] *Masterpiece Comics* is a unique collection where we get 65 pages of large format (9x12) parody of traditional stories retold using comic techniques. For instance, the story of Adam and Eve becomes "Blond Eve" and is represented through a parody of the Sunday funny *Blondie*. Blondie herself obviously becomes Blond Eve, and Dagwood becomes Adam, with other characters taking on alternate roles (Mr. Dithers is God). Another example is the classic tale of Faustus being retold using *Garfield*, where Garfield becomes Mephistofield. Beckett makes his first appearance in a full page "advertisement" for AC International Comics "Raskol" brand. He is grouped with Kafka and Camus, the latter the only other smoking depiction. Others in the series of "finest ... classic entertainment" include Dante, King James and even Voltaire. Clearly, this parody is not using stereotypical representations of high culture. Beckett's representation is the standard floating head depiction, here with de rigueur turtleneck and cigarette.

The comic genre is perfect for stereotypical renditions of Beckett as many of his creations *are* comic characters, and much academic work has been done regarding Beckett's use of comic tradition. Even his "doodles" or marginalia in his manuscripts are filled with comic renditions, notably Joyce himself in the *Murphy* manuscripts.[4] And this is the point of Sikoryak's Beckett/Bushmiller correspondence parody: the comic strip *Nancy* already *is* Beckettian because Beckett is already operating in the comic medium both with his imagery and dialogue, just primarily on stage. In *Waiting for Godot*, the usual suspect, the language and interactions between the characters are stripped down into syllables that are perfect for the confined spaces of the stage and the comic panel structure. Most comic representations will neglect the profundities of Vladimir's tragic awareness, but jokes about hanging oneself and all that follows are perfect for parody. And that is what Sikoryak gives us with "Gogo and Didi in Waiting to Go." Beavis and Butthead become the latest incarnation of Vladimir and Estragon in 15 panels.[5] Beckett's story is remarkably complete in such a short format, even Lucky and Pozzo walk through two panels without speaking. Gogo and Didi mistake them for "Godot," possibly, and the final panel is the two characters not leaving, not "go"-ing anywhere—not even speaking, fulfilling the faithful representation of Beckett's play. What we are left with is a compelling, intriguing (re)presentation of Beckett that in no way diminishes or trivializes his play. The play is suddenly opened up to a new audience. Maybe there is something to the comic genre and its engagement with culture.

The second manner in which Beckett is integrated into the comics genre is as a character in a biographical representation, usually connected with the much larger draw of James Joyce. Even though Beckett did have experiences around World War II that would seem to be suited to visual representation, Joyce's rather pedestrian story has been more frequently illustrated. Here, Mary and Bryan Talbot's *Dotter of Her Father's Eyes* and *James Joyce: Portrait of a Dubliner*, by Alfonso Zapico, are notable examples.

Mary M. Talbot writes a doubled autobiography of her story and how Lucia Joyce, James' daughter, has a similarly troubled relationship with her father, Talbot's own father being noted Joycean scholar James S. Atherton whose works are still in circulation today. Using different coloring techniques to illustrate the temporal shifts, Beckett is introduced through an outside perspective: "In October 1928, James had a new devotee—a willing scribe and all-purpose errand boy."[6] And it is this depiction of Beckett as a "secretary" for Joyce that is the usual other popular representation, even going back to the Largely Literary t-shirts and mugs in the 1990s which featured Joyce as a gifted writer and Beckett as first Joyce's secretary, and only later an enigmatically focused writer who also happened to win the Nobel Prize. Joyce's shadow is large. Mary Talbot, however, uses Lucia's biography to depict Beckett in more than the usual Joyce/Beckett popular renditions, so the Beckett we have depicted is first of all personable and social, two characteristics that are not in the popular imagination regarding him. Talbot's Beckett is always smiling and a supporter of Lucia, hinting at the complexities of their personal relationship that led to their falling out and Beckett's banishment from the Joyce house for several years. Lucia later refers to that "Beckett swine" when he is invited back to celebrate Joyce's birthday,[7] but Beckett is not the focus here, rather Lucia's fragile mental state. Talbot's depiction is a refreshing take on Beckett: it is not often we get to imagine a Beckett that is removed from the detached, solitary writer engaged in complex existential investigations. Here we have a young man who is engaging and personable. We can see why Lucia might have been attracted to Beckett. Talbot's Beckett is ready to hear about Lucia's dancing and enthusiastic about it and her, as opposed to the depiction of Joyce and Nora who are tolerating or openly discouraging it. Aside from the dictation "come in" and "Let it stand" legend of Joyce and Beckett working on *Work in Progress*, Beckett's conduct on the Déjeuner *Ulysse* lunch is probably almost as famous, and here Talbot depicts him as "the drunken Irishman" who "needs to piss" and in so doing, gives all the men another chance to hit the bar, and all the women a reason to get upset at the men. Historically accurate, Talbot's depiction maintains its authenticity as Beckett then reappears as a continuing supporter of Lucia until she accuses him of using her like an "hors d'oeuvre," a "tasty morsel" to be had before Beckett sees her father: "You utter bastard!"[8] The depiction of Beckett reflects this tense, hostile accusation, with him becoming stern and starting to take on characteristics of his later public imagery: mainly just a head; circular glasses; stern, studied expression. For a little while though, we received a glimpse into the Beckett that might have existed outside his public persona.

Alfonso Zapico's *James Joyce: Portrait of a Dubliner* is a comprehensive visual biography of Joyce, using much material from Joyce's texts and other literary biographies. As such, it picks up many of the same stories of Beckett that are in the popular realm: his relationship with Lucia, his role as secretary for Joyce, and the Déjeuner *Ulysse* debacle. The depiction of Beckett is likewise stereotypical, with a recognizable shock of hair already taking place and a thick scarf under a greatcoat as the typical uniform of Beckett. This is the Beckett who will later become represented in the popular imagination.

Zapico's depiction of Beckett is the Beckett of academic biography, the Beckett that is a dedicated intellectual who doesn't really *exist* outside of these characterizations. It is, in many ways, a one dimensional depiction. Zapico visualizes many of the same events as Talbot, so a direct comparison is useful. For instance, Zapico has Beckett instigating the Déjeuner *Ulysse* debacle by wanting a drink, and then getting left behind, being "dumped outside a roadside inn" while he yells "Jooooyce" after the departing bus, and Joyce yells out "Beckeeett,"[9] shades of Joycean wordplay by Zapico. Although the depiction doesn't stray far from the accepted events, it is quite comical and shows the affinity Joyce and Beckett might have had for each other, and the drink.

Much like Talbot introduced Beckett with objective narration, Zapico does the same with the Lucia/Beckett relationship: "Lucia was completely in love with Samuel Beckett."[10] The relationship with Lucia is not depicted as in depth as in Talbot, so Beckett remains an unassailable figure, showing how he is not responsible for Lucia's illness. He is encased in his uniform of scarf and greatcoat and doesn't contribute anything to the dynamic, other than a few phrases that all trail off into ellipses. Here is the great author of minimalism being at a loss for words. Beckett's popular persona is already rewriting the past and creating his image.

Finally, Zapico illustrates one of the only two remaining defining stories of the Joyce/Beckett dynamic: turnips (the overly small shoe legend being the other). Joyce and Beckett are at a literary gathering and Joyce is annoyed at the discussion, preferring to talk about turnips: "Hmph! Let's get out of here, Beckett," he says in one panel. Then, in the next panel as they are walking in the street, Joyce says, "If that idiot had at least talked of turnips.... Turnips are interesting."¹¹ What is interesting in this depiction is Beckett again is in his uniform and he doesn't say a word. He is just a foil to Joyce's genius, and Joyce is right: turnips might be more interesting than this rendering of Beckett.

If stereotypical representations of Beckett and parodies of *Waiting for Godot* are the norm in most comics, Art Spiegelman's use of Beckett stands out from usual depictions. *Maus* is a groundbreaking work that is generally regarded as redefining the role of comics—or comix—and largely creating the genre of graphic novels that can be traced all the way back to the woodcuts of Lynd Ward. *Maus* appears to be the story of Vladek, Art's father, his experiences during World War II, his survival of Auschwitz, and his later experiences as an immigrant to America, particularly how his relationship with Art develops. As is well-known, *Maus* is drawn with the Jews as mice and the Germans as cats. *Maus* is, however, more complex than just Vladek's narrative. As Part II opens, we learn Vladek has died and Art is torn over whether he should continue with trying to illustrate Vladek's narrative. As readers, we then get to see that much of the story is actually Art's story, not just Vladek's. To try to help himself through this dilemma, Art goes to see a psychiatrist, Pavel, also a survivor of the Holocaust. In yet another layer of complexity, the Art and Pavel characters are wearing their mouse masks, exposing the metacritical layers in which the text operates. It is during one of Art's meetings with Pavel that the Samuel Beckett reference is made, and it is the only reference to a literary figure in the entire two volumes. Art Spiegelman's reference to Beckett is an early connection with the Holocaust that anticipates later directions in Beckett scholarship.¹²

The reference to Beckett occurs in *Maus* at a key time structurally. Art Spiegelman is trying to continue with his story against overwhelming obstacles. The first part of *Maus* has been published and he is under pressure to commercialize it; his first child is about to be born; and he is grieving the loss of his father. Pavel is trying to help Art get past his blockages, and Pavel says, "but look at how many books have already been written about the Holocaust. What's the point? People haven't changed...."¹³ Of course, what Art Spiegelman is attempting to do with *Maus* is radically different than the volumes already written, much of which Art was familiar with, but he still feels the futility. As Pavel says, "the victims who died can never tell THEIR side of the story, so maybe it's better not to have any more stories." Art agrees in the next panel: "Uh-huh. Samuel Beckett once said: 'Every word is like an unnecessary stain on silence and nothingness.'" With Pavel's affirmation in the same panel—"Yes"—we then get a blank panel where they are both smoking and contemplative. This is significant: it is the only wordless panel in the whole of *Maus*. Even other panels that break conventional grammar and bleed into the present, such as Vladek and Anja's arrival at Auschwitz, have narration, usually Vladek's, on them.

Accepted comics grammar defines wordless panels as potentially increasing intensity, duration, and clarity.[14] Art Spiegelman is uncompromising in his deliberate composition of his panels, their size, structure and illustration. Frequently, there is more going on in the shadows of his panels than a quick perusal will reveal. Thus, a panel with no words is very intense, especially given the subject matter surrounding it: can the Holocaust be described and what does it feel like? What is the point of "going on"? That Beckett is the reference for this wordless panel also increases the intensity of the connection. The reference is from the last chapter of Deirdre Bair's biography *Samuel Beckett* and refers to a purported comment Beckett made about the necessity he felt to write.[15] The comment itself is rather suspect as it is part of the type of scholarship that creates the hagiographic Beckett, rather than the real Beckett,[16] but it is clear why Spiegelman is attracted to it. Spiegelman, like Beckett's characters, must write, must "go on." He must tell his and Vladek's story even though he doesn't want to given the subject matter and personal issues he has. The reference also tends to reflect Adorno's "no poetry after Auschwitz" idea and becomes a matter of psychological torment for Spiegelman.

As wordless panels also increase the duration, the amount of time we might spend on any given panel, Spiegelman is also paralleling early Beckett in his letter to Axel Kaun, where "language is most efficiently used where it is being most efficiently misused," to the point of dissolving the "word surface" to link "unfathomable abysses of silence."[17] Although this is the standard view of Beckett, Spiegelman actually gives us a representation of Beckett's ideas here. The medium of comics allows us to see Beckett's ideas in ways that his prose cannot. Even Beckett's theatre pieces are logocentric with the stage directions necessary to communicate his ideas. There is no alternative in his mediums, but there is in Spiegelman's. Again, this harkens back to the woodcuts of Lynd Ward that tell whole stories without language. We spend more time on this panel, which increases its significance, its intensity, and allows us to reflect on what has just been mooted: is another story about the Holocaust necessary? Thankfully, Spiegelman finishes his and we can say, unequivocally, yes, it is. Outside of the Bair reference, Spiegelman transforms Beckett from reductive stereotypes of the author himself or parody of the usual *Godot*-esque variety into a larger thematic concern. What is the value of more work on certain subjects; is this new work worthwhile, or is it just so much more cultural litter? These are questions we could see Beckett himself weighing throughout his career, given, for example, the "fatigue and disgust" of the remnants of *Watt*. And these questions can be fairly asked of much of the Beckett adaptations in comic strips and on the internet. However, in the hands of a talented artist like Spiegelman, adapting Beckett becomes a significant advancement to both writers: we might now think differently about Beckett and his works after the War. And this is what Spiegelman is attempting to get us to do with his work: to cut through the clutter and think differently. Sometimes the only thing that might cut through the clutter as Sikoryak and Spiegelman show us is a blank panel, and this is the "common language and experience" that Sir Patrick Stewart was indicating is the benefit of a "company," and why Beckett is good company for graphic novels.

Notes

1. http://www.mckellen.com/stage/godot/broadway-2013/. Retrieved August 26, 2014.

2. R. Sikoryak, *Masterpiece Comics* (Montreal, Quebec: Drawn and Quarterly, 2009).

3. By A.S. Hamrah and R. Sikoryak. Although originally published in *Hermenaut* No. 15 (1999), the complete "correspondence" and illustrations can be found at http://theamericanreader.com/the-beckettbushmiller-letters/.

4. Joyce and many other representations, even a golfing doodle which anticipates the Irish Film Board's "Pitch 'n' Putt": http://www.bbc.com/news/entertainment-arts-27687121.

5. Continuing the parody, Sikoryak has "*Masterpiece* Queries" on the facing page, where "Professor Scholar" answers letters from readers. The last letter is about "Waiting to Go" and its resemblance to the long running The Katzenjammer Kids comic strip. Here is "Prof. S's" response: "I suppose so, but we were thinking of the Mike Judge's 1992 duo, the stars of television, film, and books. Their world and complex relationship precisely echo those in Samuel Beckett's 1952 modernist play ... these two may resonate to some degree with Hans & Fritz Katzenjammer, as well as Mutt & Jeff, Fred & Barney, Archie & Jughead, the Thing & The Hulk ... but perhaps that's a discussion for another time." We can also add Nancy and Sluggo as is made clear from the Beckett/Bushmiller work.

6. Mary M. and Bryan Talbot, *Dotter of her Father's Eyes* (Milwaukie, OR: Dark Horse Books, 2012), 62.

7. *Ibid.*, 81.

8. *Ibid.*, 78.

9. Alfonso Zapico, *James Joyce: Portrait of a Dubliner* (Dublin: The O'Brien Press, 2013), 182.

10. *Ibid.*, 192.

11. *Ibid.*, 205.

12. One out of many recent essays on Beckett and the Holocaust is David Houston Jones "From Contumacy to Shame: Reading Beckett's Testimonies with Agamben" in *Beckett at 100: Revolving It All*. Eds Linda Ben-Zvi and Angela Moorjani (Oxford: Oxford University Press, 2008), 54–67. Marjorie Perloff indicates that Beckett "takes his responsibility to be *showing* rather than the making of ideological points" (original italics) in

connecting his works to his war-time experience ("'In Love with Hiding': Samuel Beckett's War" *The Iowa Review* Vol. 35, No. 1 [Spring, 2005]: 99). It is this "poetic" representation that might indicate Beckett's wide-ranging appeal in dealing with such horror.

13. Art Spiegelman, *The Complete Maus* (New York: Pantheon Books, 1997), 205.

14. Scott McCloud in many works outlines how comics work: *Understanding Comics* (New York: HarperPerennial, 1994) 102–103 and *Making Comics* (New York: HarperCollins, 2006) 47–49 are two good examples.

15. Deirdre Bair, *Samuel Beckett* (New York: Harcourt Brace Jovanovich, 1978), 640. The full quote from Bair is "Over and over again, he has said, 'I couldn't have done it otherwise. Gone on, I mean. I could not have gone through the awful mess of life without having left a stain upon the silence.'"

16. Bair's source for the direct quote from Beckett is as follows: "In one form or another, he had made this remark to DB and others" (723).

17. Samuel Beckett, "German Letter of 1937" in *Disjecta: Miscellaneous Writings and a Dramatic Fragment* (London: John Calder, 1983), 171–172.

"a mollycoddled little git from Foxrock"
Beckett in Irish Pop Music

CAMERON REID

"he blew my mind"

April 2006. Beckett's centenary. The tributes pour in, online and elsewhere, so too the performances, festivals, readings and retrospectives, seminars and symposia—all things Beckett. In Dublin, a seminar on "Beckett and Music" grapples with matters of influence:

> What influence has Samuel Beckett had on composers worldwide? What affect has he had on Irish composers? Did Beckett use music in his own works? Does he still affect contemporary music?[1]

The question of Beckett's engagement with, and effect on, contemporary music is an interesting one, but what of music's engagement with Beckett? How do songwriters and musicians *intone* the man and his work? And why? What do they want from him? What do they get?

In contemporary music circles, invocations of the author (not only in lyrics, but in raps, poems, performances, interviews) pull a kind of "Beckett" into focus—one imagined or hoped for. Such a "Beckett" does the lazy work of metaphor and symbol for musicians and songwriters, and in the context of Irish pop, renders those same musicians heralds of a retrograde nationalism.

Back in 2006, Bono, U2's protean front man, becomes the questionable choice to open Beckett's centenary. Before a media-junket, the pop star makes his case for the job: "I'm a fan. I don't know what he's on about half the time but I have enjoyed not knowing…. He blew my mind, that's all I can say. He shrank language, minimalist, all that stuff. It is great that he's Irish."[2] Other than shared Irish roots and a "blown mind," Bono's connection to the one he calls "maestro" (in the circuitous title to the poem he would perform for the centenary's opening night) appears limited to a few cultural collisions: (1) an offer to Beckett, late in his life, of a signed copy of U2's *The Unforgettable Fire*[3]; (2) a strange rap about Beckett—one that oddly traverses Wordsworth's poem "The Leech-Gatherer"—inserted into a live performance of U2's "Where the Streets Have No Name" in the days following Beckett's death (in 1989); and (3) an offer to headline the centenary by the Artistic Director of Dublin's Gate Theatre, Michael Colgan—an offer that Bono, at first, resisted.[4]

In 2006, an editorial published in the *Irish Examiner* openly mocked the idea of Bono as the centenary's opening act: "Who do we choose to open [Beckett's] centenary celebrations? Bono. Obviously. Who else would we ask? Not an infinitely more suitable literary figure? In our scrambling attempts to claim back our national writers whom we now recognize as marketable commodities, we once again drag this narcissistic, glorified pop star back into the limelight."[5] But Bono didn't go looking for the job: Michael Colgan did the *dragging*, from one limelight to another. He guilted Bono into versifying his affection for Beckett. But why? Because Beckett had to leave Ireland in the 1930s, disgusted as he was by his country's "sterilization of the mind and apotheosis of the litter"[6]—(*Trans.*, Ireland's newly invoked censorship laws and its banning of contraceptives). In contrast, Bono—who might actually have been Ireland's reward for banned contraceptives, a poster-boy for the cause—was able to stay in-country and make it big. So, according to Colgan, "He [Bono] owed it to Beckett to do this"[7]—and to do this, I would add, even if Ireland's praise for Beckett, of the one who had so soundly denounced a philistine Ireland as a "Paradise peopled with virgins, and the earth with decorticated multiparas,"[8] was a bit of a whitewash. Laura Salisbury comments on Beckett's difficult relationship with his homeland: "Skating close to the discourses of eugenics with which many modernist writers were both concerned and enamoured, Beckett is clear that a state [like Ireland] that makes a virtue out of rural illiteracy and a fertility unhampered by contraception is incapable of realizing that its philistinism cannot partake of the joke; as such, it simply becomes [the joke]."[9]

But let's forget about all that! Why mar the 100th with a lot of silly talk about eugenics and the like. Bono, according to media reports, killed that night, "wow[ing] a roomful of eggheads, luvvies and random seekers of 'culcher' in Dublin Castle."[10] Not everyone was so enamored, though. That aforementioned critic of having chosen Bono to open the centenary, by labeling the gesture as "yet another example of misguided Irish self-importance at its parochial best," described the rock star's "Un homage du Bono au Maestro Samuel Beckett" (Bono's French!)—still a shortened version of the title—as "stomach-churningly awful." Really? That seems harsh. On Bono's own admission: "I don't know what he's on about half the time..."—so we concede the homage was likely 50 percent clueless. But let's take a closer look.

The full title of Bono's poem—or actually his *pastiche* (meant as a kind of ventriloquism in the style or voice of Beckett)—which, according to Michael Colgan, was written in just one day (cause, why fuss?), reads,

> Un homage du Bono au maestro Samuel Beckett, starring un homage du Mannix Flynn, à Barry McGovern—or a piece what I wrote called.... Waiting for Colgan.[11]

Delicious! Voicing the homage, Bono sometimes speaks *about* Beckett and, at other times, *as* Beckett—or, more accurately, in the style or voice of Mannix Flynn, doing Barry McGovern, doing Michael Colgan, doing Beckett (an objective surely obvious to the night's attendees). The homage, itself, makes liberal use of this idea of "waiting"—16 mentions in the 4-minute pastiche. Beckett is said to be *waiting* around, *waiting* to answer the phone, *waiting* "to be fuckin' understood," even waiting for the centenary (e.g., "I've been waiting / Waiting a long time / 100 years"). Bono, in fact, really grooves on the whole birthday thing (e.g., "they kick a banana ball through the splits / On your birthday"; "It's your birthday, it's your birthday"), and on Beckett being 100, *waiting* to be 100.[12]

From there, the pastiche plays out a pat comparison between Beckett and Joyce, and their respective uses of language. Beckett, for his part, is "waiting for language to turn to liquid"; and, of language, itself, Beckett "made a fart out of it, made a fart out of everyone who didn't like the smell of it." So, for Beckett (a.k.a., the *maestro*), language is a smelly, liquid fart.

At one point, the pastiche turns to *The Unforgettable Fire* incident, clearly still on Bono's mind, and maybe a point of friction between the two? A kind of *Bono-Beckett* hybrid takes the microphone (where Bono, speaking *as* Beckett, channels the unfeeling sentiments of the author toward Bono): "remember you gave me a signed copy of the unforgettable fire? / I told you I loved it? / I lied, I never listened to it." Maybe he listened? He might have been listening at the end? A few tracks—a little "*Pride (In the Name of Love)*"? We just don't know.

Finally, Bono-Beckett reveal their collective fatigue with "All those PhDs" who keep asking, "Where's Godot? Who's Godot?"

—It's true! We're so lame that way!

But what interests us here (in light of Bono's earlier pronouncement to the media, when introduced as centenary headliner: "It is great that he's Irish") is (1) the phrase, repeated twice in the homage, that *Ireland* "wins the triple crown on your birthday"; and (2) the idea that Beckett, in one of the many acts of *waiting* mapped out in the pastiche, seems to be waiting for the native voice of the Irish to re-emerge (i.e., "Waiting for language to be our own again")—we will engage such sentiments moving forward.

"half of Beckett"

French philosopher Gilles Deleuze, speaking on what he deems France's woeful literary legacy, weighs-in on this question of Beckett. Believing that France has produced so few great writers (e.g., Proust, Gide, among them), Deleuze claims, "All we've got in France is Artaud and *half of Beckett*"[13]— "half," but no more. Beckett lived in France 50 years, and sometimes wrote in French; writing in another language may have helped him to *hear* the words, the language, more clearly, and thus escape (or, as Deleuze would say, *exhaust*) the tired rhythms and refrains of his own language.

But, whatever. Beckett wasn't a French writer, per se. So France only gets *half*.

Curiously, Bono's title for the pastiche uses words like "un" and "à" and the phrase, "Un homage du Bono au maestro Samuel Beckett...." He seems to give a little back to France, a continental shout-out. Or maybe he's just screwing with them? But where so many in Ireland wrestle with their country's cultural exodus, a few notables in the Irish music scene, perhaps those most unwilling to tear Beckett to pieces across the English Channel, like Van Morrison and Bono, have spoken out. They want his heritage re-affirmed, and so too their proprietary hold over the legacy, literary or otherwise. They want him *home*. They loathe, for example, the notion of a French-Beckett, caught between worlds, carved in "half" and strung between France and Ireland. So a battle ensues over the Beckett *corpus*: a body (of work), the (textual) remains of the man (affections and possessions). *Battlefield Beckett*.

Case in point: Van Morrison's bluesy hymn, "Too Long in Exile"—a song in which the Irish Morrison laments the loss, or *repeated* losses of refugee artists like Samuel Beckett (not to mention James Joyce, Oscar Wilde, George Best, Alex Higgins, etc.), a who's-who of Irish ex-pats, owing to their collective exile. Morrison punctuates each refrain with the recurring, titular lament, "too long in exile"—a phrase that in its dogged return echoes the anguish of longing and regret felt by many in Ireland about their country's loss of so many literary icons.

The ex-pats Morrison names in the song (including Beckett) are not only lost and lonely, but also fighting for their lives and livelihoods on foreign shores. They are struggling to succeed, to thrive, to be respected. Yet no one, says Morrison, understands them the way *we* (the Irish) do. No one cares for Beckett like we do. (This hardly seems fair. Remember, France is willing to take *half*.)

But this is an old story in Ireland—the myth of the exile. Irish artists (e.g., songwriters, poets, dramatists) have long thematized this issue of Ireland's cultural diaspora, and have done so through any number of well-known (if not, well-traveled) literary tropes: "Irish emigration had been one of the great unspokens of political life, while simultaneously being one of the great themes of Irish drama, fiction and poetry."[14] "The Irish Exile," a traditional, 19th-century Irish ballad, asks, "Oh! Where has the exile his home?" And then locates that "home,"

> Where the mountain is steep,
> Where the valley is deep,
> Where the waves of the Ohio foam;
> Where no cheering smile,
> His woes may beguile,
> Oh! There has the exile his home.

Of note here is the idea, not lost on Van Morrison, of the Irish in exile overcome by anguish and "woe," precisely for having been exiled, or for having being cut off from their *real* family—the Irish. Morrison's dirge further bemoans the feelings of the Irish, and especially those, like Bono or even Morrison himself, left to fill Ireland's cultural potholes in the wake of its historic literary migration.

With Beckett gone, some, like Indie singer Eliza Day, mourn the loss of Beckett's *voice*. In her curious little song, "Samuel Beckett's Telephone," Day invokes the image of Beckett's old phone, now housed at the Dublin Writer's Museum, with its flashing green and red lights (i.e., green accepts calls, red blocks them), and later points to the notorious scene from *Waiting for Godot* where the tramps excitedly contemplate hanging themselves on a nearby tree, given the promise of autoerotic asphyxiation. In general, the song bemoans a sort of disconnect with Beckett—whatever that "disconnect" might be for contemporary German singers disseminating their music through *MySpace*. It might be exile or the death of the author at issue, but the old phone, forever silenced and in a museum, provides an apt symbol of disconnection. In the song, the image of a severed phone line fuels the singer's displeasure over not being able to *call-up* a literary hero—even though her call would likely have flashed red on Beckett's phone.

Comparatively, Kevin Rowland, Dexy's Midnight Runners' lead-man, in his passionate, punk-inspired anthem, "Burn it Down" (off the album, *Search-*

ing for the Young Soul Rebels), points to writers like Beckett as evidence of Ireland's greatness. Born to Irish parents himself, and a staunch defender of Irish nationalism, Rowland is contemptuous of those who would denigrate the Irish, and is ready to rub the country's literary behemoths in the *fat faces* of all who would be so unkind. In addition to the writers noted by Morrison, in "Too Long in Exile," Rowland further acknowledges the likes of Sean O'Casey, George Bernard Shaw, Eugene O'Neill, Laurence Sterne, and others—all named in the song. But unlike Morrison, Rowland's target, conveyed with inimitable punk ferocity, is what he deems ignorant, anti–Irish sentiment and those who need to shut their *fucking* mouths about the Ireland they don't understand.

"like one whom I had met with in a dream"

Poet Eaven Boland, in "The Emigrant Irish," envisions a way the Irish might reclaim their exiles, by following the "dread, makeshift example" of these people—i.e., their spirit and "fortitude," their grit in the face of loss and hardship, their nothing-to-lose attitude—and in such a way that "their possessions may become our power." This suggestion mirrors the cynical blueprint of musicians like Bono, wanting to reclaim Beckett for Ireland (or really, for themselves), and finds its fullest articulation at a U2 concert in December 1989, at Point Place in Dublin. Some four days after the death of Beckett, and just as the recognition began to hit home that one of Ireland's literary treasures would *never* be returning, Bono makes the case for a different kind of proprietary hold over Beckett: not the Irish Beckett, but the *exiled* Beckett. Unlike Morrison, Bono doesn't necessarily need Beckett to come home. Instead, he finds power in the figure of an itinerant Beckett (i.e., Beckett as exile), and in the related notion that Beckett's exile was *chosen*, not forced. His reasoning, delivered before a screaming Dublin audience—an audience not likely chastened by thoughts of a dead author—requires a little unpacking.

In a moment of poetic revelry, leading up (one would assume) to a stirring performance of "Where the Streets Have No Name," Bono makes a peculiar, maybe even counter-intuitive, reference to Beckett, by way of William Wordsworth's poem, "The Leech-Gatherer."[15] In the poem, the poet (or poet-narrator), referred to as "a traveller upon the moor," reflects repeatedly upon the profound highs ("such a happy Child of earth am I") and lows ("Solitude, pain of heart, distress, and poverty") of being a poet. Those feelings of despair and despondency are mitigated in the poem itself by a chance encounter between the poet-narrator and the leech-gatherer: "The oldest man he seemed that ever wore grey hairs." In a familiar Wordsworthian conceit, the poet-narrator—after asking, "How is it that you live, and what is it you do?"—discovers a source of hidden value in the leech-gatherer's words: "Choice word and measured phrase, above the reach / Of ordinary men; a stately speech."

It is at this point that Bono—speaking both *to* and *of* Beckett—takes up a key line from the poem and begins to recite a little Wordsworth before the screaming throngs:

> But now his voice to me was like a stream
> Scarce heard; nor word from word could I divide;
> And the whole Body of the Man did seem
> Like one whom I had met with in a dream…

Prophetic! Bono would re-package these same sentiments some 17 years later with the words: "I don't know what he's on about half the time." But what was the intent back in '89? Why Wordsworth and "The Leech-Gatherer" as a memorial tribute to Beckett? While it seems unlikely that he (Bono) would be suggesting some sort of comparison between the figure of the leech-gatherer and Beckett himself, these lines can be read in just that way. That is, Bono believes that Beckett (or the more folksy "Sam Beckett," as Bono calls him in his pre-song rap) speaks—just like *any* good leech-gatherer would—in the authentic voice of some rustic everyman. He speaks, as Wordsworth would elsewhere say, as one who communes daily with "the essential passions of the heart," and in a "language really used by men."[16] He, the leech-gatherer, speaks with economy and precision; and Bono will one day say the same about Beckett: "He shrank language, minimalist, all that stuff." And because Beckett's language, according to Bono, has the weight and presence of a "smelly, liquid fart"—well, what is more *essential* than that?

Let's assume Bono's self-proclaimed, fractional, "I don't know what he's on about half the time" understanding of Beckett is paying off at this point. By invoking "The Leech-Gatherer," Bono—who, much like Wordsworth's poet-narrator, seems "deified" by his own spirit—truly *finds* Beckett; he discovers, however vaguely or indiscriminately, something elemental or truly stupefying in the writings of his erstwhile countryman ("He blew my mind, that's all I can say"). Put another way, Bono, by invoking these phrases from "The Leech-Gatherer," tries to forge a kind of *Wordsworthian* bond between himself and his compatriot. What began in 1989, with Beckett not yet 4 days in the ground, would come to fruition some 17 years later at the centenary, as the *Bono-Beckett* hybrid.

So one could imagine Beckett to be the leech-gatherer in this scenario, but does that really mean that Bono, by default, becomes the poet-narrator? Maybe. Wordsworth's poem clearly sought to explore the subterranean bonds between those who collect leeches (for medicinal reasons) and the poet's own search for his creative quarry. Connections like this would certainly be appealing to Bono. But another interpretation could be that Bono is *leech* to Beckett's leech-gatherer. Bono is the mindless, instinct-driven bloodsucker ("I don't know what he's on about half the time but I have enjoyed not knowing"), exsanguinating the newly dead Beckett. Beckett, for his part, unwittingly offers up his naked, Irish leg for Bono to suck on ("It is great that he's Irish").

Whatever the case, one would have to assume that Bono (like Wordsworth's poet-narrator, or like any *actual* leech) is not listening to Beckett, as evidenced by his deliberate deployment of Wordsworth's phrase, "Scarce heard"—which might only mean that Bono is not so much a reader, but more of a Beckett enthusiast ("I'm a fan," he says). But no matter. Beckett's words and works conveniently flow together, "like a stream," for the U2 chanteur—a stream that (shall we say?) drowns Bono in the roiling, agitated undertow of the Beckett oeuvre, even if that body of work were only imagined, not understood; also a stream that lays waste to whatever *distinctions* (in particular, linguistic or spoken—recalling Wordsworth's poem: "nor word from word could I divide"—but also, creative, temporal, political, even corporeal) that may separate the two men from one another, despite being fellow Irishmen; and finally a stream that conflates worlds, where Bono, in a near totalizing identification, merges with "the whole Body of the Man"—i.e., Beckett, the leech-gatherer—"a man," as Wordsworth goes on to say in the poem, "from some far region sent / To give me human strength, by apt admonishment."

But the most relevant bond that unfolds between these would-be blood-brothers seems to be socioeconomic in nature. Back in 1989, in the same pre-song rap discussed above, Bono suggests, "Sam Beckett dreamt of other roads ... of other lands ... of another home." I think he's talking about France. But really what he's talking about, as the song-title suggests, is "Where the Streets Have No Name"—a reference to Bono's own desire to disassociate himself from places (like Ireland) where a person's religious affiliation or financial status might be determined by little more than their street address. Discussing the song, Bono claims,

> [...] it's a sketch—I was just trying to sketch a location, maybe a spiritual location, maybe a romantic location. I was trying to sketch a feeling. I often feel very claustrophobic in a city, a feeling of wanting to break out of that city and a feeling of wanting to go somewhere where the values of the city and the values

of our society don't hold you down. An interesting story that someone told me once is that in Belfast, by what street someone lives on you can tell not only their religion but tell how much money they're making—literally by which side of the road they live on, because the further up the hill the more expensive the houses become. That said something to me, and so I started writing about a place where the streets have no name.[17]

In the lyric, Bono wants to leave, to escape. He proposes as much in the band's autobiography, imploring *everyone* (which includes Beckett, right?) to take up residence in what he calls "that other place," that *romantic* place of soul and imagination: "Do you want to go there? Because if you do, I'm ready to go there with you, to that other place. Call it what you like, a place of soul, a place of imagination, where there are no limitations."[18] So, in that place "where there are no limitations," he (Bono) will go there, with Beckett in tow, and will do so through the workings of the imaginary, or some sort of specular identification; he (Bono) dreams the writer and, in turn, dreams himself. The two men fuse, not so much by their respective Irish heritage (though that is clearly on the table in Bono's varied encounters with Beckett), but by a kind of otherworldly welding, a *felt* and fully sovereign bond, fuelled by the mutual dream of another home. This is a chosen exile—a romantic place, one that sheds its marks of socioeconomic, national, or religious identification.

Of note are the songwriter's ritual duplications in his poetic addendum to "The Leech-Gatherer." Bono repeats, "Sam Beckett," "Sam Beckett"; "dreamt of other roads," dreamt of other lands"; "of another home," "of another home." These echoing, ethereal phrases iterate and reiterate Bono's ever-deepening merger with the "one whom [he] had met with in a dream"—a merger that *sucks* "the whole Body of the Man" into the U2 imaginary, or at least into the sort of spiritual domicile where Beckett, himself, might have held the same political and socioeconomic motives as Bono. With Beckett compelled to seek other places the two merge in some place of the soul, as part of some *imagined* community, "where the values of the city and the values of our society don't hold you down." In the end, Bono (the *apparent* itinerant and honorary exile) will walk together with Beckett—*Bono-Beckett* is born.

Maybe Bono was right all along, that Beckett would have wanted to reside in the kind of place "Where the Streets Have No Name," where Bono awaits him? But whether or not Beckett would have recognized any of this, or whether ascribed motives such as these would have actually had any purchase for the man, seems beside the point. It's the battle for Beckett (body and soul) at play here.

"what is it to be at home?"

So one wonders what Beckett's take on these proprietary matters might have been? Anthony Cronin relates a story—possibly apocryphal—about a conversation between Becket and literary critic Martin Esslin, in which Esslin is said to have asked Beckett "point-blank why he lived in Paris and if he had anything against Ireland."[19] Beckett quickly replies, "'Oh no. I'm a fervent patriot and republican.'" But as Esslin then presses the issue further—"'Why do you live in Paris then?'"—Beckett is said to have answered, "'well, you know, if I were in Dublin I would just be sitting around in a pub.'" Cronin further points out, "there was a standing cliché that in Dublin people went to the pubs rather than to their desk or table or easel." But, as we know, there certainly was a more weighty rationale for why Beckett had wanted to leave Ireland. Something like the feeling of dread, oppression, or cultural paralysis associated with having to *stay* in such a deadening place. However, journalist Sean O'Hagan writes that, unlike Joyce, "It was Beckett who gave voice to the exile's dilemma of not belonging ... of spiritual and cultural displacement"[20]— a dilemma that has obvious roots in the myth of the exile. While getting inside Beckett's head on these matters seems unlikely, his character, Mrs. Rooney, from *All That Fall*, may offer an interesting insight: "It is suicide to be abroad, but what is it to be at home, Mr. Tyler, what is it to be at home? A lingering dissolution."[21] In a sense, it's suicide either way; but staying at home is to linger, to drift (toward death?). Decay is inevitable, but somewhat protracted. And that may be the reason why most of us just *wait*?

Bill Marshall, in his song, "My Poor Woman of Ohio," invokes the name of Beckett and various images and themes from *Waiting for Godot* to make the case for why the woman he names in the song ought *not* to leave, why she should wait. That is, she finds beauty in gestures that preserve connection, community, or mutual support. But recalling Mrs. Rooney on the matter, she finds beauty in the "lingering dissolution" of staying home. In fact, *Waiting for Godot* is only superficially about waiting or staying behind, and really not at all about community. The real question is: *how* do you leave? Or, *why* can't you leave? Or, in the case of Lucky: how do you escape slavery and denigration? Staying behind or *waiting* have much to do with this question of "lingering dissolution" in Beckett. *To wait* is to avoid or, at least, to sidestep the problem of escape or departure. So, why don't they leave? Why can't they leave? It's the struggle to leave or escape that, at least in part, defines the modern condition for Beckett. The sort of soulful sentimentality or mawkish beauty that overcomes the woman in Marshall's song only protracts the suffering in a Beckettian world.

"a mollycoddled little git from Foxrock"

But there is one final point to consider. The aforementioned ballad, "The Irish Exile," asks a question about the exile's return and, in turn, puts forward a somewhat counter-intuitive response to that question:

> Oh! when will the exile return?
> Oh! when will the exile return?
> When our hearts heave no sigh,
> When our tears shall be dry,
> When Erin no longer shall mourn;
> When his name we disown,
> When his mem'ry is gone,
> Oh! then will the exile return.

So, *when* will the exile return? When the Irish no longer care if they do. They'll return, the ballad suggests, when "mem'ry" of these people dissipates; they'll return when their names and identities are wiped from Erin's (Ireland's) ledgers. They'll return when Erin "disown[s]" them; or when they no longer have cause to think about those absences; or when they lose all interest in grieving their losses, as a nation. These verses *can* be read, albeit somewhat irreverently, as a big "Fuck You!" to Ireland's exiles. But in Beckett's case, some (like Morrison) want him back. Of course, they want him back at the centenary—but only if his reasons for leaving be kept hushed during the festivities.

However, because Irish nationalism, if not the various stereotypes associated with sentimental Irish ballads, may be a retrograde gesture for some, not all Irish musicians long for that lost past. A case in point is The Pogues, a London-based group of Irish descent who "wrote songs that were hard-edged and unsentimental, featuring rent boys and hooligans, rather than romantic heroes dreaming of their lost homeland."[22] While acknowledging The Pogues present an image of themselves that mirrors the more archetypal image of the classic *paddy* (hard-drinking, ill-mannered, etc.), authors McLaughlin and McLoone argue that the band's music offers up a "critique, through parody, of national stereotypes. They rant about the absurdity of nostalgia for Ireland and twist and bend sentimental ballads."[23] In the end, "nostalgic associations are wrenched out of their context" in The Pogues' music.

With that agenda in mind, it is hardly surprising that when the question of Beckett is put on the table in an interview with The Pogues' notorious lead singer, Shane MacGowan, the singer makes no mention of a wistful longing for Beckett's return:

"We haven't talked about writers yet, what do you think of Beckett?"
Shane [MacGowan] grins, suddenly.
—"Yeah, I'll talk about Beckett. The reason why he's such a depressing, miserable bastard, so unlike any other Irish writer—cause any of the other Irish writers got some humor in them at least, y'know? I mean you could say Beckett had humor in him, but it's such black humor that it doesn't count as Irish humor, y'know?"[24]

He goes on to add, "If I had to shoulder the ambition of wanting to play cricket for Ireland, I'd be a miserable, fucked-up old cunt like Beckett, as well."[25] So, as he says, "wanting to play cricket for Ireland" drove Beckett's decidedly non–Irish humor into dark places, and left him, MacGowan concludes, "a mollycoddled little git from Foxrock."

Contrary, then, to the praises we've seen (e.g., "It is great that he's Irish!"), MacGowan would be happy to repatriate Beckett, that "mollycoddled git," and we have reached the point where Beckett's Irish credentials come into question. His humor doesn't fit. He's "a depressing miserable bastard," and cricket made him that way. He's "a miserable, fucked-up old cunt." But, in the end, maybe we could strike a deal, where Deleuze and various Irish musicians (now haunted by the words of Shane MacGowan) could sit down and hammer out the terms: "half of Beckett," for France; the Irish get the other half. Let him tell his jokes to the French, like some sort of existential Jerry Lewis. He plays cricket on weekends. Chop him up; pass him around. *Everybody's* happy. Or as Bono puts it, everybody's "flappy, happy, happy, clappy … [because] It's hard not to be happy when you feel the sappy in someone else's veins."

Notes

1. "Samuel Beckett and Music," *The Contemporary Music Centre (Ireland)*, March 27, 2006, http://www.cmc.ie/news/2006/beckett-and-music.html.

2. "'I'm a Beckett fan,' Says Rocker Bono," U2www, March, 29, 2006, http://www.atu2.com/news/im-a-beckett-fan-says-rocker-bono.html.

3. In that same press conference, Bono would wonder aloud if the author had had time for a listen, as Beckett hadn't been forthcoming with a review of their sound: "I gave it to him, I'm not sure he ever listened to it, but that is my connection. I am very proud he had a copy of *The Unforgettable Fire*."

4. "Bono, Me … and That Big Mouth of Mine," *Independent IE*, March 31, 2006, http://www.independent.ie/unsorted/features/bono-me-and-that-big-mouth-of-mine-26397058.html.

5. Nuala Walsh, "Beckett Honour Should Have Been Given to a Writer," *Irish Examiner.com*, April 5, 2006, http://www.irishexaminer.com/archives/2006/0405/ireland/beckett-honour-should-have-been-given-to-a-writer-260330281.html.

6. *Disjecta: Miscellaneous Writings and a Dramatic Fragment* (New York: Grove Press, 1984), 87.

7. "Bono, Me..."
8. *Disjecta*, 87.
9. *Samuel Beckett: Laughing Matters, Comic Timing* (Edinburgh: Edinburgh University Press, 2012), 44.
10. "Bono, Me..."
11. The complete text of Bono's 650-word pastiche was published on April, 29, 2006, in *The Irish Times*, under the title: "Where's Godot? Who's Godot?" (http://www.irishtimes.com/news/where-s-godot-who-s-godot-1.1045074). All excerpts that follow are from this source.
12. Here's a snatch: "One hundred years, one hundred bum steers, one hundred and seventeen thousand black beers before your peers / One hundred years / One hundred ears flappy happy happy clappy ears / It's hard not to be happy when you feel the sappy in someone else's veins." On and on.
13. *Negotiations (1972-1990)*, trans. Martin Joughin (New York: Columbia University Press, 1995), 23. My emphasis.
14. Sean O'Hagan, "Ireland's Emigrants Sing Songs of Exile that Echo Through the Generations," theguardianwww, February 28, 2010, http://www.theguardian.com/world/2010/feb/28/ireland-exile-culture.
15. *William Wordsworth—The Major Works* (Oxford: Oxford University Press, 2008), 260-65. All subsequent references are from this edition of the poem (alternatively titled "Resolution and Independence").
16. "Preface" to *Lyrical Ballads*, *William Wordsworth—The Major Works*, 597.
17. U2www, accessed July, 25 2014, http://www.u2.com/discography/index/album/albumId/4031/tagName/. This is an excerpt from Bono's interview with *Propaganda 5* (August, 1987).
18. U2 and Neil McCormick, *U2 by U2: Bono, The Edge, Adam Clayton, Larry Mullen, Jr.* (New York: Harper Collins, 2009), 231.
19. *Samuel Beckett: The Last Modernist* (New York: Harper Collins, 1997), 265.
20. "Ireland's Emigrants."
21. *Collected Shorter Plays of Samuel Beckett* (London: Faber and Faber, 1984), 15.
22. O'Hagan, "Ireland's Emigrants."
23. "Hybridity and National Musics: The Case of Irish Rock Music," *Popular Music* 19 (2000): 191.
24. Shane MacGowan and Victoria Mary Clarke, *A Drink with Shane MacGowan* (New York: Grove Press, 2001), 251-52.
25. *Ibid.*, 252.

B Is for Beckett
Babies and Baby Naming

TANYA PAWLIUK

I am not an expert on Samuel Beckett, but I know men who are, and for this reason I have spent the last seventeen years with an eye and ear open to popular culture Beckett references both common and delightfully obscure. In 2006, my child[1] was born, thereby making baby names suddenly interesting and relevant to my own experience. I began to notice a rise in the use of the name Beckett as a celebrity baby name. Celebrities like Conan O'Brian, Stella McCartney, Melissa Etheridge, and Natalie Maines were naming their boys Beckett. To someone attuned to all things Beckett, this raised the obvious question ... why Beckett? When these boys were bestowed with the name Beckett, were their parents thinking of Samuel Beckett, bee cottages[2] or perhaps sports trading cards? Do any of these possess nameable properties? Does the growing popularity of this name signify a generational reverence for the renowned author? Does it signify the importance of "cultural cachet" in our modern society, and if so what does Samuel Beckett have to do with it?

What's in a Name? The Theory Behind Baby Naming.

Recently, the public interest around baby names has reached a fevered pitch with the naming of the Kardashian-West baby in June 2013 and the Royal baby in July 2013. "What is she wearing" and "who is he dating" seem to have found an equally important popular query in "what are they naming."

Baby naming is a task rarely taken lightly and as such names are rich in history, tradition, religion, meaning, and creativity.[3] Names also appear to be related to the levels of income and education of the parents naming.[4] Research demonstrates that what we are named influences our sense of self as well as how others think about us well into adulthood.[5] Parents want to believe that the name they select for their children will provide them with a positive sense of self. Further, the names we choose for our children indicate to others how we want our children to be perceived, as well as signal to them and the world who we want them to become. Parents seem to innately understand this and therefore naming is usually done thoughtfully, and with an eye to the child's future. Levitt and Dubner posit that parents want to believe they are making a difference to the person their child will become, and this power begins with the name bestowed (181). Baby naming books support this focus on the future when naming in the present. Consider the advice offered to parents when considering traditional boys' names:

> Of course, there is absolutely nothing wrong with giving your son one of these traditional names. In fact, it can benefit him. These names carry a certain prestige and positive connotation that more unconventional names have not yet earned. The traditional names represent strength, intelligence, valor, and power. We associate these names with upstanding young men, with good providers, with family men, with those who are firmly grounded and solid as a rock. After all, isn't this what we want for our sons to grow to be? We have high hopes for them, and if giving them traditional names will help them to move them ahead in the world, and at the same time instill family pride, why not? [Bolton, 27]

As this essay focuses on baby naming in popular culture, it is helpful to consider the evidence for attributing baby names to popular culture. Both Levitt and Dubner, and Bolton in her book on baby naming reflect on the birth and explosion in popularity of the name Madison and offer the movie *Splash* as directly influencing its growth in popularity. In addition to Madison, Bolton offers the name of Emma as evidence that baby naming can be heavily influenced by popular culture:

> For example, prior to the movie *Splash*, with Darryl Hannah, the name Madison was virtually non-existent as a girl's first name. After this movie, Madison started gracing birth certificates of American female babies, and rose in popularity from there, reaching the number-three spot in popularity in 2000. Even more recently, the show *Friends* popularized the name Emma, which made it to number two in 2004 [205].

Despite the obvious pop culture connections offered in the examples of Madison and Emma, Levitt and Dubner propose that it is not celebrities that drive popular growth in a name, but the more affluent family down the street, suggesting that some of these popular names begin with more highly educated families:

> But as a high-end name is adopted en masse, high-end parents begin to abandon it. Eventually it is considered so common that even lower-end parents may not

want it, whereby it falls out of the rotation entirely. The lower end parents, meanwhile, go looking for the next name that upper-end parents have broken in [205].

In a sense the name goes viral, catches on among high-income, highly educated parents, becomes overused as it works its way down the socio-economic ladder, and eventually becomes exhausted.

Naming Baby Beckett

So what does this mean for Beckett—the name? Happily, Levitt and Dubner reflect on the growing popularity of the name Beckett, see a similar pattern of development, and predict the future of the name. In 2006,[6] Beckett is identified as fifteenth on a list of "the twenty white boy names that best signify high-education parents" (200), and by 2015 they predict that Beckett will make the list of the most popular boys' names (206). As someone attuned to Beckett references in popular culture, I too noted first the use of Beckett as a baby name to celebrities, and then the growing trend of the name Beckett in our local newspaper's birth announcements, playgrounds, and references to children named Beckett in the lifestyle coverage sections of the *Vancouver Sun* newspaper.

Nameberry credits Melissa Etheridge[7] with beginning this baby-naming trend: "Melissa Etheridge jumpstarted the name in 1998, followed by Conan O'Brien, Stella McCartney, Malcolm McDowell, Nicole Sullivan, and Natalie Maines" (Nameberry). Other celebrities have also used the name before and after Etheridge, including Irish actor Pierce Bronson,[8] Shonda Rhimes, and Diane Farr. And although celebrities may not be solely responsible for the growth of this name, it is interesting to note that some parents attribute hearing the name first with celebrities.

If we accept the premise that naming is aspirational, what qualities are baby Beckett's parents hoping to imbue their Beckett with? Is Beckett an inspirational name? Is it aspirational? Does their choice in a unique name result in a unique individual? The answer to this question may be yes, but not for the sake of the unique name: for the parenting style of the adults who have chosen Beckett's name and will parent Beckett into adulthood:

> Names serve as social signals that can indicate either cultural or economic "wealth," in which liberals are more interested in signaling cultural wealth while conservatives prefer to signal economic wealth. In particular, they indicate that liberal parents are more likely to choose uncommon, culturally obscure names (e.g., "Namaste," "Finnegan," and "Archimedes"), possibly a reflection of liberals'

tendencies toward openness, while conservative parents are more likely to choose culturally traditional names (e.g., "John," "Thomas," and "Catherine"), possibly reflecting their tendencies towards conscientiousness.[9]

It seems that Becketts named in the image of Samuel Beckett will be parented with the author or at least what the author signifies to them in mind. And perhaps this is best demonstrated in increased use and applicability of this surname turned first name. The name is now identified as a name for boys and girls.[10] It is interesting to read the baby names blogs and see posts advocating Beckett as a boy's name and not a girl's name. Even author Chris Knopf attributes his dog's name, Sam, to Samuel Beckett.[11] Of course, we must not forget the characters named "Sam Beckett" from the hit TV show *Quantum Leap* and *China Beach*. Finally, Beckett is a name and aesthetic being used to market media products such as the *Teletubbies*[12] and consumer goods such as Stella McCartney's Beckett purses,[13] J. Crew's Beckett Boots,[14] and Pottery Barn Kids Beckett baby doll. Beckett is no longer just a baby name: it is a lifestyle signifier.

Although perhaps not academically rigorous, baby-naming blogs provide us with both the overwhelming evidence of how much time and consideration parents put into naming as well as some insight into why people have chosen the name Beckett for their own children. Some of the comments include choosing the name for its uniqueness because it sounds strong and cool. Others attributed the name to Samuel Beckett as an original source:

> My son's name is Beckett and was born in 2003. We were looking for an unusual name from literature and we both like the works of playwright Samuel Beckett. I loved that it was unique and not a lot of boys have the name. Looks like it is gaining in popularity. I also read *Freakonomics* so time will tell if it is all the rage in 2015. I really hope it's not the next Tyler and Taylor, but if it is, I'll tell my Beckett he was a trendsetter.—Jun. 19, 2009[15]

Others attribute the name to Samuel Beckett, but acknowledge that other celebrities were responsible for bringing the name to their attention:

> I named my son Beckett in 2004. I found it in a celebrity baby names book.... Melissa Etheridge had a son named Beckett. Now it is on the popularity chart at #678 due to many other celebrities choosing the name. I haven't met anyone else who has used the name, yet. The response is almost always favorable with many people saying that it's a cool name and wondering how I came up with it. The one downside would be that most everyone asks me to repeat his name because they think I say Becker.—Oct. 17, 2008

Another blogger continues the celebrity endorsement:

> We first heard the name when I was looking for an Irish name and Conan O'Brien's son is named Beckett. We liked the name a lot and wanted something

unique. My only concern is that he'll get teased and called "Becky."—May 20, 2009

And the trend continues:

Grandson named Beckett in November 2008. My daughters and I all made boys name lists and Beckett was on all 3. Paired it with Lee as both parents have that as middle name. Had heard of course of the playwright Samuel Beckett and also Melissa Etheridge's son. Have also heard Conan O'Brien's son.—Aug. 11, 2010

The originality of the name—as well as its growing popularity—has come to the attention of *Freakonomics* readers and baby name bloggers alike:

We named our son Beckett, born Nov 2011. We found it in our baby name book from 2007 (from our daughter) and it just stuck. I think it is still gaining in popularity, and we knew about *Freakonomics* too—and took the risk anyway. I heard of 3 other Becketts right after he was born—sons of friends, not direct friends. We also had another Beckett in his daycare class—that was unexpected! I will probably always call him his full name, as his mom—but other family members do call him Beck too.—Jun. 4, 2013

While the blogs illustrate the growing popularity of Beckett, records indicate that 4,715 boys in the United States have been named Beckett since 1880. The greatest number of babies were given this name in 2012, when 1,037 people in the U.S. were given the name Beckett. Those Becketts are now one year old.[16] That Beckett is a popular name seems undeniable, and what this means in relation to Samuel Beckett is interesting.

What Does Using the Name Beckett Imply?

If we also accept the premise that names are bestowed on us to influence our sense of self as well as how others see us, is it not worth asking what association does the name Beckett carry within popular culture? What does this name represent? How will these Becketts be received if Samuel Beckett is part of that association? If Beckett is a lifestyle signifier, what are we signifying?

Nameberry describes the name Beckett as "a handsome name with an attractively brisk sound, and rich in literary associations via major Irish playwright." This seems positive; however, other popular culture references suggest a more challenging association. In a recent stage review, Beckett's humor is referred to as "bleak and perversely misanthropic"; and his observances are referred to as "astute," and drawing further attention to his "sensibility for the absurd" (Hood). In a reflection on his movie *127 Hours*, Hollywood actor/writer/scholar James Franco is asked whether or not literature inspired his role. Franco responded, "I always thought when first signed on that it was like a Beckett play with a happy ending." He continued about the director Danny Boyle, "that's Danny's real contribution, so it's like a Beckett movie that's entertaining and dynamic and has a happy ending" (Ryzik). And, in an interview with actor David Duchovny, the actor and the journalist discuss his senior thesis on Samuel Beckett. Duchovny asks the writer "you read my thesis on Samuel Beckett? Is it horribly pretentious?" To which the writer responds, "Naturally. It is after all, a serious thesis about Samuel Beckett" (Heath, 40). Thus, with these generally poor "reviews" of Beckett, it might seem incongruous that one would name a child Beckett.

The connection the child's name Beckett has to Samuel Beckett is perhaps best seen in an extreme example. In Germany, a mother won the right to name her son Godot after a year-long legal battle. A lower court initially supported the denial of the use of Godot because "it was not a first name but a fantastical literary name," further, "people associated Godot with death, guilt, salvation or God because of the play *Waiting for Godot* by Samuel Beckett and that the child would be exposed to ridicule as he grew up if given that name" (*International Herald*). Of course, here we are reflecting on the use of Godot, but how far a leap is it to consider it in relation to the man best known, if not only known, for this work?

Do these comments reflect the popular understanding of who Samuel Beckett is? A man who possesses the ability to make astute observations, and has a bleak and perversely misanthropic humor? A man who could be more entertaining, more dynamic, less depressing and less pretentious? Is this aspirational?

What would Beckett himself think of this naming trend? Would he be flattered, or would he be annoyed? Would the dilution of his name—from a one of a kind literary genius to one of four in the class—be amusing or dismaying? Although Beckett cannot comment on this naming trend, perhaps his work can provide us with some insight.[17] Beckett's work often focused on the nameless and the uncertainty of naming. This is a premise that challenges the very nature of establishing a desired outcome through careful consideration of a name.

Is the growing popularity of this name signaling a generational reverence of Samuel Beckett and his work, or is it simply a signal of cultural cachet? Is there still a connection between Samuel Beckett and the en masse use of Beckett as a baby name? I would suggest yes, and I believe the baby blogs support this. Beckett's image as a man who was singularly unique and unwavering in his commitment to his vision and his literary integrity is familiar in some of the discussion on the Beckett name.

Is the popular use of Beckett a signal of a generation's esteem for the author or is it something else? Is having a child named Beckett a sort of unspoken signal to others that I am intelligent, I am well read, I am unique, and my child will be too? Does baby Beckett provide us with a shorthand opportunity to signal our intelligence to others without having to prove it ... instead of having to do the work involved in producing genius does Baby Beckett absolve us of the work?

So what is it? Is it his perceived inaccessibility? Beckett's work is challenging, and perhaps using the name signals an intellectually advanced parent and family who value high culture? Is it his public image, that brilliant unyielding distant man? A hero when he needs to be? A man considered an uncompromising intellectual? A man uninterested in what others think of him, but instead committed to his intellectual and literary pursuits. Damned to fame.

Is naming important? Does it matter if Samuel Beckett has inspired some who inspired many to use his name? As with every name there are some positive connotations as well as negative connotations; however, what would it mean to Beckett fans to know that the man who has inspired the name of their child is a façade ... a construction in the most modern sense. If we consider the opinion of Stephen John Dilks, who suggests that Beckett was much more involved in the management of his image and that some of the very traits Beckett fans have considered in naming their futures are more affected than had previously been considered, what does this mean?

Why Beckett? A pro-Beckett popular culture imagery includes the vision of a man who is artistically uncompromising, brilliant, a man who possesses a sensibility for the absurd, is devoid of commercial interest, and significantly intellectually challenging for many. For some, Beckett offers the dual purpose of possessing the characteristics of a true artist, qualities only those of high intellect and high culture can appreciate. Everyone else is alienated by these very qualities, reassuring Beckett fans of their intellect and literary taste.

While the idea that this image is more managed than reality and could compromise the views of some, it doesn't appear to have influence with Beckett fans who have embraced the real/mythical "floating head." Have they embraced the image of Beckett as a "floating head" without scratching the surface of why this image of Beckett exists and how carefully constructed this image is? Of course, the problem is not in the construction—one must admire Beckett's astute management of his literary career and public self (honestly, there are lessons for modern celebrities here)—the problem is the lack of transparency with fans who have named their futures for a genuinely uncompromising intellect, a revered talent, and a commercially and publicly disinterested artist, not a managed one.

While some have chosen Beckett as a child's name without an interest or awareness of Samuel Beckett—"it's my son's name and he is as cool as his name! He was born September of 2006. Have never heard of any others" (May 23, 2009), others have chosen the name with appreciation or even reverence of Samuel Beckett. That some find him boring, pretentious, bleak, or depressing is not a concerning factor. Those descriptors only work to reinforce the choice of the name.... Beckett is a genius, and you have to be really smart to get it! Naming your child Beckett is a signal to the world: We get it! We are high intellectuals, and our baby will be too.

Like many, I can enjoy the works of Samuel Beckett, and I hold an interest in seeing how his work is used by the popular culture institutions; however, with more than 17 years of consuming books, television, movies, papers, magazines, and other opportunities with an eye or ear open for a Beckett reference, I have learned that it is not Beckett's literary contributions that emerge in these opportunities, but his image and his reputation as unyielding, challenging, intellectually elitist, commercially inconsumable, and ultimately incomprehensible to all but the most intelligent of us. I suggest that it is this image of "the floating head" (unchallenged and unexamined) that has inspired and motivated the naming of baby Beckett(s). The hope that in this current media society their child will be strong, intelligent, and self-possessed enough to stand in defiance of what's popular, and what's easy. Beckett(s) never sell out.

Notes

1. She is not named Beckett or Samuel. In fact her name is not related to the man at all.
2. Nameberry.com.
3. Lesley Bolton, *The Complete Book of Baby Names* (Naperville, IL: Sourcebooks, 2013), 8.
4. Steven D. Levitt and Stephen J. Dubner, *Freakonomics: A Rogue Economist Explores the Hidden Side of Everything* (New York: Harper Perennial, 2006).
5. Jeanna Bryner, "Baby Names Have Long-lasting Effects, for Better or Worse," *The Christian Science Monitor*, 14 June, 2010. Web. 22 April, 2015.
6. Notably also Samuel Beckett's centennial year.
7. Yes, this could be just a coincidence, like so many babies named Beckett, even by faculty at my institution; however, a deeper investigation into the Etheridge baby makes the coincidence less, and the connection stronger. Etheridge and Cypher's sperm donor is none other than musician David Crosby. David Crosby also plays John Larroquette's AA sponsor in *The John Larroquette Show*, a show that is very Beckettian and direct in its usage of the writer's aesthetic, at least in the early, less popular episodes. She also named her eighth studio album *Lucky*, similar to Beckett's Lucky in *Waiting for Godot*, with the song having strong metaphoric similarities to a symbolic interpretation of Lucky in Godot.
8. Interestingly, Pierce Bronson's youngest children with Keely Shaye Smith share

names rich in literary tradition. They are Paris Beckett Bronson (2001) and Dylan Thomas Bronson (1997)

9. Gregg Murray, "Baby Names: 2 Reasons We Name Our Kids What We Name Them." psychologytodaywww. psychologytoday. n.d. Web. 22 April 2015.

10. http://www.thinkbabynames.com/meaning/0/Beckett.

11. 9http://coffeecanine.blogspot.ca/2009/06/chris-knopf-sam.html0.

12. Interestingly there are even Beckett inspired media and products being marketed to children. Dr. Eckart Voigts-Virchow in "Samuel Beckett: Endless in the Year 2000," (*Beckett Aujourd'hui/Today* 11 [2001]: 210–218) has suggested that Beckett's 1981 plays *Quad 1 & 2* have inspired the British children's series *Teletubbies*:

> Whereas the hooded figures of *Quad* exemplify Beckett's strategy of consecutive excorporation—the intellectual denial of bodily representation, a purge of human semblance and human interaction—the *Teletubbies* suggest elementary and technologized group bodies. If one brackets reference, one may watch both the *Teletubbies* and the hooded *Quad* figures in 'aesthetic' terms as electronic presences in anarchic rhythms. Repetition and heteronomy govern both works, as the colour figures are wholly dependent on either a mysterious direction expressed in a mathematically permutated, automatic course, avoiding a dangerous center (*Quad*), or the fantasy of an enigmatic technological adult regime (*Teletubbies*) (2001).

He is not the only one to note that the *Teletubbies* appear inspired by Samuel Beckett. One blogger noted, "*Teletubbies* is pure bliss. The show has a formal elegance rare for TV: a minimalism as rigorous as those of early Phillip Glass or late Samuel Beckett" (http://www.shaviro.com/Blog/? p=212).

13. Although some might attribute the name of the purse to her child, the shape and color of the purse emulate Samuel Beckett's minimalist grey granite grave marker in Montparnasse.

14. Jenna Lyons identifies her son Beckett as a major influence in her day-to-day dress (Lyons & Whitney 2013) and, like Stella McCartney, has elevated the name "Beckett" from nom du jour to aspirational brand status. Like Beckett himself, these products—named after a man and boys gifted with influential and discriminating taste—offer a cool and unattainable vibe for cool and unattainable customers.

15. http://www.babynameshub.com/boy-names/Beckett.html.

16. *Ibid*.

17. On naming with a child's destiny in mind, Beckett's quote, "what do I know of man's destiny? I could tell you more about radishes" (Beckett, "Enough") may be relevant. And on naming in particular, Beckett's work offers us this to consider:

> And even my sense of identity was wrapped in namelessness often hard to penetrate, as we have just seen I think... Yes, even then, when already all was fading, weaves and particles; there could be no things but nameless things, no names but thingless names. I say that now, but after all what do I know about then, now when the icy words hail down upon me, the icy meanings, and the world dies too, foully named (Beckett, *The Unnamable*).

In Fashion
Literary Wardrobes and the Marketplace

JENNIFER MURPHY, TANYA PAWLIUK,
P.J. MURPHY *and* NICK PAWLIUK

> Le CLIENT: Dieu a fait le monde en six jours, et vous, vous n'êtes pas foutu de me faire un pantalon en six mois.
>
> Le TAILLEUR: Mais Monsieur, regardez le monde, et regardez votre pantalon.[1]

Beckett's subtitle and epigraph for "La peinture des van Velde ou le Monde et le Pantalon" are reprised in Nagg's "story of the tailor" in *Endgame* (1958). Nell doesn't want to hear this old chestnut yet again—her mind is on a romantic scene on Lake Como the day after they had become engaged. The bare bones of the joke as cited above are greatly embellished, especially in terms of particular problems faced by the tailor, namely, making a "mess of the seat," a hash of the crotch," and a "balls of the fly."[2] Hamm then breaks into their dialogue and orders his progenitors "bottled." Nell's last word to Clov as he closes the lid of her bin is "Desert!" This in turn leads directly to the opening words of stage direction in *Act Without Words* which was published along with *Endgame*, as a sort of double-bill: "Desert. Dazzling light" (87). In this existentialist vaudeville routine, a man is "flung backwards on stage" and a series of objects are tantalizingly lowered down to him only to be whisked away at certain junctures. The most interesting object is a "pair of tailor's scissors," which echoes Nagg's story while also fulfilling Nell's apparent *non sequitur*, "Desert!" The man first employs the scissors to trim his nails (with tailor's scissors! shades of Beckett Scissorhands?); later he begins to cut a piece of rope with them; and, in the final allusion, "he runs his finger along blade of the scissors, goes and lays them on small cube, turns aside, opens his collar, frees his neck and fingers it" (90). Any suicidal act is thwarted as the scissors disappear in the flies.

Nagg's joke about the quality of the tailor's trousers when compared to the mess that has been made of the world could also be regarded as a sort of existentialist fashion statement, one more concerned with questions of ontology, of Logos, than designer logos. Though, as we will see in the marketplace sections of this chapter, Beckett's status in our celebrity obsessed culture carries a certain cachet ("*cashet*"), a host of fashionable products being marketed under his name as itself a sort of "logo." *GQ* even went so far as to name Beckett as one of the 50 most stylish men of the past 50 years in a 2007 special edition, one year after his centenary celebrations.[3]

The crux of the matter is that Beckett as artist-tailor posits that there is an inherent "misfitting" among our bodies, our clothes (and accessories), and the world which not even the most talented tailor can overcome. In our introduction to this study, we focussed upon the very foundation of the "clothes make the man" line of thought: the recurring image is of characters tormented and tortured by shoes and boots that simply do not fit, are most decidedly out of joint, from poor Belacqua in *Dream of Fair to Middling Women* to the boot-business of *Waiting for Godot* and the later works. Beckett also saw "how worn out and threadbare was the conventional language of cunning literary artificers."[4] It is indeed the very question of language that distinguishes Beckett's richly textured comments on clothing—his sartorism—from other writers who have employed it as an encompassing trope.

Swift's *A Tale of a Tub*, for example, is often described as two-fold in its structure, "two threads on which an immense comic embroidery is woven"[5]: firstly, the satire on religion, the three brothers with their three coats, and the elaborate theology of clothes; secondly, the series of digressions mocking "modern learning" as expostulated by a mad narrator (Beckett's *Watt* exhibits its influence in this regard). The Tubbian world is presided over by a God cast in the classic pose of a Tailor:

> a Sect arose, whose Tenents obtained and spread very far, especially in the *Grand Monde*, and among every Body of good Fashion. They worshipped a sort of *Idol*, who, as their Doctrine delivered, did daily create Men, by a kind of Manufactory Operation. This *Idol* they placed on the highest Parts of the House, on an Altar erected about three Foot: He was shown in the Posture of a *Persian Emperor*, sitting on a *Superficies*, with his Legs interwoven under him [349].

Such worshippers "held the Universe to be a large Suit of Cloaths," "Man himself but a *Micro*-Coat." But the subversion of logic characteristic of the Tubbian world determines "that the outward Dress must needs be the Soul" (351), thereby reducing religion to a mechanical production. Such materialism undercuts, indeed unravels any credible ethical function of religious belief.

Beckett's own "philosophy of clothes," as we trace its development, summarily rejects any such grand allegorizing of a systematic nature and moves instead towards the sociological and ontological. A telling point is that what Beckett takes most directly from Swift has nothing to do with his theology of clothes, but a "fashion tip" of a pragmatic nature Beckett appropriates from *Gulliver's Travels*, "A Voyage to Lilliput," where Gulliver, after a shipwrecked landing on shore, discovers that his hat, which he had "fastened with a String" (35) to his head, has been lost. Both Molloy and his doppelgänger Moran use variations on Gulliver's strategies to keep their hats on.

Thomas Carlyle's *Sartor Resartus* (*The Tailor Retailored* [or "Patched"]) is cut from some of the same cloth employed by Swift. Under the influence of German Idealism, Carlyle, however, turns upside down the Tubbian world's materialism: for Carlyle Spirit is the only reality and visible things are but the manifestations or "clothings" of Spirit. In this regard, all forms are deemed "clothes" and Carlyle emphasizes how indispensable such vestments are since without them any cognitive apprehension could not take place and society itself would fall into disorder. The key distinction Carlyle points out is that whereas the foolish assume such vestments exist for themselves, the wise see them as necessities without autonomous functions. In short: whereas clothes have made us, their influence is such "they are threatening to make clothes screens of us." To forestall such a consequence, Carlyle's "Editor" of the Great Clothes Philosophy of Diogenes Teufelsdröckh concludes that "the beginning of all wisdom is to look fixedly on clothes ... till they become transparent."[6]

Postmodernist readings of *Sartor Resartus* contest the Idealistic rhetoric so often superimposed upon the text and, in what might be deemed a more "Swiftian" mode, challenge this new type of "modern thinking" and the at times questionable mental balance of the Editor and his patchwork rendering of the great Philosopher of Clothes. Such an approach brings Carlyle's thought much closer to Beckett's in a number of instances: namely, the so-called clothes philosophy seems at most a "patching" since we are left in ambiguity and uncertainty. As Colin N. Manlove develops the postmodernist reading of *Sartor*, he proposes that it is perhaps most aptly termed a "panegyric" in praise of the complexities of being, one which acknowledges the darkness and silence which enshrouds this sense of being and just how "evanescent" and "ghostly" it is when the overblown rhetoric is stripped away. We are then left with a contradictory awareness that the clothes philosophy is not "the key to all the multifariousness of life," instead it "leaves us with that life more manifold and complex and chaotic than ever before."[7]

Faced with such complexities, Beckett's sartorism develops in a patchwork fashion. Literally so: Beckett's first two important works, the short story "Assumption" (1929) and the dramatic monologue "Whoroscope" (1930), are *centos*, a Latin word for patchwork garments, compositions made up in large part of quotations from other authors. The development of Beckett's philosophy of clothes is intimately connected with the outfitting of the artist-figure and the stripping away of conventional literary language in order to devise more suitable styles to accommodate his vision.

Let's take stock of the essential items hanging in Beckett's literary wardrobe, focussing chronologically on the fiction. *Dream of Fair to Middling Women* (1931; published 1992) is primarily concerned with ideals of Beauty, ones which have nothing to do with female beauty as promoted and advertised in fashion magazines. Beckett's Belacqua is obsessed with versions of Beauty which transcend the merely physical and, in a dialogical engagement with Joycean renditions of "claritas," seeks a "radiance," of sorts. There are a few synecdochic details such as his Smeraldina's béret, which "the sun had bleached from green to a very poignant reseda,"[8] but for the most part clothing is regarded as merely external trappings. The most striking sartorial image in early Beckett is found in "Draff," the last story of *More Pricks Than Kicks*, the "retailored" version of *Dream of Fair to Middling Women*. Here we encounter the Smeraldina busy at her worktable retailoring her favorite dress ("black and green had always been her colours") so that it will serve as her widow's weeds for the funeral of her dearly departed Belacqua: "Soon the floor was strewn with the bright cuttings."[9]

Murphy is much more down-to-earth about clothing, its third sentence stressing that the art of dressing and undressing is the very *sine qua non* of quotidian existence: "Here for what might have been six months he had eaten, drunk, slept, and put his clothes on and off."[10] On the "jobpath," "stalking about London in a green suit" (technically, "aeruginous," as pointed out by the narrator), Murphy is a strikingly grotesque figure. His jacket is described as a "tube" and "entirely non-porous" (72). Clothing does in this novel embody the central issues: that engaging "gaga" Mr. Endon, an inmate at the mental hospital in which Murphy works, "did not dress, but drifted about the wards in a fine dressing-gown of a scarlet byssus faced with black braid, black silk pajamas and neo-merovingian poulaines of deepest purple" (187). Mr. Endon would seem to be outside all fashions or conventions, the designer of his very own line of clothing. Murphy spots him in his cell "squatted tailor-fashion on the head of his bed, holding his left foot in his right hand and in his left hand his right foot" (241). Murphy can never hope to penetrate Endon's inner world, and in the dénouement he divests himself of his uniform as he makes his way towards his rocking chair, where he meets his explosive end.

This pattern is repeated with significant variation in *Watt*. Mr. Knott is an Endon-type figure of an essential negativity and the clothes he wore were "very various, very very various," so much so that the glimpses Watt caught of him were "seldom of the same figure" since he was indeed "so various."[11] The key variation, however, is that, unlike the expendable Murphy, Watt is a prototype of the Beckett artist-figure as he makes ready to depart Mr. Knott's. The sartorial sign of this is that Watt wore a greatcoat ("still green here and there"), "of a very respectable age," bought second-hand by Watt's father, with quality material "exempt from perforation" (217), just as Murphy's suit was advertised as "hole proof." This stamp of parental authority—with an Edwardian retro-look—is topped off with a block hat (Irish for a bowler) and, voilà, the characteristic outfit of the Beckettian artist-figure.

Before the full unveiling in *Molloy*, *Mercier and Camier* warrants a brief appraisal of the clothing motif for it makes a radical proposal of a rather immodest nature for a refitting of Beckett's "world and trouser" analogy:

> The male trouser has got stuck in a rut, particularly the fly which should be transferred to open trapwise, permitting the testes, regardless of the whole sordid business of micturition to take the air unobserved. The drawers should of course be transfigured in consequence.[12]

Remarkably, this bold design for a fundamental retooling of the male trouser has not, alas, been taken up by any fashion house. Even though trouser is indeed a word of Irish-Gaelic origin, there is clearly no danger of the Irish wresting the yellow jersey of any Tour d'Haute Couture from the French or Italians.

The Beckett artist-figure emerges fully dressed in the eponymous *Molloy*, but it is in part II with the "undressing" of Moran that the way is cleared for this make-over. Moran declares that when it "comes to the clothes that cleave so close to the body and are so to speak inseparable from it, in time of peace" he is "sensitive to the clothing, though not in the least a dandy." A good bourgeois, he proudly maintains that his clothing was "tough and of good cut."[13] Vivian Mercier in the "Gentleman/Tramp" chapter of *Beckett/Beckett* is an astute critic of the dress code of middle class Dubliners, especially when threatened by a fall into the category of the down and out.[14] Hilarious examples of such a comedy of manners are the rotting away due to incontinences of Moran's drawers and the seat of his breeches. He clings to his shirt, while discarding his hard collars, and refuses to jettison his tie which he knotted around his bare neck, "out of sheer bravado" (170). Clothes have served to camouflage Moran's identity to this point and without them he now maintains he has a clearer sense of it than before. On the other hand, Molloy is panicked over the loss of his clothes when he is held captive at Lousse's. Initially, he believes that they have been "burnt," and in the meantime must make do with cross-dressing, wearing Lousse's undergarments until his own are returned. And the most important item is, of course, his greatcoat, which, with its various pockets, is front and center in the famous sucking stones episode.

The greatcoated-figure ostensibly disappears by the end of *Three Novels*, the Unnamable having been reduced to a talking ball. Clothing itself as both material reality and metaphor virtually disappears in the next phase of Beckett's fiction. In *Texts for Nothing* the world "below" is peopled with anonymous pronoun references and in the world "above" there are just glimpses of various effigies. *How It Is* is a much more extreme example of the "unclothing" in some of Beckett's later works. The mise-en-scène is an excremental underground in which a great chain of naked crawlers, armed with a sack of tinned provisions and a can opener, take turns as victims and torturers. (There is one exception—an image of a crawler "clad in a sack bottom burst.") It is as if the threads which had formerly tied these underground denizens to the world above have been cut. One of the most powerful images of the man, clothing, world analogy invokes the Fates:

> great shears of the black old hag older than the world born of night click clack click clack two threads a second five every two never mine[15]

In *The Lost Ones* (1970) the setting is a hermetically sealed "Abode where lost bodies roam each searching for its lost one."[16] All the threads have been cut, all the bodies are totally unclothed. There are no "scraps" here whereby a semblance of a life outside could be patched together.

There is, however, in Beckett's final phase ample confirmation that the greatcoat remains the indispensable signifier of creativity. The most dramatic confirmation comes towards the conclusion of *Company* (1980), which might be regarded as Beckett's literary autobiography (a redressing of Deirdre Bair's first Beckett biography). On "A strand. Evening. Light dying" the Beckett "You," "back to the wash," listens "as it slowly ebbs":

> You lean on a long staff. Your hands rest on the knob and on them your head. Were your eyes to open they would first see far below in the last rays the skirt of your greatcoat and the uppers of your boots emerging from the sand. Then it alone till it vanishes the shadow of the staff on the sand.[17]

The echoes of Shakespeare's Prospero are not intended merely in an ironic way. Beckett's "retailoring" acknowledges a literary debt while at the same time altering the original to fit his own design.

The next two works in Beckett's second trilogy, *Ill Seen Ill Said* (1981) and *Worstward Ho* (1983) also prominently feature the greatcoat figure as essential to the narratives' very being. In the former, the old woman who makes her pilgrimage to the lost one's cairn is vouchsafed memories of him: "Dark greatcoat reaching to the ground. Antiquated block hat. Finally the face caught full in the last rays." "Hanging from their skirts two black greatcoats" (60) serve as a curtain within her dwelling. The central image in *Worstward Ho* is an old man and child, conjured into existence "bit by bit," lives patched together by their outfits:

> Black greatcoats to heels. Dim black. Bootheels. Now the two right. Now the two left. As on with equal plod they go.

Even if the image is sheared off, the synecdochic details still suggest a wholeness:

> Head in hat gone. Greatcoat cut off higher. Nothing from pelvis down. Nothing but bowed back. Topless baseless hind trunk [77].

In Beckett's final fiction, "Stirrings Still" (1988), the "he" sees himself "rise and go," and it is a stringently eloquent and moving summary of the underlying story of Beckett's fiction: "Seen always from behind whithersoever he went. Same hat and coat as of old when he walked the roads."[18] The situation in the second part is, however, quite different: the "he" emerges "in the guise of a more or less reasonable being" as he enters the "outer world" (262). It is as if Beckett has finally attained that state of insight which Carlyle had pointed to as the ideal resolution of a problematical clothes philosophy: "to look fixedly at clothes ... till they become transparent." That is: clothes would be assumed to be there, but there is no need to call attention to them for the ontological parable is concentrated on more essential matters.

Nevertheless, in the great works of Beckett's middle and later periods he fashioned an aesthetic that grew out of his "retailoring" of the fundamental analogy of "le monde et le pantalon." Beckett's greatcoat is indeed comparable to Prospero's magic robe, a fabulous creation which became the defining marker of his visionary exploration of language and being. Literary descendants might declare someday: "we all come out of Beckett's greatcoat," echoing what Dostoyevsky had said of an earlier generation of writers: "We all come out of [Gogol's] 'The Overcoat.'"[19]

The evolution from literary wardrobes (Beckett's greatcoat) to the marketplace has been infused with the aesthetics of fashion in addition to the iconography of Beckett as impenetrable and unknowable, encapsulated in the following quote from a t-shirt box which contained a white t-shirt with an unflattering caricature of Beckett's face: "Samuel Beckett is one of those great writers few of us have ever read" (Largely Literary Series). The idea that Beckett's fashion credibility rests with his "mystery" is a familiar refrain in the fashion world. This manufacturing of "mystery" is a well-established tactic to build the idea of exclusivity. One well-known example of this is the difficulty fashionistas have in buying certain iconic couture pieces, a Hermès Birkin Bag, say, which is apparently in limited supply and only sold to "deserving" Hermès customers. The ownership of the bag denotes membership in a select "club." So too, the devotees of Beckett as a fashion icon aim to separate themselves from the herd by their naming and usage of Beckett's image within a marketplace that relies on "scarcity" and "exclusivity" as its watchword. Only those in the thick of fashion *really* understand the power of naming.

Taking this idea one step further—fashion as the grand arbiter of literary importance—*GQ* magazine in its 50th anniversary issue in October 2007 provided readers with a list, entitled "The 50 Most Stylish Men of the Past 50 Years." In a magazine filled with literary allusions to, among others, Orwell, Camus, Burroughs and Kerouac, Beckett features at Number 21, with Kerouac at Number 19 as the first literary icon in the list. The list is presented as a guide to men on how to dress with fashion and style, and the commentary accompanying a photograph of Beckett includes the following: "A timeless figure, both ancient and modern, traditional and (whether he liked it or not) hip, he favored black (which ignited his blue eyes) and wool or tweed coats that could have come from any number of centuries" (368). This reduces Beckett to a fashion model *par excellence*; the writer goes on to advise readers to wear a black turtleneck sweater (which is fittingly illustrated in the photograph of Beckett) which "perfectly frames your face" as long, of course, as the neck isn't "too tight or too high" (368). That Beckett's wife, Suzanne, actually chose and bought many of his clothes from flea markets in Paris is an incidental detail which does not detract from the overall picture of Beckett as fashion icon and example to emulate.

From celebrity culture which values naming as an element of fashion, Jenna Lyons, creative director at J. Crew, named her son Beckett. In a *Harper's Bazaar* column in the May 2013 edition of the magazine entitled "My List: Jenna Lyons in 24 Hours," she details a typical 24 hour schedule. In this entry, the 6-year-old Beckett functions as both fashion consultant and fashion accessory. Firstly, although Lyons herself chooses Beckett's clothes every morning: "He definitely has a preference for cashmere—I've created a monster" (101), it is her son who is allowed to choose the shoes she will wear from the 300 pairs that she owns: "The only thing is, he's got a one-track mind. I have these flat shoes, Christian Louboutin, with spikes all over them. If left up to him, I would wear them way too frequently" (101). Beckett is more than an arbiter of Lyons' daily wardrobe choices, however, he is also an accessory, a celebrity child of a celebrity mother, whose fame rests on her ability to form fashion trends for both the high street and the high end market. In fact, his daily routine is given equal billing to his mother's. He is also being "marketed" in the list as an integral part of her fashion sense and credibility; Beckett is not only Lyons' child but also a fashion icon in his own right: not shown in the column but present throughout the daily schedule from drop off at school to dinner and games of hide and seek in the evening.

Similarly invisible, the J. Crew catalogue from October 2014 introduces the "Crosby Suit" without explaining that it is named after Sidney Crosby, Pittsburgh Penguins captain and superstar (aka Sid "The Kid" Crosby). Instead, the Crosby Suit is introduced with the line "46 cm biceps are hard to come by. A suit that fits shouldn't be" (18). The implication is that further explanation is unnecessary for fashionistas in the know. A later catalogue (April 2015) provides further clues to the identity of Crosby, as a group of male models are shown wearing Crosby suits while attempting (with little conviction) to play ice hockey. They are also photographed with some members of the New York Boars Hockey team. It is tempting to see the non-appearance of Crosby in this marketing strategy as a kind of homage to Beckett: "Waiting for Crosby."

As a fitting counterpoint to Crosby's elusive presence in the J. Crew catalogue, it may also be a good marketing strategy to develop a prototype of the Beckett Greatcoat, a garment which could be promoted through its exclusivity and price. Even without its namesake as a model for the brand, the coat could be marketed as an indispensable aid to the literati and others to establish their own literary presence in the world of fashion and the marketplace. Only those with an understanding of the exclusivity of the Beckett brand would be drawn to the garment, and it could become the equivalent of the Birkin Bag for J. Crew aficionados: an item that only a few lucky or knowledgeable customers could possess. As a strategy, this could lead to long waitlists, high prices, even higher expectations for the product and, above all, a marketplace for the exclusiveness of the Beckett brand: iconic, cerebral and very, very difficult to locate.

Further, Beckett and his minimalist reach have influenced lifestyle brands in both fashion and home accessories, as Beckett seems equally represented in both the luxury and affordable mainstream brand markets. Perhaps the individual not attuned to Beckettian references in popular culture would not think much about Beckett being used as a branding strategy. These shoppers—unaware of the significance of Samuel Beckett to minimalism—may not see Beckett's specifically precise and refined aesthetics in the minimalist pieces bearing his name.

As influential as minimalism is to Beckett's work, it also appears to be equally influential to achieving a personal signature of style that is unyielding in its precisely refined editing and exclusive discerning taste, and Beckett's uncompromising image appears to be a part of this marketing. This shouldn't be surprising as luxury brands depend on an association with exclusivity, quality and authenticity, as a well as the ability to "sell an experience by relating it to the lifestyle constructs of consumers."[20] In essence, these products help consumers to define, refine, and signify their personal identities, and Beckett provides a ready image and shared commitment to this exclusive aesthetic. The relationship between products and brand concepts is well established:

> values are abstract representations of desired end-states that serve as guiding principles in people's lives. Shared abstract human values are transformed into concrete and material reality when embodied by brands. Marketers imbue brands with human values to evoke the sense that the brands can benefit consumers' lives in ways that are meaningful, not merely utilitarian.[21]

This confirms that the consumer's drive to obtain a lifestyle that projects an image consistent with her values and goals may, in fact, be persuaded by products that are so in line with minimalism that they embody the name if not the very image of the man. "Austere" and "minimalist" are descriptors as easily used to describe Beckett-type accessories as they are commonly attributed to the man himself. An easy correlation between these sparse, elegant, refined products and the author himself is made, and buying Beckett ensures these purchases are meaningful and translate the aesthetic to the aspirational minimalist consumer. We must be clear when we are reflecting on these Beckettian style products: these are handsome and exclusive pieces, unique in their stark simplicity and quality materials. We are not conjuring the worn work boots and ill-fitting, poor-conditioned costumes of his characters or even the second hand selections worn by the author himself, but instead an image most reflective of the disembodied author Samuel Beckett selected to represent his public self.

One may question the relevance of Beckett to fashion as well as the likelihood that the imagery associated with Samuel Beckett has been influential to fashion designers in establishing their design aesthetic; however, there is evidence—both direct and inferred—to support this association. In regard to these direct associations, consider the retailer Beckett Simonon, makers of dress and casual shoes for men, who attribute their styling directly to the author:

> Why the name Beckett Simonon? Have you ever imagined a character that combines the sharpness and strength of Samuel Beckett with the rebelliousness and

style of Paul Simonon? Well, there you go. We have always admired both of them, their personalities, and their work. We created Beckett Simonon around self-confidence, authenticity, cleverness, and refinement; values inspired by these two gentlemen.²²

Patagonia advertises its ultra-light down jacket as being like a "Samuel Beckett novel, minimalism is the name of the game."²³ With such a direct attribution to Beckett's imagery, is it fair to consider the more indirect or conjured effects Beckett's minimalist imagery may also have had in both luxury and mainstream fashion companies, such as Isabel Marant, Ann Taylor, Ugg Australia, Diane von Furstenberg, Dr. Martens, Stella McCartney and Carlos Santana? In Spring 2015, a scan of some of the fashion and home market place saw Stella McCartney selling Beckett sandals, a Beckett cork shoulder bag, Beckett wallet and even a Beckett key ring. Dr. Martens are selling a black boot with a floral pattern by the name Beckett. A quick check on net-a-porter features a Stella McCartney faux-leather Beckett shoulder bag and Isabel Marant Beckett suede concealed wedge sneakers.²⁴ Beckett's influence moves past fashion into toys,²⁵ and even furniture where Beckett's name is being used to build brand identities for rugs,²⁶ sofas, ottomans, and loveseats.²⁷ As the Beckett label moves from luxury brands to more mainstream brands, we begin to see the disconnect between the Beckettian name and the minimalist message. However, in these cases it appears it is "Beckett" and not "exclusive Beckett" that is being sold,²⁸ a less exclusive more inclusive Beckett for the masses.

Stella McCartney is interesting in that the Beckettian brand has been attributed to a variety of her products, suggesting the name is congruent with the exclusive lifestyle her company and her customers aspire to achieve. In reflecting on the company's marketing successes, *WWD: Women's Wear Daily* quotes Francois-Henri Pinault as attributing the success of Stella McCartney's non-leather goods to "consistency of message and matter" as well as producing products that "reflect her principles,"²⁹ and one wonders if we could not relate this commitment of a consistency to message and matter to the Beckettian aesthetic she appears to espouse. Many of Stella McCartney's products bear the name Beckett and each product is consistent in her lauded minimalist expression: "bringing relaxed, yet utterly polished and elegant shapes and super-versatile shades, the newest Stella McCartney spring 2015 rtw [ready to wear] collection targets the modern woman, who loves to make a statement with her iconic minimalist and effortless style."³⁰ Stella McCartney is a celebrated minimalist taste maker whose commitment to her aesthetic is echoed in her person, her company, and her products. Stella McCartney's products and related imagery signify an exclusive, discerning, and cool customer ... much like Beckett himself.

Naturally, not every minimalist will love Beckett, and not every Beckett enthusiast will embrace minimalism in every aspect of her life,[31] but associations between Beckett products and the consumed minimalism of the day (clothing and home fashions) and a recognized shorthand to exclusivity, authenticity, and minimalist imagery in Beckett seem irrefutable. If a minimalist effect—and all it represents—is the purchasing endgame, then Beckett the label seems like a trusty shorthand for discerning customers to rely on.

Polonius tells Laertes that "the apparel oft proclaims the man; / And they in France of the best rank and station / Are of a most select and generous chief in that" (1.3.558–560). Thus, it should be no surprise that a French writer is used to market fashion. But Beckett? Beckett as number 21 in *GQs* Best Dressed? This is surely incongruous unless we remember how unique his texts are. "Ay, and there's the rub" Hamlet would say: most of these designers and fashionistas have likely never read much Beckett. What people are buying into is nothing: a gap where meaning should be is just a carefully constructed image that does not correspond to the reality. After all, Beckett's second-hand clothes should really be called "vintage" and we should recognize that he was just trend-setting—again. When Kerouac and Beckett can become fashionable—both anti-materialist, the antithesis to the fashion industry, we can see how desperate the industry is for marketing campaigns. And this brings us full circle in the hagiography of Beckett (and others): we are left worshipping an image bereft of meaning, which is what fashion does best. Beckett would appreciate this, however, as "How can one better magnify the Almighty than by sniggering with him at his little jokes, particularly the poorer ones?"[32]

Carrying around an exclusive clutch that symbolizes—or may not depending on one's interpretation and proximity to Beckett scholars—the grave of Beckett is the final act of negation perfectly suited to fashion. And what is surprising is Beckett seems to have recognized this: Even Winnie wonders what she would do without her accessories if she was left on her own: "What would I do without them, when words fail" (53). Of course, she is referring specifically to her "Brownie," her Browning pistol, and parasol, but she knows the value of these items, and the value of keeping up appearances: "Is that not so, Willie, that even words fail, at times? What is one to do then, until they come again? Brush and comb the hair, if it has not been done, or if there is some doubt, trim the nails if they are in need of trimming, these things tide one over" (24). All of these items, save the parasol, come from her Mary Poppins–like carpet bag, her "capacious black bag, shopping variety" (7), notably distanced from a thousand dollar clutch, but it could still hold her "Brownie." And maybe, in a way, there is something inside the clutch anyway. Let's negate the man (do we actually know anything he stood for? Vaclav Havel anyone?) and negate his works (reading them is such hard work when there's a funny cat clip on YouTube). This is what fashion does: it consumes everything for a sale of the new season's must have catalogue item, even one's soul if one is not careful which is what Swift recognized. But in this negation *is* liberation, and Beckett knew this: Just like Joyce had his artist-God figure removed, indifferent, paring his fingernails, Winnie pares hers, the tailor's scissors are ripped away into the wings: when there is nothing left, before the stories return, one must go on. And that is where fashion fits in, although perhaps a little mis-fit for Beckett (but it suits him). The words eventually come back, but in the meantime there are accessories, fabrications: context. The words: "clean lines with a clean conscience," "purist," "dignified," "elephant grey hue."[33] Exclusive(ly) Beckett or Beckett-lite? Or both? Here we have the rupture of signifier from signified, leaving us with nothing, so let's fill the gap with something, some thing. A coat, a clutch, a pair of boots, a suit? Nothing is more real than nothing.

Notes

1. Samuel Beckett, "La Peinture des Van Velde," *Disjecta: Miscellaneous Writings and a Dramatic Fragment*, edited and with a foreword by Ruby Cohn (New York: Grove Press, 1984), 118.
2. Samuel Beckett, *Endgame, A Play in One Act*, followed by *Act Without Words, A Mime for One Player* (New York: Grove Press, 1958), 22.
3. GQ (*Gentlemen's Quarterly*), 50th Anniversary Issue, October 2007, "Icons of Cool: 50 Most Stylish Men of the Past 50 Years and What You Can Learn From Them," 357–384. Beckett's entry at number 21 is on page 368.
4. Samuel Beckett, "Dante... Bruno. Vico.. Joyce," in *Disjecta*, 30.
5. John Middleton Murray's description cited by Philip Pinkus (editor) in his "An Approach to 'A Tale of a Tub,'" in *Jonathan Swift: A Selection of His Works* (MacMillan of Canada, 1965), 289. All references to Swift are from this edition.
6. Thomas Carlyle, *Sartor Resartus* and *On Heroes and Hero Worship*, with an Introduction by W.H. Hudson (New York: Everyman's Library, 1967), xi, xiii.
7. Colin N. Manlove, "'Perpetual Metamorphoses': The Refusal of Certainty in Carlyle's *Sartor Resartus*," in *The Critical Response to Thomas Carlyle's Major Works*, edited D.J. Trela and Rodger L. Tarr (London: Greenwood Press, 1997), 44.
8. Samuel Beckett, *Dream of Fair to Middling Women*, edited Eoin O'Brien and Edith Fournier (Dublin: Black Cat Press, 1992), 4.
9. Samuel Beckett, "Draff," in *More Pricks Than Kicks* (London: Calder and Boyars, 1970), 191.
10. Samuel Beckett, *Murphy* (New York: Grove Press, 1957), 1.
11. Samuel Beckett, *Watt* (New York: Grove Press, 1959), 200.
12. Samuel Becket, *Mercier and Camier* (London: Calder and Boyars, 1971), 72.
13. Samuel Beckett, *Three Novels (Molloy, Malone Dies, The Unnamable)* (New York: Grove Press, 1958), 170.
14. Vivian Mercier, *Beckett/Beckett* (New York: Oxford University Press, 1977), 46–72.

15. Samuel Beckett, *How It Is* (New York: Grove Press, 1964), 106.

16. Samuel Beckett, *The Lost Ones* (New York: Grove Press, 1972), 7.

17. Samuel Beckett, *Nohow On (Company, Ill Seen Ill Said, Worstward Ho)* (New York: Grove Press, 1996), 39–40.

18. Samuel Beckett, "Stirrings Still" (1988), in *The Complete Short Prose, 1929–1989*, edited S.E. Gontarski (New York: Grove Press, 1995), 260.

19. The Nabokov-like character Polokov in the film *Admission* (2013) declares "Even Beckett emerged from Gogol's Overcoat." The title refers to getting in to an Ivy League University. Tina Fey as Portia Nathan is an Admission Officer at Princeton who tries to work the system so that her "son" (she's mistaken in this regard) can get into Princeton. Her "son" is named Jeremiah Belakian—a very Beckett sounding name indeed—Old Testament prophet plus a strong echoing of Beckett's first major character Belacqua.

20. Glyn Atwal and Alistair Williams, "Luxury Brand Marketing: The Experience Is Everything." *Brand Management* Vol. 16, 5/6: 338–346.

21. Carlos J. Torelli et al., "Brand Concepts as Representations of Human Values: Do Cultural Congruity and Compatibility Between Values Matter?" *Journal of Marketing*, Vol. 76 (July 2012): 92–108.

22. www.beckettsimonon.com.

23. Patagonia.com.

24. Retrieved on April 22, 2015: www.stellamcartney.com; www.drmartens.com; http://www.net-a-porter.com.

25. Retrieved on April 22, 2015: http://www.potterybarnkids.com.

26. Retrieved on April 22, 2015: http://www.potterybarnkids.com/products/beckett-rug.

27. Retrieved on April 22, 2015: http://www.woodleys.com/Bernhardt-Interiors-Beckett-Loveseat; http://www.livingspaces.com; http://www.houzz.com/photos/504774/Beckett-Sofa-contemporary-sofas.

28. For more information on how the name moves from exclusive to less exclusive markets consider the previous essay "B Is for Beckett: Babies and Baby Naming" by Tanya Pawliuk

29. Jessica Iredale, *WWD: Women's Wear Daily*, Nov. 28, 2012, Vol. 204 Issue 111, 4.

30. Retrieved on April 22, 2015: http://www.fashionisers.com/fashion-news/stella-mccartney-spring-summer-2015-collection/.

31. Retrieved on April 22, 2015: http://www.trendhunter.com/trends/waiting-for-godot.

32. Samuel Beckett, *Happy Days* (New York: Grove Press, 1961), 31.

33. Describing Stella McCartney's "Beckett faux leather clutch" ($698) on mytheresa. com. 24 April 2015. Web. In the typical gender portrayal, the model is the antithesis to the floating head of Beckett: she is decapitated above the lips so you too can look as good as she does, in feminized Beckettian uniform: black, black and more black. You really should look this up, the clutch *is* Beckett's grave marker, fulfilling Polonius' advice: "costly thy habit as thy purse can buy, / But not express'd in fancy; rich, not gaudy" (1.3.556–557).

The New Dedalus
Avatars and Identities in Online Social Networks

Mark Rowell Wallin

As Anja Muller and Mark Schreiber note in their essay "Sam 2.0: Appropriation, Interpretations and Adaptations of Beckett on YouTube,"[1] the opportunities presented by video file sharing tools radically undermine the all-too-frequent attempts of authors, directors, creators and publishers of all stripes to create and codify unified heroic author-figures. Beckett's own obsession with the "fidelity" of adaptations of his work and his Ozymandias-like obsession with his authorial legacy are shown to be the trappings of a bygone era where the illusion of control could be considered to reside in some sort of romantic personification of genius. They point to Stephan Porombka's argument that the kinds of amateur video productions posted to hosting sites like YouTube shift "the focus away from the text—what is being said—to the self-performance of the author" (13). While this is undeniably true, the larger revolution in adaptation represented by social media goes well beyond a shift from textual fidelity to permanent performativity; social media platforms of this type represent the front line of the latest battle in the ongoing struggle for authorship in a world quickly turning its back on the myths of the author-as-solitary-genius. Rather, social media presents everyone as co-creators, elaborators and adaptors.

Adaptation studies has begun to pay attention to the battle between authors inherent when one text claims the title or structure of an antecedent, but has been slow to do so largely because the majority of adaptative relationships examined tend to be literary/cinematic ones. Both these modes have been, with few outliers, deeply invested in the enlightenment and romantic projects that placed single authors and artists as the brands that unify and sell products. Film, in its attempt to gain legitimacy and cultural capital, enthusiastically embraced Truffault's auteur theory that worked to enshrine the equivalency between the director of the film and the author of the novel. Such models worked well in structuring early film and media studies departments to mirror literature departments as they set about building a new canon with "directors" as the organizing term. This evolution, while eminently logical given the constant need for new technologies to dress and act like the old in order to be considered part of the in-crowd, pushed back the reckoning for the author-figure until technology and economics made the cracks in the edifice too glaring to continue with any seriousness. The collaborative nature of media production was always an awkward issue as the devotees of canon discussed directors while the corporate ownership of "texts" (films, books, video games) made a mockery of the philosophical underpinnings of intellectual property, and as copyright lawyers dutifully quoted Immanuel Kant to justify multinational conglomerates suing teenagers for works of fan fiction. But the architecture and design of social media platforms have not only spawned a brood of "unauthorized" adaptations, but also mortally stung the lingering pest of the unified author and revealed it to be nothing more than an image—a mirage that can be appropriated and adapted in and of itself.

This new reality is, as I've suggested, particularly ironic when we examine Samuel Beckett's avatar as he has been ripped from the stable moorings of authorized use and set adrift in the tempestuous seas of social media. Given the lengths Beckett himself went to control the works that bore his name, the anarchist in me derives no small amount of pleasure that his image and decontextualized phrasings are strewn hither and yon on the internet by any nerdy teenager with a fascination for existentialism or corporate tycoon with a mobile phone and a twitter account. These images and words are part of the complex matrix of online identity and user profiles across various media platforms, from Facebook, to YouTube and Vine, or Twitter to Tumblr. What we find is that the carefully crafted image Samuel Beckett created of himself is as proprietary as his work; that is, not at all. The rapacious process of adaptation has accelerated with the advent of social media and "maker culture" to the point where "the text" breaks down into shards of a mirror. There is no point where one can differentiate what exactly is being adapted: the limited vision of "the source" or its author's image. In her work on adaptation, Linda Hutcheon[2] rightly works to clearly define what she means when she takes up the notion of adaptation. Her project is vested in the conceptualization of adaptation as a "sustained" project of equivalence; presumably in this alchemy, a 300-page novel is roughly equivalent in aesthetic heft a 1.5-hour film. The problem is that adaptation doesn't end with "the text." While it certainly makes things more convenient to create a limitation on what constitutes adaptation, ultimately, such definitions are more for the convenience of those examining the adaptation, rather than fearlessly staring into the fractal abyss that threatens to overwhelm us when we begin to look carefully at the process.

What is important to understand about Beckett on the internet—particularly on social media—is that he is used, appropriated, twisted, distorted, and adapted. Not only his literary work is so abused but, perhaps more importantly, his image and persona. Beckett's scowling black and white visage becomes a digital sock puppet by which users can take on any number of roles: solitary genius, misunderstood artist, random spewer of zen-sounding maxims, photogenically intense and really, really ridiculously good-looking male model with cavernously chiseled cheekbones. As Stephen John Dilks[3] rightly points out, Beckett's obsession with the marketing of his own brand has created a constellation of cultural associations around his identity and image that linger. In an online world where identities are as easily obtainable as a cut and paste image and a recognizable quote, Samuel Beckett comes with a ready-made persona; for the brooding artist, the existential dabbler, the cultural critic, the sneering aesthete, the lure of the Beckett brand becomes irresistible. He looks how we want to look, writes how we want to write, poses how we want to pose. In short, we want to be him. The structure of social media platforms allows for just such plasticity of identity and the ubiquity of the brand provides the fodder for the assemblage. Consequently, Beckett has been posting on Tumblr since 2011, has had a Facebook page for years, and prolifically tweets (and is, in turn, widely retweeted). At the same time, at any given moment, endless numbers of users "wear" his iconic avatar in all social media, and by extension, all their posts are read in terms of the Beckett brand.

Rather than delving into another analysis of YouTube postings, I'm more interested here in that aspect of social media that makes it social: its interactive element. While Paul Levinson's book *New New Media*[4] is most often a tedious study in self-aggrandizement (I have, in all honesty, never read another book where the preponderance of citations are from the author's previous work. Gilderoy Lockhart would be proud!), but upon one salient issue he is spot on: what defines the next generation of new media is not its digital or computer basis, but its interactive element. Without the comments section, YouTube is just another video posting board. What makes social media distinctive is the capacity for users to engage with each other directly, often over some sort of "text." Users may directly comment or engage with each other—as in YouTube and Facebook—or repost, like and/or augment—as with platforms such as Twitter, Vine, Tumblr and Pintrest. In the world of social media, the process of adaptation occurs less in the formation and deployment of texts in the way that Hutcheon defines them, and more at the level of the persona, or creation of the "author-figure." These performances tend to fall into two broad types: the appropriation and modification of an artist's work, and the actual co-opting of the artist's image in order to shape and sculpt a user's identity.

While some work has been done picking over the exuberant proliferation of overt textual adaptations on sites like YouTube, I will focus my attention on the ways that the carefully crafted fiction of Samuel Beckett has been adapted and deployed in social media. The structural design of social media, by and large, places limitations on what can be adapted. One cannot, for example develop an equivalent and sustained Twitter adaptation of *Murphy*. But, if we proceed down into the comments section of Nigel Tomm's YouTube excerpt (titled "Green Screen"[5]) from his more "sustained" adaptation of *Waiting for Godo*t ("Green Screen" a 55 second taste of the full 1:12:15 version available on IMDB[6]) one finds various invocations of the person of Beckett, from his presumed response to iconic representations of Beckett himself or references to his work. For example, the user murcurialohern claims that "this 'adaptation' makes baby samuel beckett cry"—an interesting notation that constructs Samuel Beckett as having the holiness of Jesus Christ. This quote is common to the genre of social media responses: short, pithy, intertextual and frequently sarcastic. The line plays upon both the acknowledgement of the canonical and reverential place Beckett occupies in both aesthetic and popular culture, while at the same time sending such adoration up as absurd in its reference to shaming children with actions that make the baby jesus cry. This association with the original "brand" is precisely the sentiment that makes images and representations of Samuel Beckett the coin of the realm in the context of social media. When all one has to represent one's self is an avatar and brief snippets of text, the fastest way to have an identity is to steal, borrow, or adapt one.

Invocation of the Slogan: Beckett's Epic Fail

In the comments section of the game playthrough (a recorded video of a person playing a video game) entitled "Pokemon Fire Red Omega Part 13: Speeding Through Cerulean Gym"[7] the video's poster begins the description section with the ubiquitous Beckett quote "Try again. Fail again. Fail better." Such a deployment is common in the digital world; the epigram is more popular than it has ever been. But what makes this particular moment revealing is that the first comment below the video, from a user named "Chevitile," asks about the quotation, wondering if the quotes are "planned?" Feratrox interprets the question to be an inquiry as to where the quotation is from and responds, "I just look up a relevant quote on wikiquote, wisdom quotes or just some of my magazines." Such meta sources for quotations have allowed people who have no background in literature or avant-garde culture to widely reference authors like Beckett. But as is apparent from this example, such uses are frequently decontextualized. There is no indication whatsoever that Feratrox has ever read or seen Beckett's work, nor that invoking the maxim in this context would encourage the poster to engage with the work. The upshot of this accessibility and decontextualization is a general tendency to the aphorism or slogan. Beckett's work seems uniquely suited to these maxims that seem designed for the structural limitations of social media contexts.

The Samuel Beckett Twitter account has spewed forth no less than 78,140 character Beckettisms, at the time of this writing. The account has nearly 4,400 followers. What is particularly interesting about the twitter feed is its complete and utter decontextualization. Unlike many other attributed aphorisms, the Samuel Beckett twitter account does not cite its slogans in any way, assuming perhaps that since one has chosen to "follow" Samuel Beckett, one would assume all the tweets are attributable to the namesake. But the effect of such radical decontextualization is that it conveys the sensation, not that Beckett said these things, but is *saying* them. This is the power of the social media technology: it resurrects the past and drags it into the present in a way that creates the illusion of immediacy and intimacy. In the currency of the Twittersphere, "retweets"—or people who chose to post your tweet on their account—are an indication of success. What is interesting about the Samuel Beckett twitter account is that despite beginning in early June 2010 with a flurry of tweets, but with little attention, averaging 3–5 retweets per. Three months later, on October 22nd, the retweets suddenly take off with "My mistakes are my life" (with 87). That same day sees the two most popular tweets of the account with "You're on Earth. There's no cure for that" (299) and the ubiquitous "Nothing else ever. Ever tried. Ever failed. No matter. Try again. Fail again. Fail better" (174). These three represent the high water mark for Samuel Beckett's twitter account. Apparently Mr. Beckett lost interest in early 2012 because after a flurry of activity in 2010 and 2011, the account has gone silent. It is no accident that the two most popular retweets are the ones associated with failure.

But this sense of the immediate present, of the continuing life of the avatar is not just a matter of twitter. On Facebook, we find competing profiles for Beckett. One Samuel Beckett, who lives in Rennes, France (and who seems to be originally from Turkey) has only one post, a black and white of

Beckett with the "Fail Better" tagline, but who apparently is a fan of the Besiktas football club and likes BBC Turkey and The Style Brothers. Despite this rather tired and flat presentation, Mr. Beckett has 159 friends as of this posting. Another profile has Samuel Beckett currently working at the French Red Cross in Paris, while accurately noting that he used to work at Trinity College, Dublin, is married and is originally from Dublin. Alas, this, slightly more accurate digital personification of Samuel Beckett has garnered only 16 friends in the last 4 years, although arguably, the poverty of numbers is offset by their international flavor whereas Rennes's Beckett is befriended almost entirely by Turkish nationals. Paris's Beckett posted several times in 2011, mostly in the form of classic, black and white Beckett images of various headshots. The 2011 activity closes out with an announcement of marriage (March 30, 2011). Since heading off into matrimonial bliss, Paris Beckett's only other activities are a persistent tendency to play WordTornado and a fairly decent score in Candy Crush Saga.

Tumblr, an image-based blog platform, hosts several Samuel Beckett pages and countless references to his work. In the Tumblr "fuckyeahsamuelbeckett" an outside poster named "rustbeltjessie" posts an exchange with another poster named "jools-holland" where the latter asks "should I make a cake in honor of Samuel Beckett's birthday or just sit around contemplating whether or not I should make one for the whole day"—an obvious reference to *Godot*. But rustbeltjessie takes the post in a different direction by suggesting that "I would recommend making a terrible cake, then making a second, even worse cake. That way both cakes fail, but the second one fails better." We see here the two essential Beckett slogans playing out in a single exchange, without direct reference to the works in question. Rather, both seek to express an abstract or diffuse "sense" of what constitutes "Beckettness" in the popular consciousness.

One of the more interesting phenomena on Tumblr is the "beckittns" page, which appropriately consists of visual "mash-ups" of two highly memetic forms: quotations from Samuel Beckett and the ubiquitous and universal appeal of cat images. Most frequently, beckittns uses lines from *Godot*, some of them over and over with myriad amusing cat imagery. Citations are done in hashtag format—that is, rather than directly attributing a quotation to Samuel Beckett and a particular source, a series of "hashtags," or systems of grouping like information, are used so that if one of the cat images references *Worstward Ho*, one can click on the hyperlink for #worstward ho and be taken to all the Tumblr pages that use the same hashtag. Almost unanimously, the attributions to this particular work are of the same quotation. One of the earliest iterations, though, is a "gif" (or short, looping video) of a cat attempting to jump from one counter to another and plummeting, accompanied by the "Try again. Fail again. Fail better" quotation.

What these myriad exchanges on social media seem to indicate is that Samuel Becket is profoundly and successfully wedded to the beauty of failure. Perhaps even more than *Waiting for Godot*, "Fail better" has become the essence of Beckett in social media context. This association may arise because of the pre-existing association of new media with the concept of "the fail" or the expression of disapproval, usually deployed in an imperative form (as in "Fail!"). When one combines the existential pessimism and sloganeering that appears to characterize Beckett's more quotable phrasings with the scathing penchant for irony that defines many social media users, the possibilities for parody at the meme-level are almost limitless. The beckittns phenomena is only one part of a larger constellation of user-generated mockery, using standard meme-formats like the "inspiration" poster, or "keep calm" phenomenon.

Bending Beckett: Avatar as Identity Adaptation

There are, of course, many Samuel Becketts to be found on Facebook, most assiduously avoiding any connection to the author-figure with a penchant for brooding black-and-white portraiture. This, of course, belies the many, many people who use the myriad images of Beckett to either invoke in posts, in indirect *acts of association*, or as profile pictures in direct *acts of identification*. By and large, these two different approaches to the image mark all the social media approaches to the appropriation of Samuel Beckett's avatar. Acts of association tend to be minor acts of adaptation, as the image is often associated with a quotation from Beckett himself, or framed in such a way as to ascribe credit to his oeuvre. The adaptive element in this case arises from the decontextualization and transplant of large and complex ideas into a single image. Acts of identification, however, are more radical appropriations, where the image stands for the person claiming it. The use of Beckett's image as an avatar suggests a "one-ness" of the artist and the profile: that I AM Beckett in some capacity. At the same time, the adaptation of the image in the context of identity creation obscures the "everyday" identity of the user. Just as the political/hacker group Anonymous uses the image of Guy Fawkes to simultaneously project an ideological position and protect their physical identity from political reprisal, so the invocation of any online avatar performs this dual function.

What makes this process particularly easy in the case of Beckett's images is precisely the degree to which Beckett managed to control his "brand." There is a uniformity and recognisability to the Samuel Beckett image that is distinct from all others: the black-and-white image with high contrast, the black or dark turtleneck sweater, the intense gaze, the deeply lined face and chiseled features. Thus, the uniformity of the brand makes appropriation simple. Additionally, it is precisely this uniformity and recognisability that makes it particularly enticing to social media users, as it has become a distinct "meme." First popularized in Richard Dawkins's *The Selfish Gene*,[8] the notion of the meme is akin to a thought-virus or an idea that replicates itself over and over. The term has become synonymous online with a set format, usually in the case of an image or design, that facilitates linguistic play at the level of audience expectations. Memes are constantly appearing as current events and popular culture offers opportunities for mockery and distinctiveness. The reason the Beckett brand makes itself so available to this mode of adaptation is precisely its set form and predictability. The very things that allowed Beckett to control his identity are the same things that make that identity irresistible to those who seek to appropriate and modify it. This tension in the Beckett-image between control and adaptation is distinct from say the aforementioned Guy Fawkes mask or even fan-motivated avatars (I myself have sported various Twin Peaks avatars over the years). Beckett's awareness of and concerted effort at control over his own image and his treatment of himself as proprietary makes any "unauthorized use" of that image a fundamental challenge to the larger branding project. In this way, Beckett avatars point to the tension at the heart of Beckett's art/life: the careful cultivation and control over the projected image of the bohemian rebel aesthete. With the click of a mouse and a breach of copyright law, you too can be as bad-ass as Beckett.

In posting images of Beckett in blogs or Facebook status lines, the image associates the poster with the cultural connotations of the brand. This kind of association places one in the company of other aesthetic figures of similar cultural capital. The *act of association* is a process by which one accrues *ethos*, or credibility, by acting in a particular way—in this case, by posting images of Samuel Beckett and associating my social media identity with them in some capacity. The act of identification, where the poster uses the image of the Beckett brand as a part of their "profile," creates a direct line of connection between the poster and the image. In this case, Beckett's image becomes an avatar, or stand-in for the poster. On the one hand, this use creates a double-distance between the poster and their audience insofar as the "profile" is generally understood to be (to one degree or another) an invention. The social media profile is by no means a "true" representation of the poster. Most users of social media have several accounts on any given platform under a number of names. Many users are more comfortable operating in anonymity and therefore resist having names or images that can be associated with their off-line identity.

But the image is not only used as a direct identity avatar or *acts of identification*. More often, the image is used as part of a larger project of identity bricolage, or the assembly of various images, phrases, links and connections that constitute an online profile: acts of association. In keeping with the invocation of the rhetorical term ethos above in terms of the direct avatar connection, we should see this type of assemblage approach to online identity-creation as a *hexis*, or disposition. One's hexis, or patterns of behavior, creates a character for the public to observe and offers a way to interpret new posts that follow. According to Hauser,[9] "As we observe [the rhetor's] public behaviour, we see their habits revealed in the choices they make. From observing their habits, we draw inferences about their character, or ethos" (97). The hexis[10] is constantly produced by action as it is simply synonymous with being—"a permanent condition as produced by practice" (Miller 311). But character is not fixed and stable; there is no "true self." Rather, "the nouns habit and character are not static—are not states or conditions of existence, but rather they can be only dynamic states, that is, states involving action" (315). These dynamic states are created deliberately and in turn project an image of the creator.

When we think in terms of the identity assemblage of social media life, these acts of association can be seen as objects of self-attribution, or perhaps *digital identity possessions*: bricolage that we continually acquire for the sole purpose of projecting an image of ourselves. This concept of assemblage is in keeping with more traditional translations of the term hexis as "possession" as well as its Greek verb-root (e.g. "having"). Of course, all this talk about social media users creating piles of digital possessions in order to adapt an identity runs straight into the carefully crafted and assembled monolith of Beckett himself. The process of hexis is precisely what makes a brand, and by extension, what constitutes our understanding of who Samuel Beckett is to our culture; it is no wonder Beckett took such pains to control it. But the very structure that allows for users to shape themselves by means of identity possessions allows them to do so independent of, and at times at the expense of, Beckett's own identity-intentions. Most often, the act comes at the direct expense of the property rights of the image-owner. Social media users, for the most part, ignore issues of copyright as they post and repost images. Because of the ubiquity of the pilferage and the fact that users rarely monetize their use, image owners rarely take legal action against digital identity possessions. But the fact remains, the users of social media who trade in the social and cultural capital of Samuel Beckett's image directly undermine the edifices of authorial control that have worked to create and maintain the Beckett brand.

On the social media site, Pinterest, users "pin" images to their "board" in order to form portraits of their interests and personalities. The site is primarily a means by which users identify found objects to create a bricolage identity, emphasizing images over text, as opposed to other blog sites that emphasize the accumulation of identity by means of creation and composition at the levels of poetry, prose, or visual elements. On Pinterest, users can navigate by theme or by "following" other users that they know. When one encounters images that one finds appealing, one selects the push-pin icon in order to "pin it," thereby creating a link between the original poster and one's self. Users can develop multiple, thematically organized boards, but what is interesting is that the default titles for these boards are based on consumption: "places to go," "things to buy," "recipes to make," etc. When I entered a search for "Samuel Beckett" the search result confronted me with a relatively homogenous assemblage of almost entirely black-and-white images of Beckett. As I scrolled down, I came across three color photographs in total (of hundreds of pins), all of which were taken surreptitiously, or candid shots of Beckett by private citizens. What is interesting among the images are the smattering of "Becket with…" shots that situate him in time and culture. The most frequent of these is the invocation of Buster Keaton, particularly two black-and-white images of them speaking, looking like Vladimir and Estragon.

If one looks for Samuel Beckett boards (or the segregated "folders" users make to group their pins), one finds, again, the same assemblage of images and phrases that define the online presence of Samuel Beckett. But those who take the time to devote not just a single "pin" on a more general board (about themselves, or with a more generic title such as "authors" or "playwrights") but a whole board to Beckett alone are invoking a particular level of commitment to the identity. These clusters and constellations of images suggest a weight and gravity of digital identity possessions that, while homogenous in composition and character, adapt Beckett's fixed brand into a project of identity formation, putting these images in association with other boards in their profile to create a composite representation of the poster.

Conclusion

Thus, identity is frequently created in social media by means of nodal association as well as cumulative attention. One simultaneously assembles a digital self by means of linking digital identity possessions, creating an avatar of one's idealized self. But by linking and labeling those same identity possessions, one is automatically linked into a larger system of association—in this case, the association of "Beckett-ness." These links contribute to the perpetuation of the well-established Beckett "brand" by means of their uniformity and homogeneity. In other words, social media creates a profound tension between the hagiography of Beckett that venerates the author-figure as authorized, while on an individual level, users take those images and adapt them, putting them to unanticipated and iconoclastic uses. Users can either "borrow" Beckett's brand, by associating themselves with the image, or more subversively, become Beckett by creating profiles that to one degree or another, undermine the attempt at stasis the Beckett estate so carefully maintains.

At the same time as the image is appropriated for purposes of identity, the actual canonical text itself is pillaged and decontextualized. The very design of social media undercuts the prosaic and complex nature of Beckett's work; with only 144 characters, all attempts at subtlety are brought to the level of sloganeering. This adaptation of a life's work into maxims strikes at the heart of the priesthood of Beckett scholarship insofar as it appears to mock the archaeology and mining of the sacred texts as a waste of time. Countless pages have been devoted to the exposition of *Waiting for Godot*, on its intertextual references, its invocation of modernist conceits and anticipation of postmodern sensibilities, but on Tumblr, Pinterest and Twitter the triumph of modernist drama is reduced to, "—Well, shall we go?—Yes, let's go. (they do not move)." This is perhaps the biggest joke of all: that the very products of modernity (technological acceleration and identity dislocation) that seemed to, in part, inspire Beckett's work and efforts at self-monumentalism would become the very tools used to pull it down, tear it apart and recycle it into something unauthorized. Beckett himself seems to anticipate such an eventuality with his famous short play *Breath*, where heaps of garbage are assembled on the stage, without actors or linguistic script, only cries and panting. Social media has made something new of the mess it has wrought of Beckett's work. It may not be what the master intended, but life, even aesthetic life, rarely is.

Notes

1. Anja Muller and Mark Schreiber, "Sam 2.0: Appropriation, Interpretations and Adaptations of Beckett on YouTube," in *Adaptations: Performing Across Media and Genres*, ed. Monika Pietrzak-Franger (Trier: Wissenschaftlicher Verlag Trier, 2009), 173–192.

2. Linda Hutcheon, *A Theory of Adaptation* (New York: Routledge, 2006).

3. Stephen John Dilks, *Samuel Beckett in the Literary Marketplace* (Syracuse, NY: Syracuse University Press, 2011).

4. Paul Levinson, *New New Media* (2d ed. Pearson Higher Education, 2012).

5. https://www.youtube.com/watch?v=J8vFECYQ9ik.

6. http://www.imdb.com/title/tt1210845/.

7. https://www.youtube.com/watch?v=7eRDCkaodqo.

8. Richard Dawkins, *The Selfish Gene* (Oxford: Oxford University Press, 2006).

9. Gerard A. Hauser, *Introduction to Rhetorical Theory* 2d ed. (Prospect Heights, IL: Waveland Press, 2002).

10. Arthur Miller, "Aristotle on Habit and Character: Implications for the Rhetoric," *Speech Monographs.* Vol. 41. No. 4 (1974): 309–316. Accessed April 28, 2015. doi:10.1080/03637757409375855

Two Quinks for Sam

Alexander M. Forbes

I.

less more never none more less more
narrate Sam

                                        the narratives of Sam

                                        never brought Sam: upon the stage
                                        heartfelt desire but plot never factified
                                        monologue with animals etc.
                                        write Sam

                  the amanuensis transcribes his portion
                  of the sparkling dialogue speaking his
                  memorable lines rapidly lest he forget
                  them before handing his pen to his
                  interlocutor that he might in turn
                  transcribe his lightsome rejoinders
                  before returning the pen to the original
                  amanuensis & so forth until they are
                  joined by a third amanuensis who
                  turns dialogue into conversation until
                  depart converse depart dialogue depart
                  monologue arrive at depart

all hologram   nightingales & moon in the trees

great distance speaker own words   white paper write Alba
own so called silent as said subject
object distance infinite

ttaw koob ssim ttaw ttonk ssim ssim
ttaw erom naht ttonk yrev das ssim
ttaw dna ttonk ssim ttaw der eson der
eson ttaw yrev das

II.

*and if you were to change the name of
Beowulf to Joe Breem his story would
still be secure in the word hoard*

hoard the pillow Beowulf carried on
  long
voyages amongst the sea monsters
  surprised
no one has commented on this the
pillow later much later carted by Breem
himself calming
story later Sam pillow

Sam: Sam lexicographers in their own
writes dictionary two parts words spaces
one dictionary two hundred years

Sam: buried to the neck in sand outside
glass house savage place two heads two
voices one pseudocouple savage place
wrong Sam wrong century dictionary
part 1 words

    standing ovations audience on their
    feet no wait for end stirred into action
    no wait foot races up the aisles critical
    strength prowess

    no better place than Coconut Grove to
    stage the play that had saved the
    theatre that had saved the play unless it
    were Vegas

    Vegas! Vulture! Vega the brightest star
    in the Lyre Vega star & vulture Las Vegas

    hungry city but buffets enough for
    famished birds & any impecunious
    student of the mathematics

    the mathematics! where games keep
    their promises fractions odds endless
    subtractions everyone learn loss no
    better place Sam festival long
    boulevard Festival of Sam infinite
    extension words on & off flashing no end

no plod no plot said the gumshoe

all allegory away endless subtractions

Sam great homeopath Sam fail down to
needful succuss no thing not nothing
school of Hahnemann subtract succuss
stir bang bottle stir

The Sporting Life

P.J. Murphy

Our fundamental strategic intervention in this study entailed a focus on Beckett "in" popular culture, eschewing in large part the complementary and sometimes overlapping consideration of Beckett "and" popular culture. The latter approach would encompass such topics as Beckett and the music hall, the circus, early modern film (Chaplin would feature prominently here), and so on; and there are to be sure many comments in Beckett criticism on the issue of Beckett "and" popular culture.[1] This final chapter on Beckett and the sporting life affords, however, an opportunity for the critical investigation of the dialogical exchanges between the "and" and "in" approaches and how such creative interplay might assist us in our reading of Beckett's works as well as our adaptations and applications of them within popular culture contexts.

Beckett's own enthusiastic engagement with a number of sporting ventures is well-known, particularly his cricket playing for Trinity College, his passion for golfing which he shared with his father, and, perhaps above all, his life-long playing of tennis. Lucky's famous pensum in *Waiting for Godot* cataloguing various sports accords athletics a central role in popular amusements. Steven Connor's "My Fortieth Year Had Come and Gone and I Still Throwing the Javelin: Beckett's Athletics" (2014) is the first serious attempt to explore how Beckett's sporting interests are significantly connected with his work, are indeed much more than merely incidental features of his cultural background, such as his Anglo-Irish sporting activities versus those sanctioned by the Gaelic Athletic League.

Connor summarizes various efforts at establishing a relationship between modernism and sport, concluding with an emphasis upon a fundamental dichotomy:

> The huge expansion of competitive sport in the twentieth century brings about a new form of stand-off between scrawn and brawn. On the one hand there is the modernist body, frail, tremulous, hysterical, but infinitely sensitive: on the

other hand there is hiking, mountaineering, the Olympic ideal and the cult of the Aryan superman.[2]

Connor then considers the application of such divergent attitudes towards the body in Beckett's work, drawing attention to the debate between what used to be an influential "commonplace of Beckett criticism," namely, "that his work retreats progressively from embodiment," while "more recent criticism has tended to stress the stubborn irreducibility of the body in Beckett's work" (17). Both of these views do, however, share an emphasis upon an inevitable deterioration in the corporeal realm, as underlined in Lucky's famous "think" on our sporting culture:

> man ... wastes and pines ... in spite of the strides of physical culture the practice of sports such as tennis football running cycling swimming flying floating riding gliding conating comogie skating tennis of all kinds dying flying sports of all sorts autumn summer winter winter tennis of all kinds hockey of all sorts ... and ... simultaneously for reasons unknown to shrink and dwindle in spite of the tennis I resume flying gliding golf over nine and eighteen holes tennis of all sorts [*Waiting for Godot*, 29].

Yet all of these images and examples of "shrink[ing]" and "dwindl[ing]" are themselves characterized by dynamic participial and gerundial exertions rather than being engulfed by passive voicing. As Connor insightfully puts it, "Beckett's corporeality is kinetic, in the way that one should expect of an athlete or dancer" (20). No wonder Lucky slips in "conating" as a sport, of sorts: Spinoza's concept of conatus entails a motivational drive towards affirmations of being in time.[3] Whereas a game is abstracted from such a reality continuum, sport is kinetically embedded in it. For example: "Assumption"'s comment on how the "supreme manifestation of Beauty" must perforce be experienced in its physicality in the modern world; "we are taken up bodily and pitched breathless on the peak of a sheer crag: which is the pain of Beauty" (*Collected Shorter Prose*, 4). From "Assumption" (1929) to *Worstward Ho* (1983), over the course of Beckett's career, the driving need, in my estimation, was somehow to find the means of *realizing* human presence within the field of language—a project in which the embodied reality of sports was bound to play an important role. *Worstward Ho*'s reiterative exhortation, "Try again. Fail again. Fail better," hammers home the point: conation, from *conari*, to try. This very late text's "Never by naught be nulled" and "Naught not best worse" (*Nohow On*, 106) swerves counter to a great deal of Beckett criticism that was based, in large part, on a misreading of how Beckett made use of the philosophical tradition, in conjunction with the ready-made rhetoric of the "art of failure" school which has so dominated critical studies.

Steven Connor's groundbreaking study of Beckett's athletics has helped clear the way for further speculations which could extend and expand his key points about physical embodiment and the primacy of kinesis in Beckett's ontology of sports: "For Beckett, sport provides the impetus for the utter seriousness of a gaming in which everything, mind, body, world, is in play, which is not in the least to say up in the air but rather to say risked, wagered, at stake" (25).

There are, however, a number of points in his concluding remarks on "Having Done with Losing" which are problematical:

> The losing that Beckett has in view is not defeat; rather it is an active striving and contriving to outwit, or win out against winning. In the end, the athletic qualities I have made out in Beckett—endurance, expertise, equipoise, exertion of will—are not simply exercised through his work, but are themselves put into play, or sported with by it.
> What kind of athleticism is this, so expertly unsure of its capacities, so supple in its mock-incompetences, so alertly self-defeating, so dextrously maladroit, returning with such indefatigable fatigue to the being that is questioning its being?
> A kind of its own [26].

As I argue, Beckett's formulation of the key terms in any game or sporting venture, namely—winning and/or losing, can be stated much more affirmatively in terms of engagement with the world. Connor's penultimate paragraph questioning "What kind of athleticism is this" seems to turn in on itself and to back away from his key points about the kinetic nature of Beckett's writing about athletics. Such self-reflexivity, albeit eloquent in terms of its own verbal athleticism, is, however, strongly reminiscent of similar set pieces throughout the history of Beckett criticism in which a perplex of oxymoronic pairing is all too neatly packaged. Furthermore, "A kind of its own" underlines a sense of self-absorption within a particular game's own boundaries rather than the full opening up to a world with which others might also engage.

First of all, it could be argued that the athletic and aesthetic are more intimately connected in Beckett (as testified to by the reference from "Assumption" on "Beauty" and being "pitched bodily" cited earlier) than Connor allows: "There is no display in the play involved in sport, no il-lusion or al-lusion. It is in this sense that Beckett's work is sporting rather than ludic, athletic rather than aesthetic" (23). Nowhere is this more obviously *not* the case than in the very title of Connor's essay, which is taken from the last line of "Fizzle 2" ("Horn Came Always"): "My fortieth year had come and gone and I still throwing the javelin" (*Collected Shorter Prose*, 231). For here is embedded an allusion to the famous parable of the javelin-thrower in the section on "Boundlessness of universe" (lines 950–983) of the first book of

Lucretius' *On the Nature of Things* (*De Rerum Natura*). Lucretius begins with an Epicurean assumption that it matters not

> Where you may take your stand in the cosmos. The place you take leaves the rest unbounded,
> Extending equally in all directions.[4]

And the arresting image of the javelin-thrower embodies the idea of the limitless nature of the universe. Lucretius proposes that if someone arrived at a supposed boundary and let the javelin fly it would either go on or be blocked:

> You must choose one of these alternatives,
> But either one will cut off your retreat
> And force you to grant that the sum of all
> Extends unlimited [...][5]

Connor sees a "revulsion against sport" in the two sentences from "Fizzle 2" which precede the powerful kinetic image of the javelin-thrower: "What ruined me at bottom was athletics. With all that jumping and running when I was young, and even long after in the case of certain events, I wore out the machine before its time." Connor has, arguably, missed the real import of these sentences and how they connect with the main ideas developed in "Fizzle 2." The narrator greets his visitor Horn, a Gaber-like go-between à la *Molloy* I, only at night, in the dark. The little story the narrator now tells is, however, about a number of significant changes in his own behavior: that after five or six years in which no one had seen him, he has now decided "I'll let myself be seen before I'm done. I'll call out, if there is a knock, Come in!" Shades of Joyce and Beckett for this scene reprises Richard Ellmann's anecdote about Beckett taking dictation from Joyce and inadvertently including Joyce's response to a knock on his study door.[6] Now the roles are reversed and it is the Beckett narrator who welcomes and incorporates the contingency of the outside world.

More importantly: just before the concluding sentences about athletics and throwing the javelin, the narrator states that in addition to being seen he has also now taken "to getting up again" from his bed, taking a few faltering steps, and that he has *not*, in fact, made his "last journey": "But the feeling gains on me that I must undertake another" (230). In other words, this Beckett narrator is really in a situation now analogous to that of Lucretius's javelin-thrower: it is a liminal experience, on the threshold of a boundless boundary line, so to speak, one located in "outer space," open to the universe at large. Beckett's "I" is figuratively still "throwing the javelin," testing out the boundaries of his world and acknowledging the materialistic contexts of that world, albeit replete with voids.

As a philosophical allusion, as a "sporting" invocation of the literary tradition, this narrator might more accurately be said to have been "saved" not "ruined" by "athletics." To live in the world is perforce to be drawn to an endless throwing of the javelin.[7] Earlier Malone had cited "Suave, mari magno" (*Malone Dies*, 218) from the opening lines of Book II of *The Nature of Things*: "When winds churn up a heavy storm at sea / It is a pleasant thing to watch from land / Another's mighty struggles with the waves."[8] For the I-narrator of "Horn Came Always" life is no longer merely a spectator sport. The opening invocation of Horn could also be taken as an echoing of the parable of the two gates at the conclusion of Book VI of Virgil's *Aeneid*:

> There are two gates of Sleep, one said to be
> Of horn, whereby the true shades pass with ease,
> The other all white ivory agleam
> Without a flaw, and yet false dreams are sent
> Through this one, by the ghosts to the upper world[9]

In "Horn Came Always" the narrator is drawn out of the "ivory tower" of his skull and its solipsistic realm towards the outside world when Horn came knocking.

Such a reading of this short later work goes against the grain of most Beckett criticism which still sees Beckett's writing as being essentially framed within a series of negations and failures inherent in the very nature of expression, or, much more rarely, as in Connor's case, a number of new insights are proposed, only to be, in the final analysis, subsumed within the well-established boundaries of the controlling rhetoric of Beckett criticism.

Connor's discussion of athletics in "Fizzle 2" lacks the necessary particularities of literary context, most telling with the reference to the Lucretius image of throwing the javelin. On the other hand, much Beckett criticism is limited by a myopic focus on particular details which are often subsumed within an ideology of negativity which is *assumed* to be the common sense or "natural" way in which Beckett's works are to be received. A painful case in point is the explication of "Horn Came Always" in *The Grove Companion to Samuel Beckett* (Ackerley and Gontarski, 2004); namely, they propose Horn "suggests sexual tension, the narrator perhaps a cuckold, still 'horny.'" The myth of Psyche in search of a lost lover is briefly touched on, only to be dismissed since "this is difficult now, because (in an anticlimactic non sequitur) his body has been ruined by athletics ('throwing the javelin' may imply onanism, but the tale lacks definition)."[10] Without any critical contextualization of *Fizzles* and this work in particular in terms of the directions of Beckett's fiction after *How It Is*, the interpretation is bound to lack "definition," serving primarily as a pretext in this instance for an excursion into psychoanalysis. What would these critics have made of "shaking-the-spear"? A primal "Shake-scene,"[11] most likely.

Connor concludes his discussion of Beckett and athletics with his own Didi-Gogo-like exchange of volleys: "What kind of athleticism is this...?" answered with "A kind of its own." Well, not quite; certainly not when it comes to the depiction of Beckett and the sporting life "in" popular culture. Whereas in academic Beckett criticism the very engagement of Beckett's words with our world is regarded as highly problematical, this is definitely not the case when it comes to the appropriation and adaptation of Beckett's works within the contexts of popular culture. (It is a nice irony, even if merely coincidental, that in North America *Beckett's* is the name of a sports compendium magazine with encyclopaedic inventories of the major professional sports.) The following two testimonials, both rooted in the sports world within Canadian contexts, focus on the ethical and ontological dimensions of Beckett's reception in popular culture.

Charles Foran tells the curious tale of how "Hockey + Beckett = Inspiration" as the Irish writer became "the man within my head":

> In 1979, I was playing for the Brebeuf College hockey squad in North York. It was a Jesuit high school then, all boys, a team photo of future doctors and lawyers, sturdy business and family men.
> Our coach, Jim Barry, was also our English teacher. He achieved the near impossible that winter, turning a Toronto suburban cohort into Samuel Beckett devotees, given to arena recitations of the great Irish modernist's best-known work.
> Here is the scene: a home game against powerhouse St. Michael's College. Brebeuf boys line both sides of the rink. As I idle in my crease, closing (echoing?) sections shout across the ice to each other. "Let's go," one side says. "We can't," the other side answers. "Why not? The first crew asks. "We're waiting for Godot!" the second crew answers. "Ahhh," both sides sigh.
> They chant the famous refrain from *Waiting for Godot* for three periods, as though it is the team fight song. We win that game, but later lose to St. Mike's, in overtime, in the playoffs.
> My days as a goaltender ended with that loss. But my decades with Samuel Beckett had just begun. Or better: courtesy of Jim Barry's charismatic exploration of the universal suffering, and the universal humanity of Beckett's two tramps, Vladimir and Estragon, I found the literary mentor I needed.[12]

Foran goes on then to detail his graduate school obsession with Beckett, in particular the famous trilogy, and fixates on what he terms an "iconic photo" of Beckett he saw at a production of *Godot* at the Gate Theatre in Dublin during the centenary celebrations, drawing the conclusion that "gazing at Beckett in print isn't so morally taxing" as confronting his actual face.[13] Indeed, the extra-textual dimensions of the Beckett figure transcend sports and literature to make a number of ethical and philosophical judgments about life itself:

> Admonitions to stay mindful of suffering, to value compassion above all else, to laugh at our collective dire circumstances: This is what I mostly learn from the writer within my head. Beckett's literary mentorship has been, in effect, a moral one, and I haven't always lived up. I have to try harder—or "fail better," as he would put it. I have to keep him in there in order to keep writing.[14]

Shades of the Saint Sam (à) Beckett school of reception theory? Undoubtedly so: but the salient point surely is that somehow or other all the various Becketts Foran refers to are still somehow connected and this comes across as a genuinely moving aesthetic sentiment, not mere sentimentalizing or the appropriation of Beckett by the critic for personal aggrandizement, as is so often the case in academic criticism.

The second testimonial, in this case by a professional athlete, is eloquent in its own way in terms of the point made above about the ethos of Beckett's work for the "lay-person" with no time for and no particular interest in literary criticism. Tony Proudfoot, a star football player in the Canadian Football League (CFL) and later a sports broadcaster, was diagnosed with ALS (Lou Gehrig's disease) in 2007 and died in December 2010 at the age of 61. ALS takes Lucky's "wastes and pines" to the point *in extremis*, bodily deterioration proceeding inexorably to a total impasse. In the "twilight of his life," Proudfoot reflected on his "plight" in a number of newspaper articles. In 2010 he writes that he "chronicled a metaphor from Samuel Beckett and his *Waiting for Godot*, i.e. Waiting for Death. I spent weeks in hospital at various stages with severe infections and an exhausting battle with pneumonia. My golfing was now curtailed."[15] Later, just a few weeks away from his death, his own words were perhaps more tellingly Beckettian than the more self-conscious allusion to *Waiting for Godot*: "Well, I am still here, hanging by my finger nails while my toes are touching rock bottom and I can feel them getting a foothold."[16]

Mark Cohon, the Commissioner of the CFL, in Proudfoot's obituary in *The Globe and Mail*, hailed his contributions on and off the field: "What we ultimately learned from him is that you can grow physically weak and frail and yet remain incredibly strong and resilient. To know him was to know character. To see him battle was to witness courage."[17] Such realities cannot, in the final analysis, be mediated by literature of the modern type as advocated by Beckett and pursued throughout his writing career—this spectacle is not an old-fashioned allegory and "Proudfoot" is not iconographic of any Bunyanesque type-name. Nevertheless, both Foran and Proudfoot movingly invoke Beckett's name and works within encompassing human realms and show in quite different yet complementary ways how "Saint Samuel (à) Beckett's Big Toe" can indeed be meaningfully incorporated within popular culture.

Another means of countering some of the more "official" institutionalized readings of Beckett is, as we have seen throughout this study, via parody and pastiche, through subversive transformations within popular culture. One clever and amusing example of this, a veritable *jeu d'esprit*, is Roy Clements' *The Alternative Wisden on Samuel Barclay Beckett (1906-1989)*. Here is a small sampling of one of his many analogies with cricket:

> The novel *The Unnamable* is Beckett's no-ball (The No-ball prize?). The opening line "Where now? Who now? When now?" represents the three stumps of a wicket which he tries to knock over throughout the text using Mahood and Worm as his bowlers. Worm is the ultimate no-ball—whose existence is nothing but the oppression of his impotence to exist. (I stole that from Maurice Blanchot writing in *Nouvelle Revue Française*). In the end Beckett is frustrated and finishes with "I can't go on, I'll go on."
>
> If he had added "meself" (I'll go on meself) you would have had the impression of the captain who has tried all his bowlers and is going on to deliver the coup de grace himself.[18]

In a personal note accompanying the copy of his pamphlet which I had requested, Roy Clements commented

> I am surprised that I seem to have become the expert on Beckett and cricket on the basis of a little booklet which was designed to put to rest the incomprehensible gibberish which makes up so much of the criticism. (My next book will be on the size of full stops in *Ulysses* with particular reference to Molly's soliloquy—that should make a short treatise).

He added that "one or two people have taken it seriously—please don't." No danger there, but it was a fun read, and at times informative, to boot.

An even more *outré* example of popular culture carnivalesque is the Irish Film Board's short (two minutes and thirty eight seconds, to be exacting) "Pitch 'n' Putt with Beckett 'n' Joyce." That this is an "Irish bull" is made clear by the setting and date: namely, a "pitch and putt" course overlooking a Zurich river, the 19th of January 1922. In other words, just before the publication of *Ulysses* on February 2 of that year, Joyce's fortieth birthday, at which time Samuel Beckett would have been a ripe sixteen year old. Nevertheless, Joyce in full iconographic regalia (replete with eye patch and a yellow carnation) has already started to go "all rivery," spouting the new language of *Finnegans Wake* ("pitch and slut" gets his spiel underway). Beckett just sits there doing nothing as Joyce winds himself up in preparation for teeing off and grows increasingly impatient with his partner Beckett who appears to be waiting for their missing third who has not shown up and who Joyce insists is "not fuckin'" coming[19] and taunts Beckett about when in God's name exactly does he plan to actually hit the ball. And in a close up shot of Beckett's mouth (à la *Not I*), the Beckett figure whispers (slowly), *sotto voce*, "yes, I'll play...."

Most Beckett aficionados I have discussed this film/ette with have found it more amusing than I do. Martin Murphy as Joyce seems to be channeling the John Cleese of *Fawlty Towers* fame as his rant builds up, more so than one James Joyce and the "craic" seems to have missed the opportunity for a more pointed subversion of stereotypes of both Beckett and Joyce. This critical "tut, tut" is, however, of little relevance here: there are some genuinely funny vaudeville elements here of a cartoon-like "Mutt and Jeff" variety (one of Joyce's favorite strips), and what it lacks in wit is compensated for by its brevity. The point remains that such popular culture caricatures still serve to humanize its subjects and to place them within our world and hence open up new lines of communications, of dialogical engagement.

It is hardly surprising, given the immense growth of sports within popular culture, that Beckett's name pops up in a number of surprising as well as predictable contexts. For sports does at least supply a ready-made topic (like the weather, in this regard) for conversation. For example, when Beckett used his truck to drive to school the son of a neighbor who had helped with the building of his writing cottage in Ussy, namely one André Rousimoff, of future wrestling fame as André the Giant, young André revealed that they rarely talked about anything other than cricket.[20] Of course, metaphors from Beckett's own writing also periodically surface in sports reporting: *New York Times* "Sports Tuesday" headline (June 30, 2009) for a quarter-finals match at Wimbledon: "Under the Lights on Centre Court, Waiting for Federer." Or the unintended sporting "pun" in *The Globe and Mail* (August 18, 2008): "Blue Jays beat up Beckett," a reference to then Boston Red Sox pitcher Josh Beckett being knocked around by the Toronto baseball team. I have never heard an American baseball broadcast refer to the literary Beckett in the same breath as the pitching Beckett, whereas in ice hockey I do remember how Michael Farber of *Sports Illustrated* drew a complex analogy between the endless process of the Toronto Maple Leafs trying to trade then captain Matts Sundin and how he was our "Godot" and we were all waiting for his reappearance elsewhere. (No, he didn't turn out to be a savior for the Vancouver Canucks.)

Fast forward to the final story of *Fizzles* (1975), "For to End Yet Again," in which the last explicit sporting analogy in Beckett's prose is found in a context which has to do with the patently artificial nature of the act of writing and how the author will manipulate his creatures in order to tidy up the field of play. The little body of the "expelled" is toppled over in a wasteland setting and two white dwarfs spring forward at the author-figure's beck and call and proceed to load the fallen figure on a litter. The whole process is framed by a sporting simile: the maneuvers of the dwarfs "shape the course much as the coxswain with light touch the skiff" (*Collected Shorter Prose*, 244). The fallen body is now officially *hors de combat*, stretchered off. Here the author-figure has, arguably, committed a "professional foul" in order to win that struggle between authors and characters which I have proposed as one of the definitive features of Beckett's writing.

In the penultimate *Fizzle*, "Still," Beckett has, in dramatic contrast, presented a moving scene of a recognizable human presence in a world which we can identify with as our own. Such successful embodiments of a human presence within language will, in my judgment, become more and more the major focus of Beckett studies in its next stages. The sporting life is, in the end, about who wins and who loses and such analogies with Beckett's work can assist us in moving beyond an over-reliance upon the "art of failure" rhetoric and the ideology of negativity which have restricted us in seeing how Beckett has "succeeded."

In this regard, academic Beckett scholarship might have something to gain from a popular culture study about competition and striving to be who we are such as Matthew Syed's *Bounce: Mozart, Federer, Picasso, Beckham and the Science of Success*. Beckett appears in the index between the Beatles and Beckham and also as a footnote in the midst of the pivotal discussion of "embracing failure" as the route to "success": "Samuel Beckett, the playwright, also expresses this truth in his novella *Worstward Ho*: 'Ever tried. Ever failed. No matter. Try again. Fail again. Fail better.'"[21] The "bounce" theory of succeeding through tireless repetition and studied perseverance needs, however, to be supplemented by the creative "swerve"[22] of a particular writer's choices and adaptation. Not to mention our own collaborations with and revisions of such creations: for it is this dialogue with Beckett's work which has made it such a multifaceted and engaging phenomenon within popular culture.

Notes

1. See, for example, Martin Green and John Swan, *The Triumph of Pierrot: Commedia dell'Arte and the Modern Imagination* (New York: Macmillan, 1986), in which in the midst of a discussion of Chaplin and Keaton, Beckett is referred to as "another commedia

modernist of the theater" (135); also of interest in this regard is Mary Bryden's "Clowning with Beckett" in *A Companion to Samuel Beckett*, edited by S.E. Gontarski (Oxford: Wiley-Blackwell, 2010), 358–371.

2. Steven Connor, "'My Fortieth Year Had Come and Gone and I Still Throwing the Javelin': Beckett's Athletics," the first chapter of *Beckett, Modernism and the Material Imagination* (New York: Cambridge University Press, 2014), 16.

3. See my discussion of conation in "Beckett and the philosophers" in *The Cambridge Companion to Beckett*, edited by John Pilling (New York: Cambridge University Press, 1994), 225–228, 237. Two sporting analogies might also be appropriate in this regard: Beckett's father's next to final words to him were "fight fight fight" (Knowlson, *Damned to Fame*, 71); tennis, Beckett's favorite lifetime sport, originates from Old French *tenez*, "take, receive" (called by the server to an opponent). "Me—to play" in *Endgame* thus suggests aggression ("take that") as well as the ludic.

4. Lucretius, *On the Nature of Things* (*De Rerum Natura*), translated with an Introduction by Palmer Bovie (New York: Signet Classics, 1974), Book I, ll. 966–69, 40.

5. *Ibid.*, Book I, ll. 974–77. The "javelin" is variously termed a "dart," "missile," "spear" in various translations. In "Lucretius and the Sublime" in *The Cambridge Companion to Lucretius*, edited by Stuart Gillespie and Philip Hardie (New York: Cambridge University Press, 2007), James I. Porter identifies the "flying javelin of Lucretius' thought experiment at the end of Book I" (176) with parallel images of the sublime in Longinus and Virgil. Beckett's references to Lucretius are not mentioned in the final chapter of *The Cambridge Companion*, "Lucretius and the Moderns."

6. Richard Ellmann, *James Joyce, New and Revised Edition* (New York: Oxford University Press, 1982), 649.

7. The reference to still throwing the javelin in his fortieth year might also refer to Lucretius' own life span: his dates are ca. BC 96–55.

8. Lucretius, *The Nature of Things*, ll. 1–2, 45. C.J. Ackerley and S.E. Gontarski, in *The Grove Companion to Samuel Beckett: A Reader's Guide to his Works, Life, and Thought* (New York: Grove Press, 2004) identify Schopenhauer as Beckett's source and note that Beckett "often quoted this phrase of the theater, the spectator safely seated while the storm breaks out on stage" (330).

9. Virgil, *The Aeneid*, translated by Robert Fitzgerald (New York: Vintage Classics, 1990), Book VI, ll. 1211–1215, 191–92.

10. Ackerley and Gontarski, *The Grove Companion*, 257.

11. The phrase is part of Robert Greene's attack on Shakespeare as an "upstart Crow, beautified with our feathers," *Shakespeare: The Complete Works*, edited by G.B. Harrison (New York: Harcourt, Brace and World, 1952), 9.

12. Charles Foran, "Hockey + Beckett = Inspiration," *The Globe and Mail*, Saturday January 7, 2012, R1. The title for the continuation on R9 reads: "He shoots! He Waits! How a Young Writer Found Samuel Beckett."

13. *Ibid.*, R9.

14. *Ibid.*, R9.

15. Allan Maki, "CFL Legend Courageous On and Off the Field," *The Globe and Mail*, January 1, 2011, S14.

16. *Ibid.*

17. *Ibid.*

18. Roy Clements, *The Alternative Wisden on Samuel Barclay Beckett (1906–1989)*, Daripress, 1992, 17.

19. "Pitch 'n' Putt with Beckett 'n' Joyce," 2001, dir. Donald Clarke, Blue Light/Irish Film Board. Ironically enough, the historical Beckett did in a sense "pitch 'n' putt with Joyce": James Knowlson recounts the story of how Beckett, before he met Joyce, "felt sufficiently enthusiastic about Joyce's poems to give his golfing partner, Bill Cunningham,

a copy of *Pomes Penyeach* signed 'Yours ever, Sam Beckett July 1927'" (*Damned to Fame*, 98).

20. James Plafke, "Samuel Beckett Used to Drive André the Giant to School." themarysue.com. The Mary Sue. 11 July 2011. Web. 24 April 2015.

21. Matthew Syed, *Bounce: Mozart, Federer, Picasso, Beckham and the Science of Success* (New York: Harper, 2010), 128.

22. See in this regard, Stephen Greenblatt's exhilarating account of the "recovery" of Lucretius' *De Rerum Natura, The Swerve: How the World Became Modern* (New York: W.W. Norton and Company, 2011).

Beckett as Pop Culture Icon

P.J. Murphy

The dialogical engagements among the four epigraphs for this study progressively delineate the key points in our argument. Harold Pinter's 1954 letter makes it clear in no uncertain terms that Beckett is selling "nothing from the bargain basement, he's not fucking me about"; "he's not selling me anything I don't want to buy." Pinter further declares that he will "buy his goods, hook, line and sinker, because he leaves no stone unturned and no maggot lonely." What is so striking in this powerful *testimonio* is its emphasis upon materialist contexts, the commercial exchanges of our consumerist "buyology." Pinter maintains that we are buying into Beckett because of an identification with a number of ethico-aesthetic values, most notably his being the "most courageous, remorseless writer going." In the summing up, Beckett is portrayed as a sort of secular literary "saint," with a distinctive aura: "He brings forth a body of beauty. His work is beautiful."[1] Nevertheless, such iconic status stays grounded within the materialist contexts referenced throughout his letter.

In the second epigraph, Fredric Jameson, almost four decades later, makes a foundational point for a whole series of postmodernisms: "the effacement in them of the older (essentially high modernist) frontier between high culture and so-called mass or commercial culture." Such a "populist rhetoric" has been "fascinated precisely by this whole 'degraded' landscape of schlock and kitsch." Jameson then enumerates a series of items within popular culture that necessarily play a prominent role in our own study: namely, advertising, murder mysteries, science fiction, TV series, popular film et al. Furthermore, Jameson points out how such "materials" are now "incorporated in the very substance" of such paraliterary forms; that is, "they no longer simply 'quote,' as a Joyce or Mahler might have done."[2]

But what is perhaps most striking in our study of Beckett adaptations is the degree to which they often retain aspects of that artistic integrity which Pinter foregrounded in his mid-century modern letter. Our focus has primarily been upon reproductions of Beckett which constitute significant transformations of Beckettian views and images. Such carnivalesque re-enactments often draw upon a creative dimension inherent in "'intertextuality' or the dialogic relations among texts," as celebrated by Linda Hutcheon in our third epigraph. Moreover, Hutcheon adds two complementary points which take us to the heart of our argument: "works in any medium are both created and received *by people*, and it is this human, experiential context that allows for the study of *the politics* of intertextuality," as well as her "perhaps perverse de-hierarchizing impulse, a desire to challenge the explicitly and implicitly negative cultural evaluation of things like postmodernism, parody, and now, adaptation which are seen as secondary and inferior."[3]

As our user's guide[4] to adaptations of Beckett has so copiously illustrated, such engagement is political in so far as it entails agency in terms of the various ways in which popular culture is not only consumed but constructed. In our tripartite designation of the specific ways in which Beckett's works have been received, we recognized those particular instances of adaptation which afford creative insights in their own right and need not be regarded as "secondary and inferior," are not kitsch or schlock, nor merely pale imitations of mainstream academic views. As Stephen Brown and Charles Willeford have so insightfully and wittily pointed out in our study, Beckett's fame and celebrity are in part attributable to an anti-marketing marketing strategy. In contrast with the commercialized ethos of popular culture, Beckett's subversive approach has, ironically enough, proven to be virtually irresistible to purveyors of such productions due to Beckett's iconic status as the "great artist" who has refused to sell out his integrity and dedication to his art. Hence adaptations of Beckett's image in popular culture serve an almost "redemptive" or rehabilitative function in productions primarily driven by the corporate bottom lines required for survival in the entertainment industry. In short: "prophet" Beckett deployed to serve the interests of corporate "profit."

In *Buying In: The Secret Dialogue Between What We Buy and What We Are,* Rob Walker coins the phrase "murketing"—a blend of "murky" and "marketing" in order to highlight how the commercial persuasion industry is changing "and it is happening on both sides of the dialogue between consumer and consumed."[5] "Murketing" is most definitely not defined by any comprehensive sense of rejecting marketing, "but rather by frank complicity"[6] in which the consumer reinvents and revitalizes the consumed. Similarly, in *The Rebel Sell*, Joseph Heath and Andrew Potter underscore the fact that "anti-advertising" is not by any means against advertising itself so much as it is about "distinction" in choosing more value-enhancing images which confer a certain "status."[7] Beckett is *the* poster-boy for popular culture depictions of the high-culture artist figure, inscribing and simultaneously effacing such cross-border shopping sprees. His "brand" of iconoclastic iconicity is indeed highly marketable. No modern writer post–Joyce remotely approaches the number and variety of popular culture representations which Beckett has undergone since the mid-point of the last century. In changing measures, Beckett is deemed to be "hero," "saint" and "genius"—or combinations thereof. Harold Bloom's designation of Beckett as a "genius" in the eponymously titled study of "one hundred exemplary creative minds" is overkill in that he also terms Beckett "one of the very rare saints of literature" (even Joyce is barred from such an apotheosis).[8] At least in popular culture portraits of the artist there is often a rejuvenating comic debunking of such grandiose images, even as they also continue to be affirmed and exploited.

The next major question is how does this dynamic area of adaptations fit into the overall state of Beckett studies. A revealing case in point is *A Companion to Samuel Beckett* (2010), edited by S.E. Gontarski, who begins his "Introduction" with a rehearsal of his conflicted views on Beckett as a "global artist" in the wake of the corporate sponsored centenary celebrations of 2006. Witness his hand-wringing over the "commodification of the avant-garde," which suggests to him "its degradation, if not its annihilation." Gontarski does make astute comments about how Beckett's plays need to escape becoming "pinned butterflies under glass, audiences entering not theaters but the Beckett Museum," and also calls attention to what he terms "the new pragmatism or a return to the archives to parallel the burst of theoretical work done on Beckett during the decades of the 1970s and 1980s."[9] Gontarski appears to be suggesting that cutting-edge theoretical investigations are now in a holding-pattern since that earlier "burst," the focus now being on archival studies, as if such work could actually take the place of rigorous creative-critical thinking. Is Beckett studies perhaps in danger of becoming a "soft option"?

On the contrary, I would argue that such an assumption of a consensus about what Beckett is really about, a sort of "pax Beckettiana," is founded on a number of stereotypical views that need critical revision. Gontarski's lynchpin for the consensus argument is (yet again) the oft-cited statement to Israel Shenker in which Beckett ostensibly distinguishes his own art from Joyce's, rejecting the latter's "heroic" for his own "impotence, ignorance."[10] Here we have what could be justifiably termed one of the most influential instances of the intentional fallacy in twentieth-century literature, one which has greatly impeded critical investigations in Beckett studies.

In *Beckett's Dedalus*, I proposed, in a series of detailed analyses, particularly with reference to the prose, that this so-called Beckettian "confession and all-out embrace of artistic impotence,"[11] as Gontarski terms it, is a gross oversimplification. I hasten to add that my counter-critique has nothing to do with other Beckett scholars adopting my own lines of thought but everything to do with encouraging others to engage in their own reassessments of the party line about Beckett's "negativity" and "artistic impotence." The Joyce question is in a host of ways absolutely central to the narrative trajectory of Beckett studies. As I have argued, Beckett's views about Joyce are much more complex than previously assumed—in effect, dialogical; everything changes if this is recognized: more affirmative dimensions of his art might then justifiably warrant our attention in the next period of Beckett studies.

One of the most provocative and innovative essays in Gontarski's collection is H. Porter Abbott's "The Legacy of Samuel Beckett: An Anatomy," particularly its middle section, "Recombinant Beckett" that deals with adaptations and from which our fourth epigraph is taken. Abbott very neatly encapsulates how such a "legacy" or "afterlife" of the Beckettian oeuvre is an important supplement: "In quantitative terms, this will be, in fact already is, Beckett's most abundant, most diverse, and most haphazard legacy, since it trades on his availability to any and all users."[12] This is evident with reference to Beckett's plays, but Abbott identifies them as only "a small fraction of a 'memetic' explosion of all Beckett-related things large and small."[13] Such "memes" or units of cultural meaning replicate and transform various aspects of Beckett's iconicity. Abbott is intrigued by some of these permutations and relishes cataloguing them (unlike Gontarski who tends to dismiss them as merely epiphenomena). For instance: "'*Worstward*,' *Ho!* The punk rock CD by Shinobu"; the Wine Detective ad, "Krapp's Last Bottle"; as well as a plethora of Godot-inspired nomenclature, ranging from "Godot, the online art Gallery, Godot Technology, Godot the Go-playing applet, and the comic book hero Buck Godot, Zap-gun for hire."[14] Abbott concludes with a Hutcheonesque optimistic view of "all this hubbub of recombination" and appropriations:

> The works of Beckett, along with what we think we know of Beckett, have become and promise to continue to be, a powerful collection of instruments for art, thought, feeling, judgment, pleasures and, yes, pain as well.[15]

Indeed, the Beckett phenomenon, memetic replications and all, could be pointing towards a "repackaging" of literary works in which "it is impossible to read the original text without reference to the many layers of popular culture that have developed around it."[16] In this regard, *Waiting for Godot* could be said to have attained the status of a touchstone text such as *Frankenstein*.

One important area which Abbott does, however, fail to mention is the YouTube clip. Anja Müller and Mark Schreiber in "Sam 2.0: Appropriations, Interpretations and Adaptations of Beckett on YouTube" (2009) focus on the "vast archive of clips inspired by Beckett and his literary and dramatic oeuvre" and, more pointedly, that this "may turn out to be an ideal medium for Beckett plays to adapt and multiply."[17] Of particular relevance to our argument about dialogical engagements with Beckett in popular culture are their seminal remarks about the dynamic nature of such "production and reconstruction," a process which they identify (following Axel Bruns) as perforce engaged in by "PRODUSERS."[18] Hence Müller and Schreiber conclude that "YouTube clips can be regarded as potential, perhaps even the definitive examples of adaptation per se."[19] Certainly, such media offers, in terms of our argument, a Bakhtinian liberation of a vital parodic impulse in which "users" have a "productive" relationship with Beckett's works in which they might be more rightly viewed as joint authors or collaborators, thereby circumventing the monoglossia of the Beckett Estate. "Sam 2.0" affords powerful testimony of Beckett's cultural iconicity and indeed a rich area for future studies of Beckett adaptations within popular culture.

In early August 2013, I attended the "Samuel Beckett and the 'State' of Ireland III" Conference at the Humanities Institute, University College Dublin, at which I gave a paper entitled "Boycotting Belacqua: Popular Culture Contexts at the Heart of Beckett's *Dream of Fair to Middling Women*." This was a version of the commentary on the center of "Und," the middling section of Beckett's first novel, which forms a key section of the introduction to *Beckett in Popular Culture*. The conference was stimulating as well as a lot of fun and when I mentioned that I was on the qui vive for Beckett and popular culture references, I was inundated with a host of such instances. Many Beckett scholars today move easily between so-called "serious" Beckett scholarship and the spectacle of popular culture "doublings."

Being in Dublin also allowed me to carry out my own little Beckett pilgrimage (Chaucerian pronunciation, if you please), in memory of poor Belacqua's uneasy negotiations with common culture contexts, namely, visits to the Post Office and the Bank. After a brief nod to Cuchulain, I was able to purchase at the GPO copies of two Beckett stamps. Moreover, after a helpful suggestion from the clerk at the Special Collections wicket, I was able to track down and purchase the 20 Euro commemorative gold coin to mark the 100th anniversary of Beckett's birth. And I was finally able to walk the Beckett Bridge: over the years I had followed its slow progress, which at one point had seemed material for yet another lame pun of the "I can't go on, I will go on" variety. Futuristically styled as an Irish lyre or harp, the Bridge is not in any obvious way designated as Beckett's—except for a small plaque with an inspired choice of a quotation from "The End" which details how the Liffey at this point does indeed seem to be flowing backwards.

My selected reading for this Dublin expedition was Enrique Vila-Matas' *Dublinesque*, the last third of which draws out in a surprisingly optimistic and affirmative manner a series of Joyce-Beckett linkages that strikingly deviate from the party line of Beckett having moved definitively away from Joyce's "heroic." In Vila-Matas' reconstruction of the Joyce-Beckett relationship, his narrator, the publisher Samuel Riba, spots the young Beckett "wearing the same mackintosh" as the eponymously named mystery man at Paddy Dignam's funeral in *Ulysses*. Riba regards the "reappearance of the author as an incredibly optimistic sign."[20] This extensive depiction of Beckett as a character in a novel is a much more complex and sophisticated version of similar adaptations in contemporary dramatic works such as *Calico* (the Lucia Joyce story) and *Burnt Piano* (in which the figure of Beckett mediates a domestic tragedy).[21] I was also intrigued by various conference participants' discussions about the merits of the second Happy Days Enniskillen International Beckett Festival Programme. There was a veritable cornucopia of artistic-literary events, including a host of Beckett plays by internationally acclaimed actors and directors, writer and artist talks on issues Beckettian, not to mention public art pieces inspired by Beckett—beginning with Dantean art installations of the *Divine Comedy* and ending with the "Bend it Like Beckett Festival Sports Programme." I would recommend the organizers add the "Sam and Suzanne International Mixed Tennis Tournament for Beckett Scholars." Perhaps the Festival could get Stan Wawrinka to award the trophies, with the 2014 Australian Open Champion prominently sporting his new Beckett tattoo, "Try again. Fail again. Fail better." It is as if a Beckettian Theme Park of sorts has materialized in Northern Ireland, one tailor made for Ruby Cohn's "Becketteers."[22] How about a post–Festival tour of Beckett pubs and sports bars around the world? There are certainly enough for such a pilgrimage. Too bad Beckett's Dublin Beer is *defunctus*—it would have been an ideal corporate sponsor. If *The Fast Show*'s mini-skit on how to best deal with Beckett's work is taken to heart, we could all use a quick nip to the pub.[23] Perhaps Professors David Lodge and Morris Zapp would be interested in a joint venture—"Beckett Tours International"; we could brainstorm in the Anna Livia Plurabelle Lounge, the next time our paths criss-cross in Dublin.

Notes

1. Harold Pinter, "Beckett" (letter), in *Beckett at Sixty: A Festschrift*, ed. John Calder (London: Calder and Boyars, 1967), 86.

2. Fredric Jameson, *Postmodernism, Or, The Cultural Logic of Late Capitalism* (Durham: Duke University Press, 1991), 2–3.
3. Linda Hutcheon, *A Theory of Adaptation* (New York: Routledge, 2006), xii.
4. For a very useful and insightful discussion of such matters via this engaged approach, see Susie O'Brien and Imre Szeman, *Popular Culture: A User's Guide* (Scarborough: Thomson and Nelson, 2004).
5. Rob Walker, *Buying In: The Secret Dialogue Between What We Buy and What We Are* (New York: Random House, 2008), xvii.
6. Ibid., xviii.
7. Joseph Heath and Andrew Potter, *The Rebel Sell: Why the Culture Can't be Jammed* (Toronto: Harper Perennial, 2004), 125.
8. Harold Bloom, *Genius: A Mosaic of One Hundred Exemplary Creative Minds* (New York: Warner Books, 2002), 524.
9. S.E. Gontarski, ed., *A Companion to Samuel Beckett* (Malden, MA: Wiley-Blackwell, 2010), 3.
10. Ibid., 4–5.
11. Ibid., 5.
12. H. Porter Abbott, "The Legacy of Samuel Beckett: An Anatomy," in S.E. Gontarski's *A Companion to Samuel Beckett*, 75.
13. Ibid.
14. Ibid., 76.
15. Ibid., 77.
16. Wilfred L. Guerin. et al., eds., *A Handbook of Critical Approaches to Literature* (New York: Oxford University Press, 2011), 324–325.
17. Anja Müller and Mark Schreiber in "Sam 2.0: Appropriations, Interpretations and Adaptations of Beckett on YouTube," in *Adaptations: Performing Across Media and Genres* (a special edition of *Contemporary Drama in English*), eds. Monika Pietrzak-Franger and Eckart Voigts-Virchow (Wissenschaftlicher Verlag Trier, 2009), 178, 179.
18. Ibid., 184.
19. Ibid., 186.
20. Enrique Vila-Matas, *Dublinesque* (London: Harvill Secker, 2012), 310. For another phantasmagoria of detective fiction involving both Joyce and Beckett (along with Descartes), see Stephen Bond, *Ulysses 2: Death in Paris*, 60 pages, 2013 (available only on Kindle, free on Bloomsday week).
21. Hersh Zeifman, "Staging Sam: Beckett as Dramatic Characters," in *Beckett at 100: Revolving It All*, eds. Linda Ben-Zvi and Angela Moorjani (New York: Oxford University Press, 2008), 311–318, discusses these instances as well as others.
22. Beckett depictions at the Happy Days Enniskillen International Beckett Festival remain within recognizable boundaries, quite distinct from more far out popular culture transformations. See, for example, Takayuki Tatsumi, *Full Metal Apache: Transactions Between Cyberpunk Japan and Avant-Pop America* (Durham: Duke University Press, 2006), in which one of the introductory sections is entitled "Portrait of the Japanoid Critic as a Young Cyborgian" and the conclusion is entitled "Waiting for Godzilla: Toward a Globalist Theme Park."
23. See http://www.youtube.com/watch?v=YK96IJnNse0. Accessed Aug. 9, 2014.

Addenda: Beckett Cetera
A Pop Culture Miscellany

P.J. Murphy *and* Nick Pawliuk

The following precious and illuminating materials should be carefully studied—only an embarrassment of riches prevented us from including them in the text proper. They are paralipomena, of the pop culture variety, which have their role to play in the full chronicling of the impact of Beckett's work.

Putting this section together, we were suitably amused/bemused when we came across a column Professor Werner Huber had noted in his local newspaper in Paderborn (*Neue Westfälische*, No. 182, Sonnabend, 8. August 1998):

> Men's Questions
>
> The repertory theater has a reputation for adulterating scripts. But it was left to Peter Murphy, one of Samuel Beckett's literary executors, to set certain limits to this practice. A Manchester theatre group had wanted the two male roles, those of the vagrants Vladimir and Estragon in Beckett's play, "Waiting for Godot," played by women. However, Murphy complained that Beckett's texts are executed so precisely, that they forbid any gender changes in the prescribed roles [Translated by Brigitta O'Reagan].

My co-editor (I'm Nick, he's P.J.) opined that if he were actually one of Beckett's literary executors he would have taken a much more flexible approach to such matters (do we really need to prostrate ourselves before the prostate?). How his name ever materialized in this discussion we will never know—identity theft? Transcultural osmosis? Nonetheless, we agreed that with reference to our own approach all of us are indeed "literary executors" of sorts, as we consider how Beckett's literary remains are re-deployed, re-constituted, and indeed re-created in popular culture.

Caveat Emptor: as our project neared completion, my colleague was indeed becoming more and more "Murphy"-like in that, as was the case with his Beckett namesake, he too readily succumbed to the unfortunate tendency of allowing everything to remind him of something else. Hence I had to curb his enthusiasm, temper the poor chap's lapses into "Beckettmania," that is, seeing traces of Beckett virtually everywhere. I also had to counter his propensity to see Beckett as a sort of Canadian writer *manqué*, not to mention his *ideé fixe* of Beckett and ice hockey.

"Waiting for Godot" becomes a Nintendo Wii video game. No word on when it will come out. We're still waiting.
http://www.newsbiscuit.com/2011/01/10/waiting-for-godot-for-wii-breaks-first-week-sales-records/

Editors' Note: We're still waiting for this game to be developed.

* * *

In the foyer of the Wieden + Kennedy advertising firm, there is an exhortation to staff in giant letters to "Fail Harder," consisting of over ten thousand push pins.

See http://www.youtube.com/watch?v=-xffQBxfKJg for a video of its creation, and claim that WK12 bought out all available "clear push pins on the west coast of the US."

* * *

Explanation from designer Jon Barnbrook why the Bowie album sleeve lacks color:

"The title of the [Bowie] album *The Next Day* evokes numerous reference points, notably Macbeth's speech 'Tomorrow, and tomorrow and tomorrow' which deals with the relentless onward push that any unnatural position of power requires. It also has the existential element of *Waiting for Godot* with waiting for *The Next Day*—these all seem to question the nature of existence so a monochrome palette seemed most appropriate to this feeling."

"Pseuds Corner," *Private Eye*, No. 1332 25 January–7 Feb. 2013

Editors' Note: the packaging of *The Next Day* is simply the front and back covers of the 35-year-old Bowie classic *Heroes*, with the album's original title crossed out and a white square obscuring both sides, filled by the new title (*The Next Day*).

* * *

In American First Nations author Gerald Vizenor's novel *Dead Voices: Natural Agonies in the New World*, the first epigraph is from the last sentence of Samuel Beckett's *The Unnamable*, beginning with "Possessed of nothing but my voice..." and ending with "in the silence you don't know, you must go on, I can't go on, I'll go on" (University of Oklahoma Press, 1992).

* * *

Declan Hughes' detective novel *All the Dead Voices* makes no direct reference to the famous words from *Waiting for Godot* from which it takes its title. The central character, Ed Loy, is indeed literally half of *Molloy*, but the novel as a whole is of the hard-boiled Chandler does Dublin variety.

* * *

The central character in Mudrooroo's *Wild Cat Falling* (Angus and Robertson, 1965), a young aboriginal recently released from jail uses *Waiting for Godot* as a prop while he is waiting to meet a girl, and delves into the text at various junctures, such as:
"All the dead voices."
"They make a noise like wings."
"Like leaves."
"Like sand."
"Like leaves."

* * *

Beckett is an Australian place name, as pointed out in the opening pages of Peter Temple's detective novel *The Broken Shore* (Random House Canada, 2005): "Had a call from a lady," she said. "Near Beckett. A Mrs. Haif. She reckons there's someone in her shed" (2). The GPS for literary Beckett was, however, somewhat more problematic in an earlier novel, *Black Tide* (1999): protagonist Jack Irish muses, "To carry on is all. Who said that? Rilke?," leaving the reader (perhaps) somewhere betwixt Elsinore and the ending of *The Unnamable*.

* * *

The character Manny in Robert Littell's espionage novel, *An Agent in Place* (Bantam Books, 1992), neatly combines two cultural registers in this bit of creative adaptation:

> Settling back in his wooden chair, contemplating the usual scotch on the rocks, he switched into the lazy drawl he used when afraid of being taken for an intellectual and uttered out the formula from Samuel Beckett that inspired him every time he ran into a stone wall.
> "I try," Manny growled. "I fail. I fail better."

* * *

In the television episode 3.17 ("Enemies") of *Buffy the Vampire Slayer*, Buffy says about Faith, "The girl makes Godot look punctual." This wasn't the first Godot reference in the series: episode 1.11, "Out of Mind, Out of Sight" already features the quote, "to every man his little cross. Til he dies. And is forgotten," written on the blackboard. However, they managed to misspell the author's name as "Becket."

* * *

Raymond Federman in *The Sam Book* (Two Ravens Press, 2008) recounts how the final "t" was missing on Beckett's name on the cover of his first study: "I sent a copy of the book to Sam. He sent me a note thanking me, saying he quite liked this amputated Beckett." Federman adds: "When copies of the book arrived in bookstores, they all had the T-sticker on the cover. It looked incredibly ugly" (37).

* * *

You thought the opening of *Waiting for Godot* was a bit of a bleak pastoral? Try this: Sandra Birdsell's *Waiting for Joe* (Random House Canada, 2010) opens with Joe Beaudry and his wife Laurie waking up in a stolen motorhome on the edge of a Walmart parking lot in Regina, Saskatchewan. Nevertheless, by the end of the novel, he has a Beckettian-formulated epiphany of sorts: "I don't know has become his mantra, what he says to himself when he gets up in the morning" (271).

* * *

At a Beckett Conference at the University of Stirling in the early 1980s, the late Rubin Rabinovitz, who was then at work on his *KWIK Concordance*, buttonholed me (P.J. Murphy) about what the most repeated phrase in *Three Novels* was, to which I responded, "I don't know," and to which he countered, "precisely, well done." Well,... It was just prior to this pub quiz question that he informed me in a warm-hearted self-congratulatory fashion that he had finally not only had the nerve to ask Ruby Cohn, doyenne of Beckett studies, to have a drink with him, but to quip when she accepted, "That was tough, Ruby" (a joke for Beckett aficionados).

* * *

Newfoundland writer Paul Bowdring has his character Tasker Murphy end up in a situation very similar to that of his namesake, Samuel Beckett's Murphy, at the end of a New Year's debauch:

Tasker had tucked the checkered tablecloth into his belt, mistaking it for his long shoreman's plaid. He just stood there awestruck for a moment, blinking hard at the mess at his feet with the tablecloth hanging from his waist like a failed breechcloth. Then he slumped down on his knees in the ashes and butts and glass and made a pantomimic motion with his arms, as if he were about to use them to sweep it all up [*The Night Season*, Killick Press, St. John's, 1997, 217].

Reader, Newfoundland is as close as you can get to Ireland, literally and figuratively, in Canada.

* * *

Yann Martel in *What Is Stephen Harper Reading?*, his recommended reading list for the Canadian Prime Minister (a well-known strict non-reader, except for hockey tomes and reports of the "dismal science" variety), proffers a potted summary of *Waiting for Godot*, concluding with this homily:

Samuel Beckett was with the same woman, Suzanne Beckett, *née* Descheveaux-Dumesnil, for over fifty years. And he was apparently an avid fan and player of tennis. In these two attachments, I see a contradiction between what the man wrote and how he lived. If he had the joy and energy to whack a fuzzy yellow ball over a net, if he had the joy and comfort of knowing that someone was there for him at the end of each day, what was he so desperate about? A wife and tennis—how much more did he expect from life? [Vintage Canada, 2009, 107].

Editors' Note: Yann Martel incorporates great dollops of *Waiting for Godot* in his next novel, *Beatrice and Virgil* (Vintage Canada, 2010).

* * *

Beckett would have gotten a laugh and a kick out of how some aspects of his novels are transformed in Alexander Forbes' *Oranges*, a novella for puppets, in which Sam (as in Beckett) and Ralph, the narrator, voyage forth from Vancouver to the Interior of British Columbia. In the thirteenth and final chapter, after their arrival in Kamloops, Sam finds an all-night bowling alley and exhibits a rather unorthodox approach to this sporting activity:

Sam enters at an angle, and immediately grasps a bowling ball as if it were a new idea. He carries the ball to the end of his lane, dropping it upon the assembled pins and overturning them all on his first attempt! Who would have thought it possible? [59].

And his next attempt at a strike is equally dismissive of the piffling rules of the game:

Sam, who has evidently been listing at an angle, now hurls a ball toward a second set of pins, overturning them all! And if the pins were not his own,

would it matter? It's a happy day when even one bowler is rescued from the toils of Sisyphus. But commotion and recrimination erupt from the next lane—until the commoting recriminator glimpses Sam's face [60].
(*Oranges*, Gracesprings Collective, Celista, B.C., 2010)

* * *

There is an extended parody of Beckett in Shaun McCarthy's *Lucky Ham* (London: Macmillan and Co., 1977). An Oxford College, under the terms of the Bucket bequest, has to produce annually a Lemuel Bucket play, plays which are above all deemed *contemporary* and from which dustbins (It's sort of a trademark) can't be cut. But the question then becomes, "Yes, but is he bankable?" To which the narrator responds:

> An excellent question, I thought, for future Schools papers in English Literature. "Discuss the bankability of Bucket? Or even for a postgraduate dissertation: 'O felix culpa! Bankability motivations in Bucket and Thomas Aquinas.' I'd get the girls on to it at the earliest opportunity" [89].

* * *

My mouth talks too much. Only a week earlier my mouth had soured a *New Yorker* dinner at the Caprice in London by indulging in this "exchange" with Salman Rushdie:
—So you *like* Beckett's prose, do you? You *like* Beckett's prose.
Having established earlier that he did like Beckett's prose, Salman neglected to answer.
—Okay. Quote me some. Oh I see. You can't.
No answer: only the extreme hooded-eye treatment. Richard Avedon would need a studio's worth of lights and reflectors to rig up this expression on an unsuspecting Salman. At that moment, though, a passing waiter with an Instamatic could have easily bettered it. Nobody spoke. Not even Christopher Hitchens. And I really do hate Beckett's prose: every sentence is an assault on my ear. So I said,
—Well I'll do it for you. All you need is maximum ugliness and a lot of negatives. "Nor it the nothing never is." "Neither nowhere the nothing is not." "Non-nothing the never—
Feeling my father in me now (as well as the couple of hundred glasses of wine consumed at the party we had all come on from), I settled down for a concerted goad and wheedle. By this stage Salman looked like a falcon staring through a venetian blind.
—"No neither nor never none not no—"
—Do you want to come outside?
[Martin Amis, *Experience: A Memoir*, Vintage Canada, 2000, 81–2].

Editor's Note: They do not go outside. If they had, our money would have been all in on S. Rushdie.

* * *

Molloy's famous teaser—"It is midnight. The rain is beating on the windows. It was not midnight. It was not raining."—is reprised in Don DeLillo's *White Noise* (Penguin Books, 1985), Chapter 6:

> "He wants to know if it's raining *now*, at this very minute?"
>
> "Here and now. That's right."
>
> "Is there such a thing as now? 'Now' comes and goes as soon as you say it. How can I say it's raining now if your so-called 'now' becomes 'then' as soon as I say it?" [23].

* * *

In Michael Gruber's *The Forgery of Venus* (William Morrow, 2008), there is a very creative adaptation of *Krapp's Last Tape*. The narrator abandons his acting career when he realizes that after playing Krapp he is unable to get out of character; on the other hand, his friend, the painter Chaz Wilmot, possesses the uncanny ability of virtually becoming Velázquez, hence the title of the novel. The painter opines, "Krapp was crazy, right? Or am I wrong?" The narrator replies, "It's left ambiguous I think. What does Krapp have to do with your problem?" (12).

* * *

Nick Tosches' narrator *In the Hand of Dante* (Little, Brown and Company, 2002) on the topic of books:

> They had put into my stupid fucking head the stupid fucking idea that literature was still a thing of noble fucking value. Through those books—through that shit—I had entered a different world, in which Homer and Dante and Samuel Beckett were as big a deal as my grandfather's brother, and bigger still: as big as those old-timers at the club whom my grandfather's brother used to embrace. But this was not true. And the grand irony, as I now, much later, had discovered, was that it was less true in the world of publishing than it was in the old neighborhood [84].

The conclusion being, "And there was no world where Homer moved or was revered by the masses. There was Oprah's Book Club" (85).

* * *

Randle Patrick McMurphy of Ken Kesey's *One Flew Over the Cuckoo's Nest* (1962) as an American cousin of Beckett's Murphy? Or more Merry Pranksterism…?

* * *

How does Lydia Davis's unnamed narrator in "Southward Bound, Reads *Worstward Ho*" manage to connect the world of the van in which she is riding with her reading of the Beckett text (while managing *not* to refer to the "Fail better" advertising slogan—after all, the best commercial messages are like poetry: keep it simple, compress). See *Varieties of Disturbance* (New York: Farrar, Straus and Giroux, 2007), 68–71.

* * *

'Tis (not): Beckett in American Literature, a projected study, with a nod to Frank McCourt and the narrator of Beckett's short story "Dante and the Lobster."

* * *

Newspaper report in John Burdett's *The Godfather of Kathmandu* (New York: Alfred A. Knopf, 2010), featuring Sonchai Jitpleecheep, the Royal Thai police detective with a Buddhist soul:

> Kontea, Tanzania: Not long ago Godot passed through this tiny village in the deep South of this sleepy African country. Last year, during a routine pass by a gem-hunting corporation, "gravel" was found here: a technical term referring to certain unprepossessing small pebbles the colour of raw prawns. They are near worthless members of the sapphire family, but can be and often are, indicators of their most valuable cousins. [...] Then, when it was confirmed that such sapphires as existed here were all of inferior quality with poor colouring and other flaws which made it impossible to market them profitably, the twenty-first century withdrew like a high tide, leaving plenty of detritus with the original villagers, who are scratching their heads and wondering if it had all been a dream [269].

Editors' Note: Isn't it time for a cultural history of Godotism?

* * *

In John Darnton's journalistic detective novel, *Black and White and Dead All Over* (New York: Alfred A. Knopf, 2008), Beckett's signature play is deployed to circumvent a raft of New York City regulations devised to close down porn shops:

> Sixty percent of its floor space and inventory had to be set aside for so-called legitimate entertainment materials. The owner counted the stage in this category on Wednesday nights, when it was given over to the Razor's Edge, a neighborhood theater company. The company had mounted a version of *Waiting for Godot* in which Pozzo stripped naked. An undercover cop who happened to be in the audience busted them, and so now Puss 'N Boots was going to lose its license [100].

* * *

The protagonist in John Fasman's spy novel, *The Unpossessed City* (New York: Penguin Press, 2008), draws this analogy:

> There was no here here, anyway: Gertrude Stein had said it about Oakland, across the bay from his adopted hometown, but what did she know? Had she ever seen a planned Soviet town that had outlived its empire and purpose? It was nothing plunked down in the middle of nothing because some nothing of a bureaucrat thought it was important to insulate the nothing it produced from the nothing the rest of the country produced. Towns like this make a journalist out of Beckett [87].

* * *

Aspettando Godot—Italian translation of *Waiting for Godot*—is a well-known song by Claudio Lolli. In this song, Godot impersonates the Communist revolution, that never comes.

* * *

About the song's provenance, Stan Ridgway had this to say about "bongo beatniks" (1975):

> It's a rockin' little tune. The modern poets Samuel Beckett and Allen Ginsberg and the Ramones converged here to help me write this in 1975 as a song to hear something that WAS NOT on the radio at the time. [...] I played this just once ... and a 300 pound guy with an eye patch threw a beer at me. Pretty scary, but I finished the song. Beatniks never quit.

* * *

In Stuart McLean's very popular CBC Radio show, "The Vinyl Café," Dave, raconteur of domestic misadventures, has a son named Sam whose best friend is named Murphy. Another "false positive"?

* * *

Lia and Nick Romeo's *11,002 Things to Be Miserable About* (Abrams Image, 2009) can indeed be neatly rounded off once we subtract the two nondescript references to Beckett in this bathroom "book" (an endless mind-numbing listing). Much more exciting was the attempt by North London teenagers to produce a version of *Waiting for Godot* in a public toilet for the Edinburgh Fringe festival, 2009. The Beckett Estate blocked this, but the students were undeterred, penning a new play entitled *Still Waiting for Godot* to mock the censors and to be staged, as it were, "in loo of the original" (*The Globe and Mail*, Saturday, August 29, 2009).

* * *

Beckett *testimonio* by Ibrahim Matar, a rebel fighter in the Syrian Civil War:

> When he returned to his scorched home, he headed straight for his prized library. "I saw the burned paper," he told me, and "tears came to my eyes." He had been studying for a master's degree in English translation and had maintained the library for years, collecting books by Shakespeare, Arthur Miller, Samuel Beckett. "Some say Godot is God," he said, "but I say he is hope. Our revolution is now waiting for Godot" [Anand Gopul, "Welcome to Free Syria," *Harper's Magazine*, August 2012, 40].

* * *

The main prosecutor in the video game *Phoenix Wright: Ace Attorney—Trials and Tribulations* is named Godot. Detective Lake Atmey comments that "Some people spend their entire lives waiting for him." He even looks like a manga version of Beckett, with a stylized version of that shock of white hair. The series, which originated in Japan, has sold four million plus units worldwide.

* * *

In his review of Dennis Devlin's poetry (in *Disjecta*, edited by Ruby Cohn), Beckett heaps scorn on those who need to have neatly satisfying answers to their queries, "solution clapped on problem like a snuffer on a candle, the great crossword public on all its planes" (92). It was, however, inevitable that Beckett himself would be grist for the mill; at least in this instance it is a cryptic crossword: "Across 11 Deity going back to famous no-show(s)" (Fraser Simpson, *The Globe and Mail*, Saturday, February 20, 2010, spotted and puzzled by Jennifer Murphy).

* * *

Harvard symbologist Robert Langdon in *The Lost Symbol* (Doubleday, 2009) entertains the possibility "that SBB Thirteen is the entrance to a giant underground pyramid that contains all the lost wisdom of the ancients" (132). No: "SBB Thirteen" most definitely does not refer to one Samuel Barclay Beckett (who was often attracted to the number thirteen), and any such quest for mystical knowledge leads away from Beckett's more fundamental investigation of the material culture contexts for meaning. Up the "Big Toe"!

* * *

Symbols in popular culture wherever you intend them...

* * *

We have only scratched the surface of this rich vein of material of all sorts in various genres, media, languages, and cultures.

Feel free to post your own examples and accompanying comments on the website voxpopbeckett.ca.

Bibliography

Abbott, H. Porter. "Extratextual Intelligence." *New Literary History* 28, no. 4 (Autumn 1997): 811–820.

———. "The Legacy of Samuel Beckett: An Anatomy." In *A Companion to Samuel Beckett*. Edited by S.E. Gontarski. Oxford: Wiley-Blackwell, 2010: 73–83.

Ackerley, C.J. *Demented Particulars: The Annotated Murphy*. Tallahassee: Journal of Beckett Studies Books, 1998.

Ackerley, C.J., and S.E. Gontarski. *The Grove Companion to Samuel Beckett: A Reader's Guide to His Works, Life, and Thought*. New York: Grove Press, 2004.

Atwal, Glyn, and Alistair Williams. "Luxury Brand Marketing: The Experience Is Everything." *Brand Management* 16, no. 4/5 (2009): 338–46.

Auster, Paul. *In the Country of Last Things*. Reprint edition. New York: Penguin Books, 1988.

———. *Lulu on the Bridge*. LionsGate, 1998.

———. *Three Films: Smoke, Blue in the Face, Lulu on the Bridge*. New York: Picador, 2003.

Bair, Deirdre. *Samuel Beckett*. New York: Harcourt Brace Jovanovich, 1978.

Barker, John. *Poet in the Gutter*. London: Indigo Books, 2000.

Bataille, Georges. "The Big Toe." In *Contemporary Critical Theory*. Edited by Dan Latimer. New York: Harcourt Brace Jovanovich, 1989: 135–140.

Beckett, Samuel. *Collected Shorter Plays of Samuel Beckett*. London: Faber and Faber, 1984.

———. *The Complete Short Prose, 1929–1989*, edited by S.E. Gontarski. New York: Grove Press, 1995.

———. *Disjecta: Miscellaneous Writings and a Dramatic Fragment*. London: John Calder, 1983.

———. *Dream of Fair to Middling Women*. Edited by Eoin O'Brien and Edith Fournier. Dublin: Black Cat Press, 1992.

———. *Endgame, a Play in One Act*, followed by *Act Without Words, a Mime for One Player*. New York: Grove Press, 1958.

———. *Happy Days*. New York: Grove Press, 1961.

———. *How It Is*. New York: Grove Press, 1964.

———. *The Lost Ones*. New York: Grove Press, 1972.

———. *Mercier and Camier*. London: Calder and Boyars, 1971.

———. *More Pricks than Kicks*. London: Calder and Boyars, 1970.

———. *Murphy*. New York: Grove Press, 1957.

———. *Nohow On (Company, Ill Seen Ill Said, Worstward Ho)*. New York: Grove Press, 1996.

———. *Three Novels: Molloy, Malone Dies, The Unnamable*. New York: Grove Press, 1991.

———. *Waiting for Godot: A Tragi-Comedy in Two Acts*. New York: Grove Press, 1982.

———. *Watt*. New York: Grove Press, 1959.

Blatty, William Peter. *Legion*. New York: Pocket Books, 1983.

Bloom, Harold. *Genius: A Mosaic of One Hundred Exemplary Creative Minds*. New York: Warner Books, 2002.

Bolton, Lesley. *The Complete Book of Baby Names*. Naperville, IL: Sourcebooks, 2013.

Bryden, Mary. "Clowning with Beckett." In *A Companion to Samuel Beckett*. Edited by S.E. Gontarski. Oxford: Wiley-Blackwell, 2010: 358–371.

Bryner, Jeanna. "Baby Names Have Long-

Lasting Effects, for Better or Worse." *Christian Science Monitor*, June 14, 2010. http://www.csmonitor.com/Science/2010/0614/Baby-names-have-long-lasting-effects-for-better-or-worse.

Campbell, Julie. "Beckett and Paul Auster: Fathers and Sons and the Creativity of Misreading." In *Beckett at 100: Revolving It All*. Edited by Linda Ben-Zvi and Angela Moorjani. Oxford: Oxford University Press, 2008, 299–310.

Carlyle, Thomas. *Sartor Resartus* and *On Heroes and Hero Worship*. New York: Everyman's Library, 1967.

Caselli, Daniela. *Beckett and Nothing: Trying to Understand Beckett*. Manchester University Press, 2010.

Caselli, Daniela, Steven Connor, and Laura Salisbury. "Introduction." In *Other Becketts*. Edited by Daniela Caselli, Steven Connor, and Laura Salisbury. Tallahassee: Journal of Beckett Studies Books, 2002: i–xvi.

Clarke, Donald. *Pitch 'n' Putt with Beckett 'n' Joyce*. Blue Light/Irish Film Board, 2001.

Clements, Roy. *The Alternative Wisden on Samuel Barclay Beckett (1906–1989)*. Daripress, 1992.

Colfer, Eoin. *Artemis Fowl and the Time Paradox*. London: Puffin, 2009.

Connor, Steven. *Beckett, Modernism and the Material Imagination*. Cambridge University Press, 2014.

Cronin, Anthony. *Samuel Beckett: The Last Modernist*. New York: Harper Collins, 1997.

Dawkins, Richard. *The Selfish Gene*. Oxford: Oxford University Press, 2006.

Deleuze, Gilles. *Negotiations (1972–1990)*. Translated by Martin Joughin. New York: Columbia University Press, 1995.

Denise, Mina. *The Last Breath*. London: Bantam Books, 2007.

Derrida, Jacques. *Specters of Marx: The State of the Debt, the Work of Mourning and the New International*. New York: Routledge, 2006.

Dexter, Colin. *The Remorseful Day*. London: Macmillan, 1999.

Dick, Phillip K. *The Simulacra*. New York: Ace Books, 1964.

Dilks, Stephen John. "Portraits of Beckett as a Famous Writer." *Journal of Modern Literature* 29, no. 4 (2006): 161–188.

———. *Samuel Beckett in the Literary Marketplace*. Syracuse: Syracuse University Press, 2011.

Ellmann, Richard. *James Joyce, New and Revised Edition*. Oxford University Press, 1982.

Feldman, Matthew. *Beckett's Books: A Cultural History of Samuel Beckett's "Interwar Notes."* New York: Continuum, 2006.

Friedman, Kinky. *Frequent Flyer*. New York: William Morrow and Co., 1989.

———. *Musical Chairs*. New York: William Morrow and Co., 1991.

Gardiner, Meg. *The Dirty Secrets Club*. London: Hodder and Stoughton, 2008.

Gibson, Andrew. *Samuel Beckett*. London: Reaktion Books, 2010.

Gill, Bartholomew. *The Death of a Joyce Scholar*. New York: Avon Books, 1990.

Gontarski, S.E. "Introduction: Viva Sam Beckett, or Flogging the Avant-Garde." *Journal of Beckett Studies* 16, no. 1 and 2 (Fall 2006/Spring 2007): 1–11.

González, Jesús Ángel. "Words Versus Images: Paul Auster's Films from *Smoke* to the *Book of Illusion*." *Literature Film Quarterly* 37, no. 1 (2009): 28–48.

Green, Martin, and John Swan. *The Triumph of Pierrot: Commedia Dell'arte and the Modern Imagination*. New York: Macmillan Publishing Company, 1986.

Greenblatt, Stephen. *The Swerve: How the World Became Modern*. New York: Norton, 2012.

Guerin, Wilfred L., ed. *A Handbook of Critical Approaches to Literature*. New York: Oxford University Press, 2011.

Hammett, Dashiell. "The Maltese Falcon." In *Five Complete Novels*. New York: Chatham River Press, 1986.

Harmon, Maurice, ed. *No Author Better Served: The Correspondence of Samuel Beckett and Alan Schneider*. Cambridge: Harvard University Press, 1998.

Harrison, G.B., ed. *Shakespeare: The Complete Works*. New York: Harcourt, Brace and World, 1952.

Hauser, Gerard A. *Introduction to Rhetor-*

ical Theory. 2nd ed. Prospect Heights, IL: Waveland Press, 2002.
Heath, Joseph, and Andrew Porter. *The Rebel Sell: Why the Culture Can't Be Jammed*. Toronto: Harper Perennial, 2004.
Heilemann, J. *Pride Before the Fall: The Trials of Bill Gates and the End of the Microsoft Era*. New York: Perennial, 2001.
Higdon, David Leon. "Samuel Beckett in Outer Space." *Journal of Beckett Studies* Old Series, no. 11 and 12 (Dec. 1989): n.p.
Hutcheon, Linda. *A Theory of Adaptation*. London: Routledge, 2006.
———. *A Theory of Parody*. Chicago: University of Illinois Press, 2000.
"Icons of Cool: 50 Most Stylish Men of the Past 50 Years and What You Can Learn from Them." In *GQ (Gentlemen's Quarterly)*, 50th Anniversary Issue (2007): 357–84.
Irwin, William, ed. *Seinfeld and Philosophy: A Book About Everything and Nothing*. Chicago: Open Court, 2000.
James, Bill. *Astride a Grave*. London: Pan Books, 1991.
———. *Easy Streets*. New York: W.W. Norton, 2004.
———. *Roses, Roses*. London: Macmillan, 1993.
Jameson, Fredric. *Archaeologies of the Future: The Desire Called Utopia and Other Science Fictions*. London: Verso, 2005.
———. *Postmodernism, Or, the Cultural Logic of Late Capitalism*. Durham: Duke University Press, 2001.
Jolley, Kelly Dean. "Wittgenstein and Seinfeld on the Commonplace." In *Seinfeld and Philosophy: A Book About Everything and Nothing*. Edited by William Irwin. Chicago: Open Court, 1999: 109–119.
Jones, David Houston. "From Contumacy to Shame: Reading Beckett's Testimonies with Agamben." In *Beckett at 100: Revolving It All*. Edited by Linda Ben-Zvi and Angela Moorjani. Oxford: Oxford University Press, 2008: 54–67.
Joyce, James. *Finnegans Wake*. Oxford: Oxford University Press, 2012.
———. *A Portrait of the Artist as a Young Man*. Boston: Bedford, 1993.
———. *Ulysses*. New York: Penguin, 2008.
Kenner, Hugh. *The Elsewhere Community*. Concord, Ontario: Anansi Press, 1998.
Knowlson, James. *Damned to Fame: The Life of Samuel Beckett*. London: Bloomsbury, 1996.
Koontz, Dean, and Ed Gorman. *Dean Koontz's Frankenstein Book Two: City of Night*. New York: Bantam Dell, 2005.
Kostelanetz, Richard, ed. *On Contemporary Literature* (expanded edition). New York: Avon, 1969.
Lawley, Paul. "'The Scene of My Disgrace': 'Enough' and 'Memory.'" In *Samuel Beckett Today/Aujourd'hui* 7 (1998): 259–76.
Lem, Stanislaw. *A Perfect Vacuum*. San Diego: Harvest/HBJ, 1979.
Levinson, Paul. *New New Media*. 2nd ed. New York: Pearson Higher Education, 2012.
Levitt, Steven D., and Stephen J. Dubner. *Freakonomics: A Rogue Economist Explores the Hidden Side of Everything*. New York: Harper Perennial, 2006.
Lucretius. *On the Nature of Things (De Rerum Natura)*. Translated by Palmer Bovie. New York: Signet Classics, 1974.
MacDonald, John D. *Bright Orange for the Shroud*. New York: Fawcett Gold Medal, 1991.
MacGowan, Shane, and Victoria Mary Clarke. *A Drink with Shane MacGowan*. New York: Grove Press, 2001.
Manlove, Colin N. "'Perpetual Metamorphoses': the Refusal of Certainty in Carlyle's *Sartor Resartus*." In *The Critical Response to Thomas Carlyle's Major Works*. Edited D.J. Trela and Rodger L. Tarr. London: Greenwood Press, 1997: 30–46.
Marshall, William. *Whisper*. New York: Viking Press, 1988.
Masters, Tim. "Samuel Beckett Manuscript and Doodles Go on Display." *BBC News*. Accessed April 29, 2015. http://www.bbc.com/news/entertainment-arts-27687121.
Maude, Ulrika. *Beckett, Technology and the Body*. Cambridge: Cambridge University Press, 2009.

McBride, Stuart. *Broken Skin*. London: HarperCollins, 2007.
McCloud, Scott. *Making Comics*. New York: HarperCollins, 2007.
_____. *Understanding Comics*. New York: Harper Perennial, 1994.
McLaughlin, Noel, and Martin McLoone. "Hybridity and National Musics: The Case of Irish Rock Music." *Popular Music* 19, no. 2 (April 2000): 181–99.
Mercier, Vivian. *Beckett/Beckett*. New York: Oxford University Press, 1977.
_____. *A Reader's Guide to the New Novel: From Queneau to Pinget*. New York: Farrar, Straus and Giroux, 1971.
Merivale, Patricia, and Susan Sweney, eds. *Detecting Texts: The Metaphysical Detective Story from Poe to Postmodernism*. Philadelphia: University of Pennsylvania Press, 1999.
Miller, Arthur. "Aristotle on Habit and Character: Implications for the Rhetoric." *Speech Monographs* 41, no. 4 (1974): 309–16.
Muller, Anja, and Mark Schreiber. "Sam 2.0: Appropriation, Interpretations and Adaptations of Beckett on Youtube." In *Adaptations: Performing Across Media and Genres*. Edited by Monika Pietrzak-Franger, Trier: Wissenschaftlicher Verlag Trier, 2009, 173–92.
Murphy, Dallas. *Apparent Wind*. New York: Pocket Books, 1991.
_____. *Lover Man*. New York: Pocket Books, 1987.
_____. *Lush Life*. New York: Pocket Books, 1992.
Murphy, P.J. "Beckett and the Philosophers." In *The Cambridge Companion to Beckett*. Edited by John Pilling. Cambridge University Press, 1994, 222–239.
_____. "Beckett's Critique of Kant." In *Beckett/Philosophy*. Edited by Matthew Feldman, and Karim Mamdani. Sofia University Press, 2012: 205–220.
_____. *Beckett's Dedalus: Dialogical Engagements with Joyce in Beckett's Fiction*. Toronto: University of Toronto Press, 2009.
_____. *Reconstructing Beckett: Language for Being in Samuel Beckett's Fiction*. Toronto: University of Toronto Press, 1990.
Murphy, P.J., Werner Huber, Rolf Breuer, and Konrad Schoell. *Critique of Beckett Criticism: A Guide to Research in English, French, and German*. Columbia, SC: Camden House, 1994.
Nabokov, Vladimir. "The Passenger." In *The Stories of Vladimir Nabokov*. New York: Vintage, 1997: 183–188.
Norman, Hilary. *Mind Games*. London: Piatkus Publishers, 1999.
O'Brien, Flann. "A Bash in the Tunnel." In *Stories and Plays*. Hammondsworth: Penguin Books, 1973: 201–6.
O'Brien, Susie, and Imre Szeman. *Popular Culture: A User's Guide*. Scarborough: Thompson and Nelson, 2004.
O'Hagan, Sean. "Ireland's Emigrants Sing Songs of Exile That Echo Through the Generations." *The Guardian*. Accessed April 29, 2015. http://www.theguardian.com/world/2010/feb/28/ireland-exile-culture.
Olins, Wally. *On Brand*. London: Thames & Hudson, 2003.
Oppo, Andrea. *Philosophical Aesthetics and Samuel Beckett*. Oxford: Peter Lang, 2008.
Perloff, Marjorie. "'In Love with Hiding': Samuel Beckett's War." *The Iowa Review* 35, no. 1 (2005): 76–103.
Pierson, David P. "A Show About Nothing: *Seinfeld* and the Modern Comedy of Manners." *Journal of Popular Culture* 34, no. 1 (Summer 2000): 49–64.
Pilling, John. *A Companion to Dream of Fair to Middling Women*. Tallahassee, FL: Journal of Beckett Studies Books, 2004.
Pinter, Harold. "Beckett." In *Beckett at Sixty: A Festschrift*, Edited by John Calder. London: Calder and Boyars, 1967.
Prince, Eric. "A Tempest in a Billycan: *Godot* and *Endgame* in Sydney." *Journal of Beckett Studies* 11, no. 2 (2002): 86–96.
Robinson, Michael. *The Long Sonata of the Dead: A Study of Samuel Beckett*. New York: Grove Press, 1971.
Rubbo, Michael. *Waiting for Fidel*. Montreal: NFB, 1974.
Salisbury, Laura. *Samuel Beckett: Laughing Matters, Comic Timing*. Edinburgh: Edinburgh University Press, 2012.

Schlossberg, Edwin. *Einstein and Beckett: A Record of an Imaginary Discussion with Albert Einstein and Samuel Beckett*. New York: Links Books, 1973.

Schumpeter, J.A. *Capitalism, Socialism and Democracy*. London: Routledge, 1994.

Sikoryak, R. *Masterpiece Comics*. Montreal, Que.: Drawn and Quarterly, 2009.

Spiegelman, Art. *The Complete Maus*. New York: Pantheon Books, 1997.

Stephens, James. *The Crock of Gold*. London: John Murray, 2012.

Swift, Jonathan. *A Selection of His Works*. Toronto: Macmillan, 1965.

Syed, Matthew. *Bounce: Mozart, Federer, Picasso, Beckham and the Science of Success*. New York: Harper, 2010.

Talbot, Mary M., and Bryan Talbot. *Dotter of Her Father's Eyes*. Milwaukie, OR: Dark Horse Books, 2012.

Tatsumi, Takayuki. *Full Metal Apache: Transactions Between Cyberpunk Japan and Avant-Pop America*. Duke University Press, 2005.

Torelli, Carlos J., Ozsomer, Sergio W. Carvalho, Hean Tat Keh, and Natalia Maehle. "Brand Concepts as Representations of Human Values: Do Cultural Congruity and Compatability Between Values Matter?" *Journal of Marketing* 76 (July 2012): 92–108.

U2 and Neil McCormick. *U2 by U2: Bono, the Edge, Adam Clayton, Larry Mullen, Jr*. New York: Harper Collins, 2009.

Verne, Jules. *20,000 Leagues Under the Sea*. New York: Signet Classic, 2001.

Vila-Matas, Enrique. *Dublinesque*. London: Harvill Secker, 2012.

Virgil. *The Aeneid*. Translated by Robert Fitzgerald. New York: Vintage Classics, 1990.

Voights-Virchow, Eckart. "Face Values: Beckett Inc, the Camera Plays and Cultural Liminity." *Journal of Beckett Studies* 10, no. 1 and 2 (2002): 119–35.

_____. "*Quad I* and *Teletubbies* Or: 'Aisthetic' Panopticism Versus Reading Beckett." In *Samuel Beckett Today/Aujourd'hui 7* (1998): 210–218.

Walker, Rob. *Buying In: The Secret Dialogue Between What We Buy and What We Are*. New York: Random House, 2008.

Walters, Minette. *The Ice House*. London: Pan Books, 1992.

Willeford, Charles. *The Burnt Orange Heresy*. New York: Vintage Crime/Black Lizard, 1990.

_____. *New Forms of Ugly: The Immobilized Hero in Modern Fiction*. Master's Thesis, University of Miami, 1964.

_____. *Writing and Other Blood Sports*. Tuscon: Dennis McMillan Publications, 2000.

Winks, Robin W., ed. *Detective Fiction: A Collection of Critical Essays*. Woodstock, VT: A Foul Play Press Book, 1988.

Wordsworth, William. *The Major Works* including *The Prelude*. Edited by Stephen Gill. Oxford: Oxford University Press, 2008.

Zapico, Alfonso. *James Joyce: Portrait of a Dubliner*. Dublin: The O'Brien Press, 2013.

Zeifman, Hersh. "Staging Sam: Beckett as Dramatic Characters." In *Beckett at 100: Revolving It All*. Edited by Linda Ben-Zvi and Angela Moorjani. Oxford: Oxford University Press, 2008: 311–317.

About the Contributors

Stephen **Brown** is the P.T. Barnum Professor of Marketing Research at the University of Ulster, Northern Ireland. He dreams of writing a novel featuring Sam Beckett, PI, of the Fair to Middling Detective Agency.

Alexander M. **Forbes**' poems have been published in journals and books across the United States from New York to California, and likewise in Canada from Quebec to British Columbia.

Jennifer **Murphy** is a lecturer in the School of Social Work at Thompson Rivers University. Her research interests include the reintegration into community of federal parolees, particularly the barriers facing women released from federal prisons.

P.J. **Murphy** has written extensively on Samuel Beckett's fiction and his aesthetic philosophy. He has also written extensively on prison literature and Canadian sentencing policies. His work in progress is "Beckett and Prisons: A Memoir of Sorts."

Nick **Pawliuk** teaches in the English and Modern Language Department at Thompson Rivers University. When he's not accidentally finding Beckett references, he tries to increase student engagement with innovative curriculum, pop culture, and obsolete references.

Tanya **Pawliuk** is a lecturer in the School of Social Work and Human Service at Thompson Rivers University. Her research and practice interests include permanency, adoption, and adoption preparedness.

Cameron **Reid,** Ph.D., is an independent scholar living in Vancouver, British Columbia. His research is located primarily in the fields of critical pedagogy (and its application to online education) and contemporary continental philosophy.

Mark Rowell **Wallin** is an associate professor of communication and film studies at Thompson Rivers University. His published works have addressed adaptation theory, film and video game studies, rhetoric of new media authorship and even film festivals.

Index

Abbott, H. Porter 67, 172–173
Ackerley, C.J., and S.E. Gontarski 67, 97, 161–162
Act Without Words 129
Adam & Paul 92
Admission 142
All That Fall 116
Annie Hall 89–90
Apple 19, 21, 31, 56, 67n21, 71, 83
"Assumption" 65, 131–132, 158–159
Atwal, Glyn, and Alistair Williams 142n20
Auster, Paul 60–67

Bair, Deirdre 104, 106n15–16, 134
Bandslam 96
Barker, John 49
Barr, Roseanne 70, 72, 76
Bataille, Georges 9–10, 17n10–12
Baudrillard, Jean 58
"Beckett and the Philosophers" 167
Beckett's Dedalus: Dialogical Engagements with Joyce in Beckett's Fiction 1, 5, 10, 14, 16–17, 39, 172
Berkeley, Bishop 39, 88–89
Big Night 91
Blatty, William Peter 44, 51n18
Boland, Eaven 112
Bolton, Lesley 121–122
Bono (U2) 107–109, 112, 114–115, 118, 119
Breath 153
Bürger, Peter 15
Byerly, Dick 22

Calder, John 4
"The Calmative" 55, 62
Campbell, Julie 61–62
The Canterbury Tales 3–4, 28
Carlyle, Thomas 131, 135
Caselli, Daniela 10–11, 17n13, 72
Castle 70

China Beach 71, 74–75, 123
Clarke, Victoria Mary 119n24
Clements, Roy 164
Colfer, Eoin 59–60
Company 134
Connor, Steven 10–11, 17n13, 157–162, 167n2
Cracker 70
Criminal Minds 69
The Critic 69
Cronenberg, David 96
Cronin, Anthony 116
Crosby, David 77, 127n7

David, Larry 74
Dawkins, Richard 150
Day, Eliza 111
Deleuze, Gilles 88–89, 110, 118
Derrida, Jacques 97n1
Dick, Philip K. 58–59, 65
Dilks, Stephen John 4–6, 20, 97n5, 98n12, 126, 144
Dream of Fair to Middling Women 6, 8–9, 55, 64–65, 130, 132, 173
Drucker, Peter 21

Elvis 12
Endgame 34, 43, 47–49, 70, 81–83, 129–130, 167
"Enough" 61–62, 128
Evans, Walker 16
Everett-Green, Robert 98n23
The Exorcist 44
"The Expelled" 68

Facebook 147, 149–150
Fawlty Towers 165
Feldman, Matthew 17n15
Film 87–89, 96
Finding Nemo 26, 66n8
"First Love" 9

Fizzles 162, 166
Foran, Charles 162–164
Franco, James 124–125
Friedman, Kinky 51

Gardiner, Meg 49
Gibson, Andrew 14–15
Gibson, William 54, 66*n*3
Gill, Bartholomew (Mark McGarrity) 34, 36–37, 50
Gontarski, S.E. 12–13, 161–162, 171–172
González, Jesús Ángel 67
GQ 130, 135, 140
Green, Martin, and John Swain 166–167*n*1

Hammett, Dashiell 35
Happy Days 142
Harry Potter 20, 28
Hauser, Gerard A. 151
Heath, Joseph, and Andrew Potter 170–171
Heilemann, John 32*n*5
Home Improvement 71, 78
House 80
How It Is 9, 134
Huber, Werner 18*n*22
Hutcheon, Linda 13, 57, 60, 144, 146, 170

Ill Seen Ill Said 14, 134–135
"The Irish Exile" 111, 117
Irwin, William 73

James, Bill 34, 43, 45–49, 50
Jameson, Fredric 15, 58, 67, 169
The John Larroquette Show 71, 76–77
Jones, David Houston 105–106*n*12
Joughin, Martin 119*n*13
Joyce, James 1, 5, 8, 10, 36–37, 101, 116, 160

Kenner, Hugh 33–34
Kesey, Ken 75, 182
Knowlson, James 5, 8, 14, 34, 55, 167
Koontz, Dean 56
Kostelanetz, Richard 56–57
Krapp's Last Tape 26, 86

Las Vegas 12–13
Lawley, Paul 67
Lem, Stanislaw 57–58, 65

Levinson, Paul 145
Levitt, Steven D., and Stephen J. Dubner 121–122
The Lost Ones 134
Lucretius 160–161, 167*n*5

MacBride, Stewart 44
MacGowan, Shane 119
Malone Dies 218
Manlove, Colin N. 131
Marshall, Bill 116
Marshall, William 49
Maude, Ulrika 17*n*11
McCartney, Stella 139
McCloud, Scott 106
McDonald, Ronan 4–5
McGarr, Peter 36–39
McLaughlin, Noel, and Martin McLoone 117
Mercier, Vivian 44, 133
Mercier and Camier 133
Merivale, Patricia 35
Miami Vice 69
Miller, Arthur 151, 185
Mina, Denise 49
Molloy 3–4, 35, 62, 133–134
More Pricks Than Kicks 82, 132
Morrison, Van 110–112
Muller, Anja, and Mark Schreiber 143, 173
Murphy 35, 64, 68, 73, 77, 100, 132, 146
Murphy, Dallas 49

Nabokov, Vladimir 17*n*12
Nameberry.com 122, 124–125
Nohow On 158
Norman, Hilary 49

O'Brien, Flann 7, 17*n*8
O'Hagan, Sean 116
Olins, Wally 26
Oppo, Andrea 17*n*14

Perloff, Marjorie 105–106
Pilling, John 54, 62, 66*n*7, 167*n*3
Pinter, Harold 169–170
"Pitch 'n' Putt with Joyce 'n' Beckett" 164–165, 167–168*n*19
Play 64
The Pogues 117–118
Porombka, Stephan 143

A Portrait of the Artist as a Young Man 7, 17, 36
Postman, Neil 58
Prince, Eric 97
Proudfoot, Tony 163–164
Proust 34, 42, 49

Quantum Leap 71, 78–79, 123

Radziwill, Carole 56
Reconstructing Beckett 14–15
Red Dwarf 66, 81
The Remorseful Day 51
The Riches 71, 75–76
Robbe-Grillet, Alain 35
Robinson, Michael 40–41
Roger and Me 91
Romanek, Mark 86
Rowland, Kevin (Dexy's Midnight Runners) 112
Rubbo, Michael 93–95

Salisbury, Laura 10–11, 108
Schlossberg, Edwin 56–57
Schumpeter, J.A. 32
Seinfeld 70, 72–73, 74, 76
Service of All the Dead 44
Shakespeare, William 10, 134, 140, 142n33
Shenker, Israel 5, 171
Sikoryak, R. 99–100, 105
The Simpsons 80, 84n2
Sludds, Ted 98
Smallwood, Joey 93–95
Smoke 63
Spiegelman, Art 103–105
Spielberg, Steven 24–25
Star Trek: The Next Generation 71, 81
Star Wars 69
Stargate 71
Stewart, Patrick 99
Stirrings Still 14, 26, 135
Swift, Jonathan 130–131
Syed, Matthew 166

Talbot, Mary, and Bryan Talbot 101–102, 105n6
Tatsumi, Takayuki 175n22
Teletubbies 123, 128n12
"Text 5" 62
Texts for Nothing 57, 134
Three Dialogues with Georges Duthuit 5, 40, 42–43, 51, 73
Tomm, Nigel 146
Torelli, Carlos J. 142
Tumblr 144, 145, 148, 153
Twitter 144, 145–147, 153

Ulysses 39, 43, 67, 81, 83, 164, 174
The Unnamable 27, 59, 64, 95–97, 128, 164

Van Gogh, Vincent 15
Van Sant, Gus 95
Verne, Jules 54–55, 60
Vila-Matas, Enrique 174
Voigts-Virchow, Eckart 84n1, 128n12

Waiting for Godot 16, 20–21, 31, 34–35, 38, 44, 46, 50–51, 54, 56, 58–59, 69–71, 74–78, 80–81, 86, 90–97, 99–100, 103, 109–111, 116, 125, 127, 146, 148–149, 153, 157–158, 163
Walker, Rob 170
Walters, Minette 45, 51n20
Warhol, Andy 15
Watt 41, 105, 132–133
"A Wet Night" 83
"Whoroscope" 131–132
Willeford, Charles 34, 40–41, 43, 51n15, 170
Winks, Robin W. 34–35, 50n6
Woo, John 70, 82
Wordsworth, William 112–114
Worstward Ho 14, 26, 69, 134–135, 148, 158, 166

Zangenberg, Mikkel Bruun 67n20
Zapico, Alfonso 101–103
Zeifman, Hersh 173n21

www.ingramcontent.com/pod-product-compliance
Lightning Source LLC
Chambersburg PA
CBHW032100300426
44116CB00007B/824